THE ODYSSEY OF
A HIPPIE MARIJUANA GROWER

THE ODYSSEY OF A HIPPIE MARIJUANA GROWER

A MEMOIR BY JOHN-PAUL CERNAK

LUMINARE PRESS

WWW.LUMINAREPRESS.COM

Cover Illustration by Ellen Gabehart
Cover Layout by Claire Flint Last

Luminare Press
442 Charnelton St.
Eugene, OR 97401
www.luminarepress.com

ISBN: 978-1-64388-119-5
LCCN: 2019938160

I'm dedicating this book to Ellen Gabehart for creating the cover and for being my friend. She is a gutsy lady who lives her dream.

And I'm dedicating this book to Jim Carrier (not his real name), for his brilliance and for his courage. Thank you, Jim Carrier.

John-Paul Cernak

CHAPTER 1

THE END OF AN ERA

———⟨ɞ∕ɞ⟩———

San Francisco, California
The Haight–Ashbury, 1973

FOR A LONG TIME, THE HILLS THAT GUARD THE ENTRANCE TO San Francisco Bay intrigued me. Just across the water from the city and a large population, the Marin Headlands were a doorway to a vast, mostly uninhabited region that spread north along the coast for miles. Silhouetted by the Golden Gate Bridge, I saw them clearly from the Haight-Ashbury neighborhood where I lived. They called out to me each time I looked in their direction, and we began a conversation.

"Come up for a visit," they said.

"I'm too busy," I replied.

After my divorce, my life changed and so did the dialog.

"It's time to visit, there's something up here you should see."

I awoke before dawn on a Saturday in September and with my backpack, sleeping bag, and a few provisions walked through the misty San Francisco neighborhoods and reached the Golden Gate Bridge at first light. With little traffic at that hour, an eerie silence descended over the bridge broken intermittently by the bellowing of the foghorn. Three fishing boats sailing out to sea in single file looked like toys from three hundred feet above the water and disappeared into a fogbank outside the Gate. While at mid-span walking over open water, I shivered when a large truck rumbled past and the bridge vibrated reminding me how great the distance was between the towers.

On the Marin side, I climbed the first hill into the headlands and scrambled up the to the highest point. With the risers of the bridge below me and buffeted by a stiff west wind, I stopped to catch my breath inspired by the beauty surrounding me. Across the water, the city sparkled in the morning sun, and white sails dotted the blue waters of the bay. The fog bank moving inland sent long fingers probing under the bridge. My plan was to hike all day, explore the area, and sleep under the stars. In the morning, I'd have breakfast in the small coastal town of Bolinas and hitchhike back to the city. If there was something up there looking for me, I intended to give it ample time to find me.

I didn't have long to wait.

As I turned to continue, my enchantment was instantly shattered and fear shot through me like electricity when a large cat raced past and brushed against me, and I felt the softness of it fur. It was too large for a bobcat, and it had a long tail. It was a cougar. When it stopped and looked at me, I shuttered, and it quickly disappeared over the crest of the hill. I raced down on rubbery legs and cautiously looked over the edge. A large, grassy meadow opened before me, but the puma was gone. A thicket of small trees and shrubs grew in the distance, too far for it to have reached, and there was no other place it could hide. While scanning the terrain, I saw flashes of people riding horses in what resembled a battle and felt a churning in the pit of my stomach. Everything returned to normal after a few seconds, and I was again looking at an empty meadow. Gathering myself together, I continued my hike, still a little shaky, convinced the images were a mirage. I watched for the phantom cat all day but never saw it again.

While having breakfast in town the next morning, I ran into Alex, an old friend. He gave me a ride back to the city. I told him about the disappearing cat. "How scary that it came so close," he said. "You're lucky she wasn't hungry."

"It's the strangest thing, Alex," I said. "It was an attack and yet it wasn't. It brushed against me to let me know it was there. I was vulnerable. It caught me by surprise. Had it gone for my throat, it could have easily done me in. The look it gave me was even more scary. It penetrated into a part of me I didn't even know existed. And what made you think it was female?"

He glanced at me as if unaware he made a distinction. "I don't know. I just assumed it was."

"You're probably right, but what do you make of it disappearing into thin air?"

"Sounds like a warning."

"A warning? What do you mean?"

"Like you're in some kind of danger. Be careful, Jack," he said.

Back in the city, Alex dropped me off in the Haight-Ashbury a few blocks from my print shop where I was residing temporarily. The Sunday morning traffic on Haight Street was light, and as usual, hippies sat along the street in front of cafés and restaurants. Loud music blared from an open door of a café, and a couple sat kissing passionately. With his dog at his side, a happy looking guy strummed a guitar at a restaurant down the block. Zigzagging between and around a large group that sat blocking the sidewalk, I smelled marijuana. "How you doing, man?" they called out cheerfully

It was always entertaining to walk among the hippies, and I was convinced they made a beneficial contribution, even though the vibe on the street wasn't as good as it once was. It felt gratifying they were still there and giving the finger to the establishment who wanted them gone. The Mayor claimed in his last speech they were destroying the city's image. They represented the defiance and spark of freedom I looked for from the beginning challenging authority and hoped they would be there forever. I was told all my life I lived in the land of the free. I loved the Preamble to the Constitution that said: "All men are created equal," but I never felt free until I lived in the

Haight. I was a communist for a while but quickly learned it was as big a fraud as capitalism.

Over time, my hair grew longer, and I cultivated a beard looking more like them. I even adopted their philosophy of: "Make Love, Not War," although I never thought of myself as a hippie. I remembered walking up the street smoking a doobie, and turning a blind corner, I almost bumped into a cop. He startled me, but I didn't try to hide it and kept walking as if everything was normal. "Hi. Officer," I said. He just smiled. The Haight-Ashbury was a renaissance of the human spirit and a time when I regained faith in humanity.

Unfortunately, it was coming to an end. What a beautiful trip it was while it lasted. The invasion of hard drugs like heroin and speed hastened its demise, and prostitution and thievery were common. Now when someone called me 'brother,' I checked to see if I still had my wallet, and it wasn't all peace and love anymore. To avoid being hassled by a couple of panhandlers, I crossed the street in the middle of the block and hurried along, my muscles sore after yesterday's long hike and looking forward to a hot, relaxing shower.

After walking a few block, I stopped and looked around. I'm not sure why I stopped. It must have been something I felt. When I saw the street was empty, I did a double take. A few minutes ago, it was crowded with people sitting at the cafes and restaurants, and even the panhandlers disappeared. More mysteriously, all the traffic on Haight Street ceased, and the few parked cars I saw earlier were gone. Where had everybody gone? It was a beautiful, sunny, Sunday morning in the Haight-Ashbury. The street should be crowded with hippies and with tourists slowly driving by gawking at them.

At first, it seemed insignificant I stopped in front of the Straight Theater. The hippies used it for rock concerts, and it sat empty and deteriorating. I walked past a thousand times, and it was always just a large old building. Now a disturbing vibe came from the ancient movie house filled with ghosts from the past. I remembered standing in that very spot years earlier and feeling the same confusion

I experienced that day wondering why Haight Street was empty. I winced when I recalled watching a movie there and feeling intense emotional pain, only back then it was called the Haight Theater. Suddenly, as if the dam holding them back had burst, a barrage of distressing memories flashed before me in quick succession. They were images from when I first arrived, and I felt strongly the pain and anguish from that troubled time. Their intensity caught me by surprise. Feeling the agony in my body, heart, and mine, I staggered around like a drunk. Sitting on the curb, overwhelmed, my feet on the empty street, I watched images rolling past on my mind screen and felt emotions I locked away long ago.

Suddenly it was 1963, and I saw myself on the roof of my apartment building contemplating suicide. After Lavinia moved out of the apartment we shared in the sunny Mission, I wanted to die. Although she was my first San Francisco love and my first live-in-lover, our relationship was not one made in heaven. It was a bottomless pit from hell, and I should have been glad it was over. Our battles were epic raging and screaming and smashing dishes on the floor. Our apartment manager threatened us with eviction unless we tamed down our clashes. At other times, we wouldn't speak for days. What we sought neither was capable of giving. She was looking for a father and I for a mother. Her leaving triggered long unresolved issues, and I hung on desperately from fear of living alone again and hoped to avoid another failure.

While the rents in the Mission were low, they were even cheaper in the cold and foggy Haight-Ashbury, and Lavinia moved into an apartment in an old rundown Victorian. It was probably converted into apartments during the war when housing was needed for workers at Hunters Point Naval Shipyards and for the wives of servicemen waiting for them to return from active duty. After she moved out, I started hitting the bars. Most evenings, I made the rounds and ended at a nightclub called the Mouse House. Unsurprisingly, on many occasions, Lavinia was there, and we'd spend the rest of the evening in the backseat of my car or in her apartment in the Haight.

On those cold, foggy mornings after staying with her, I remembered shivering in her living room sick to my stomach from breathing the sharp, acidy smell coming from mold buried deep within the walls of that old dwelling. I felt revolution each time I looked at the ugly rose color of the walls, the tattered rugs, and worn-out furnishings, while listening to the emotionally agonizing horn of Miles Davis. His music spoke to me of the depths of hell I experienced each night feeling lonely and unfulfilled and believing I wasn't good enough. That I was inadequate was a familiar charge throughout my childhood and the reason I ran away and moved to San Francisco in the hope of starting life over.

On a walk through the neighborhood the night before, we almost fell over the edge. All day, I pleaded and argued for her to return to the apartment we shared. She resisted. With the tension between us high, we talked strolling on a clear evening, "It's not working, Jack," she said. "We're always in conflict when together."

"I know it's me, baby! I promise I'll change. I'll make it up to you. Just come home."

She pulled away when I tried hugging her, and the more pressure I applied, the more nervous she became. As we passed a Victorian with its garage door open built up against the sidewalk, she stopped and looked into the blackness. I could just make out her expression from the lamp of a nearby streetlight, and with a look of terror, she screamed. At first, I thought some danger was coming from the darkness. I quickly realized her terror was a response to demons in her mind. Totally out of control and amplified by the large empty space, her shrieks quickly became contagious and activated a pool of fear and trepidation deep inside me I hardly knew existed. "Please stop screaming Lavinia." My pleading had no effect. Grabbing her by the shoulders, I shook her. "Stop it, Lavinia, stop it." She only screamed louder. Her hysteria was freaking me out, and I was about to lose it. "Stop it, goddamn it," and I slapped her. The shock quickly brought her out of her frenzy, and she threw herself into my arms sobbing. "I can't stand it anymore, Jack. I have to get out of here. If I stay, I'll die!"

John-Paul Cernak

"No baby! Don't go! If you leave, I'll die!"

I blamed myself for her leaving even though I knew she never liked San Francisco. Like others I knew, she was never able to adjust to the cold, dark, and foggy days. The only job she could find was a filing clerk for an insurance company in the Financial District, and her low salary gave her only enough money to eat her lunches at the Doggie Diner. Lavinia was from an established, aristocratic family in Hartford, Connecticut. An ancestor came across on the Mayflower, and she detested the restaurant shaped like a hot dog. She was petite and pretty but nervous and high-strung.

With a cab waiting on another cold and foggy morning in the Haight, I kissed her goodbye and walked for hours through the neighborhood struggling with my emotions, the rundown Victorians and the dark, overcast sky adding to my gloom. To make things worse, I lost my job and didn't even have enough money for a drink to drown my sorrows. I passed the Haight Theater in late afternoon. The movie playing was Picnic, with Kim Novak and William Holden. Searching through my jacket pockets, I found fifty cents for admission and a dime extra. With a name suggesting a gathering for fun and pleasure, I expected a light, amusing, and frolicking movie to lift my spirits. Instead, it was a deep, dark melodrama that somehow mirrored my life. I sat traumatized in an almost empty theater and identified with the characters and felt their pain and agony. When leaving, I was sure my life was over.

I huddled in the doorway next to the theater under a blanket of night and thick fog smoking a cigarette and watched the few other movie patrons quickly drive off. As the last vehicle disappeared into the night, the theater abruptly extinguished its marquee lights and plunged everything into darkness. I looked around nervously for another person. Nothing moved, except the distant flow of cross traffic on a busy street. In shock, I watched the traffic signal shining through the fog change from green to yellow to red three or four times. While many vehicles flowed past, not one turned up Haight, and the street remained deserted without even a parked car. I must have died and gone to hell.

Dazed and shivering in the cold and damp, I walked up the dark street in the eerie silence to discover most storefronts boarded up. The merchants doing business in the district for years were moving out. When I turned into the neighborhood trying to remember where I parked my car, the Victorians were dark seing only an occasional light in an upstairs window. Everything looked ghostlike in the thickening fog. Hearing someone behind me, I spun around my heart pounding, but it was only my own footsteps echoing in the empty street.

The old, run-down Victorian on the corner was large and gave off a scary vibe. I tried walking past quickly. Something stopped me. When I looked up at a dim light shining from an upstairs window, I experienced a vision and saw an old woman lying in bed and waiting to die. Her bedroom was mostly bare and illuminated by a single, naked light bulb and feeling her pain of loneliness and isolation. When the vision suddenly shifted, to my horror, I saw it was me lying in that bed waiting for eternity.

Reeling from grief and confusion, I walked blocks through the abandoned neighborhood without seeing another person or even a parked car and was beginning to believed I was the last person alive on Earth. When a dim light blinked from out of the darkness giving me hope, I came upon a tiny store, an open sign flickering in the window, and COSMIC GROCERY in gold letters across the front. How strange a shop would be open among all the emptiness. I peered in through the window, my fear held me from going inside. But cold and lonely and overwhelmed by the emptiness of the neighborhood—and the barrenness of my life—I entered feeling a strange reverence.

It was a humble little store with only a few packages of beans and spaghetti on mostly empty shelves. A Filipino woman entered from the back. She was a tiny wisp of a person, slim and not even five feet tall, but she smiled warmly. "Good evening," she said in

John-Paul Cernak

a high, squeaky voice. "What brings you out on such a cold and foggy evening?"

"Saw a movie at the theater," I mumbled.

"Hope it was a good one. Good night to be inside. What can I get for you this evening?"

"I have only a dime to spend."

She smiled. "Candy bars are only ten cents."

Her friendliness quickly diminished my fears. I took extra time looking at the meager selection under glass and basked in her warmth before deciding. She was the first person who smiled and talked with me in a day filled with loneliness and pain. I chose a chocolate bar, and as I handed her my dime, she suddenly pointed past me to the street. "Look! Look!" she squeaked, "Hippies! Hippies!"

The fog lifted, and I saw a group of odd-looking people dressed in strange clothes walking under a streetlight. They all had long hair, even the men. I never saw that before. It was a time when every patriotic American male wore a crew cut. The first Flower Children moved into the Haight. What attracted me most was their peaceful vibe that felt soothing and calm. When I turned back to face her, almost unnoticed, my gloom lifted, and I felt restored.

The Spirit led me to her store and was a shrine and spoke to me through that woman telling me I came to San Francisco to experience a revolution of consciousness, and it would change my life forever. Was the Spirit speaking to me again ten years later, while I sat on empty Haight Street telling me the revolution was over, and it was time to leave?

Feeling groggy, I picked myself up on wobbly legs and turned up Cole Street. When I saw parked cars, the world came back to the way it was in 1973. Several Victorians along the block were receiving facelifts, and I remembered the new people moving in. With increasing numbers, I saw them going to work mornings and returning evenings in a neighborhood where almost no one worked. They walked stiffly like zombies afraid to make eye contact. "It's the zombies," I said aloud. "They're buying up the great old houses and kicking the hippies out!"

At Carl Street, after coming out of the tunnel, the N Judah streetcar raced towards me, and the.motorman angrily clanged his warning when I dashed across against the red light. The block ahead changed from Victorians to commercial businesses. The Sunday morning crowd gathered at Bradley's Corner, the gay bar, and music and conversation floated out. In the middle of the block, a lone customer browsed Patrick's open-air produce stand. As I unlocked the door to the shop, several intoxicated women exited Maud's, the lesbian bar next door, and their loud talking broke the Sunday morning quiet.

<hr />

ALTHOUGH SAFELY BACK, I FELT NERVOUS AND AGITATED AND strangely annoyed after remembering Alex's cryptic remark that I was in danger. As I undressed for my shower next to my closet in the front of the building, I anxiously watched the large windows that looked out into the street. Although covered with heavy lace curtains to prevent anyone passing from seeing in, something was making me nervous. Seconds later, a woman's face suddenly appeared in the window, her nose pressed against the glass. She looked in just as I dropped my short to the floor. Standing there helplessly naked, I froze hoping she wouldn't see me. But she scanned looking around. When our eyes met, she quickly withdrew and revealed a shock of blonde hair. Feeling a strange arousal, I pulled up my pants and opened the door. She was a straight chick in her early twenties and stood pressed against the building trying to hide. "Would you like to come in and look around?" I asked. She stifled a giggle and hesitated in the doorway.

"I sometimes wait here for the bus," she said, "and because of the strange name of your establishment, I've wondered what goes on in here."

"It's a print shop and some other stuff. I'm Jack."

John-Paul Cernak

"Hi, I'm Meg." She gave me a nervous little wave and came inside. "A print shop, and what other stuff?"

"This was a graphics communication center. Everyone's gone except Frank. He lives in the studio upstairs, but I hardly see him. I'm the printer, but the shop's for sale. Someone could walk in any day plunk down the cash, and I'm gone."

As we talked, I quickly became aware she looked into my window at precisely the moment I dropped my shorts. I always believed there was no such thing as coincidence. When our eyes met, I experienced a queasy feeling that felt familiar and quickly remembered it was the same churning in the pit of my stomach when I saw the lion vanished up in the Marin Hills and experienced the vision of people riding horses. Was there a connection between the young chick who inexplicably entered my life and the cat? But when I looked at her closely, my focus changed, and any awareness I had quickly evaporated.

She was tall and busty but a little plump and awkward, as if she hadn't yet learned to live in her body. She had a round, youthful face, and her bleached blonde hair seemed incongruous on someone as young and unsophisticated. She over-applied her blue eyeliner and painted her lips beyond their natural borders making them too large and overly red. It seemed obvious she wanted to be noticed but didn't know how to dress. If I gave her a grade on her clothes, it would be an "F" for the unhappy-looking, nondescript pair of pants and jacket, along with a dumb little hat and round glasses that gave her an owlish look. Yet strangely, something about her intrigued me. She followed as I walked along the corridor. "And what are all these doors?" she asked.

"They're studios that were occupied by designers, photographers and typesetters." When we reached a door painted a different color, I opened it. "This is my studio," I said.

A multi-colored batik spread hung above a large bed in a small, lightly furnished, windowless room. She stood looking in for a long moment her feet wide apart and her hands on her hips. When she turned, one knee pointed towards me. "You live here?" she asked.

"The building has a kitchen and shower and all the conveniences of home." I put my hand under her elbow, and she moved closer at my touch. "You want to get together for a drink?" I asked.

"Sure! But I'm on my way to a women's meeting."

Bummer! She's a feminist, and I almost said forget it. I wasn't against equality, but those I knew were pushy and difficult to be around. I'm not sure why I let it ride with her. "I live in the neighborhood," she said, "and I'll be coming back this way later."

"Groovy! Stop by." The bus was pulling up when I opened the door to let her out, and when she wiggled her butt getting aboard, I felt a familiar stirring in my groin.

Under the shower, with hot water soothing sore muscles, her image danced around in my head, and my nervous agitation quickly shifted into a mood of anticipation. It was a while since I was with a woman, and I felt excited. My enthusiasm quickly tempered when an uneasy feeling rose up from deep inside and warned me she was trouble. Maybe it's best I forget about her. Strangely, I immediately ignored my intuition and said aloud: "What am I worried about? I'm not marrying the chick. She's just a roll in the hay."

———◦◦◦———

I FELT ON EDGE ALL AFTERNOON WONDERING IF SHE'D RETURN, and I couldn't stop watching the clock. Quit it, I scolded. Why am I getting uptight? She wasn't that hot. Around four, I accepted she wasn't coming, and for some reason, I felt really disappointed. The doorbell rang an hour later. Racing from the rear of the shop, I opened the door breathing hard and stared at the woman standing there hardly recognizing her. "Come in," I stammered.

Smiling, she paused in the doorway giving me a chance to look her over. Now that was more like it. Dressed in high heels and a short red skirt that showed off her long legs, she was almost as tall as I was and looked more mature and very seductive. My insides were doing summersaults. Taking her hand, I led her inside still not fully comprehending she was the same person I met that morning. She smelt delicious when I gave her a quick hug and quickly realized I overlooked some significant details. What I called that morning, "a little plump" had delightfully metamorphosed into voluptuousness, and she wasn't wearing a bra. Now with makeup skillfully applied, her blonde hair gave her a touch of sophistication. "Well!" I said, a little flustered, "Let's get going."

As evening approached, I drove to my favorite drinking establishment on Clement Street. Bill's bar was a lowbrow salon with free peanuts and sawdust on the floor, and I went there for almost as long as I lived in the city. It was a hippie hangout with friendly people and cheap beer, but mostly, I went there because it was a place without pretention. When driving up, I was stunned at seeing how everything changed. I hadn't been there for a while, and in my absence, new owners took over and give the place a remake. It looked totally different on the outside, with new signs and lighting, but the real shocker came when we walked inside.

Plush sofas and upholstered chairs replaced old rickety furniture. Beautifully framed art graced the walls and huge ferns hung everywhere. Even the name changed and shared a designation with a famous Russian novel. At the bar, I looked for a familiar face from the old place but saw only strangers. Two guys eyed Meg as I guided her past and to a far corner away from the other customers.

We sat opposite each other next to large windows in chairs upholstered in bright, colored fabrics. Feeling out of place in that glitzy new bar, I fidgeted nervously and watched a waitress sashaying her way around the furniture coming to take our order. Beautifully dressed in high-heels and ankle length skirt, her hair piled high on top of her head, she represented the new, impersonal, and indifferent direction society was taking. San Franciscans always dressed elegantly, but somehow this was different. Missing was the warmth and friendliness and the old tradition of helping and looking out for each other. Lately, the cooperation degenerated into a dog-eat-dog competition. It didn't feel good anymore, and

I longed for the friendly, more laid-back days of the 1960s.

I remembered when I arrived, the tallest buildings were around twenty-five stories. On a visit to the Financial District recently, I was lost. I worked downtown and knew it well. In the past few years, new buildings fifty and sixty stories high were added to the skyline. I called it the 'Manhattinization' of San Francisco. The corporations came in and took over similar to what was happening in the neighborhoods. Like this bar, the big money boys came in, bought up a few of the smaller operations they could buy cheaply, and drove the others out of business. Our waitress arrived wearing a Mona Lisa smile. "What'll you all gonna have?" she cooed, in a deep southern drawl.

We ordered beer. I sat back and listened to "Hey Jude" playing on the jukebox and still marveling at the young chick's transformation. She sat with her legs crossed looking relaxed and pushed her shoulder-length hair behind her ears to keep it out of her face. She smiled when our eyes met. As the song ended, our waitress brought our drinks. "Here's to you, Meg," I said, and we clinked glasses. When I suddenly remembered the warning I received about her under the shower, I studied her closely trying to pick up anything unusual. She looked at me curiously. "What's wrong?" She asked.

"Why do you think there's something wrong?"

"You have a pained look on your face."

"I don't like the changes."

"So many. Which are you talking about?"

"Take this bar for instance; it was a comfortable old place with lots of free stuff. Now it's all uppity with high prices to match, and did you get a look at our waitress?"

"She's attractive and beautifully dressed."

"I agree she's pretty, but it's all façade. She's wearing a painted on smile and emotionally remote."

"Waitressing is a tough job, especially in a cocktail bar. After a few drinks, customers become impossible."

"When it was still the old place, I came here after my divorce to

14   *John-Paul Cernak*

meet with old friends and feel good. The waitresses wore miniskirts. On slow nights, they'd sit and talk. I took one home one night, or rather, she took me home. She must have felt sorry for me."

She held my eyes in a steady gaze. "Was she pretty?"

I hesitated before answering thinking up a cool reply. "Yes, she was, but not as pretty as you are." She smiled. I scored points.

"It's strange you're living in your shop," she said, changing the subject. "Can't you afford an apartment?"

"My ex and I owned one of the Victorians near-by, and when the judge ordered it sold, I moved into the shop. It'll have to do until I decide what's next, and I don't have the slightest idea yet what next is. Well, except I've always wanted to live in the country."

"You'd want to leave this beautiful city? Aren't you an established businessman or something? What about all your friends?"

"Ah! My fucking friends." I laughed. "Bless their pea-picking hearts. After the divorce, most became her friends, and the others I don't see much anymore. Married people don't invite singles. Yeah! Since I was a kid, I fantasized about living in the wilderness. I've always believed I was born in the wrong century. I recently saw the movie, Jeremiah Johnson. He was a mountain man living among the Indians, and the flick stirred something deep inside me."

"Strange you should say that. I often feel the same. For years, I had a recurring dream of living on the frontier."

"You too! Right on! I have dreams all the time, but I can't make any sense of them."

As we talked, we looked deeply into each other's eyes, and our conversation became more intimate. I was already feeling a pleasant buzz from the beer. Holding up two fingers, I caught the waitress' eye to let her know we needed a refill.

Through the windows, I watched as night descended upon the city. As daylight faded, the day people left, and as the night people hadn't yet arrived, the bar emptied leaving only a few scattered customers. The bright sun during the day was too harsh, and the intense darkness of late night muddled my thinking. Evenings were my time of day, and I felt soothed and inspired by the low light. My mind worked best a few hours before and after sunset, and I was most in tune with my environment and the people around me.

Our talking paused when the waitress brought our drinks, and as we sat quietly for a few moments, something interesting happened. I was suddenly in her head. I could feel what she was feeling and somehow knew what she was thinking. And we were on the same page emotionally. She wanted to cuddle but was hesitant because we just met. I whispered to her with my thoughts that she was safe, and our merging together was such a beautiful way to spend the evening. It worked, and I could feel her moving closer. With desire written across her face, our lips inches apart ready to kiss, loud music blared out from the jukebox breaking the mood. She sat back looking detached. I had to do something quickly to save the situation. Impulsively, I said something I shouldn't have forgetting about the warnings under the shower. "Hey! You wanna move to the country with me."

She sat quietly, her face a blank. Slowly, a smile formed on her lips, and she beamed. "Wow! What a great idea. I'd love to! It sounds like a total gas."

Taking her hand, I pulled her close and we kissed. "Outta sight! Let's celebrate. By the way, what do you do?"

"I work for a travel agency in the Financial District."

"You sell travel?"

She smiled and shook her head. "I'm a typist."

"Is it a good job with a future?"

Her mood shifted and looked agitated. "It's a stupid job with a crappy company and a male chauvinist-pig boss who thinks he can cop a feel whenever he likes. It's another company run by men who rip off their employees. The owners make big bucks while the workers, mostly women, work for peanuts. They're all the same. I'd like to dump them all into the bay."

"If they're so bad, why don't you quit?"

"I like to eat."

John-Paul Cernak

I disliked her opinion of men but liked how she railed against the system. She's kind of young, but maybe it would work living in the country together, as long as she doesn't turn her wrath in my direction. She said yes, while the others only looked at me as if I was crazy.

On the drive back, a thousand lights shined down from the surrounding hills reminding me how beautiful the city was at night. I had an instant love affair when I arrived and knew it was where I belonged. I liked everything about her, even the fog and cold and walked every street and roamed every hill of her forty-nine square miles delighting in her architecture. The best part was I experienced her through the 1960s. It was perhaps her most glorious era in a long and celebrated history. But sadly, it looked increasingly like I'd actually leave, something I thought would never happen. I finally found someone who would move to the country with me, but instead of feeling excited, I was saddened at the thought of leaving San Francisco.

I caught a red light on Stanyon Street across from the park and waited in a long line of cars to make a left turn onto Haight. When I turned, unlike the morning, the street was crowded with people congregating in front of bars, cafes, and restaurants. They spilled out into the street slowing traffic to a crawl. The revolution wasn't over yet. In the commotion, I spotted Skye, a young hippie who lived across the street from me. He always had that far away look in his eyes and reminded me of the late Jim Morrison of The Doors. The young hippie chicks loved him, and two or three pretty little ladies always hung around ready to get it on. When I beeped, he waved and yelled back. "I'll stop by and see you, man."

Turning at the corner, I slid into a parking space. "Things are definitely slowing in the Haight," I remarked. "I wouldn't have been able to park this close a year ago."

"Where're we headed?"

"To Andy's Russian Restaurant just around the corner."

A group of young hippies sat on the sidewalk in front sharing a joint, and a teenybopper— twelve or thirteen—called out in a pleading voice. "Hey, man! Spare some change?"

Grabbing a few coins from my pocket, I dropped them into his cupped hands. They all scrambled around to see what they scored.

The restaurant was crowded and with a décor I called "Early Haight-Ashbury." Naked bulbs hung from the ceiling and food stains smeared stark white walls. None of the tables and chairs matched, and most had names and dates carved into them. We sat at the counter on stools bolted to the floor of what was once the soda fountain of a drug store, the smell of Russian food mingling with the unmistakable, potent aroma of Patchouli oil. The owner was a dour woman who always wore a babushka and badgered her husband in Russian. Although I ate there many times, she never smiled or greeted me but served some of the best ethnic food this side of Moscow at reasonable prices. The carte du jour was excellent, but mostly, I went to watch hippies.

Wearing dancer's tights, long hair, huge beard and large circular hat, the hippie freak sitting behind us at a table looked like Zorro. His lady was a slim chick dressed in all black, and leaned heavily on his arm. The longhaired dude next to us nodded as we took our seats. Although he looked good in a frilly-laced shirt open to his navel beneath a black leather vest, there was something about him that told me he was a weekend tripper and was a straight guy with a full-time job. Two attractive escorts flanked him and listened attentively. The tails of their white shirts tied in front revealed bare midriffs and deep cleavages. "But they're so beautiful," said Meg.

I moved closer to hear over the din. "What do you mean?"

"Why would anyone so pretty want to be a hippie?"

"That's the same question my wife asked when we first moved into the Haight. It's because straight is boring and hippie is fun." We sat silently studying the menu printed on a chalkboard behind the counter. "What are you having?" I asked. "I'm having what I usually have, borscht and piroshky."

"I'll have the same," she said. "What's borscht and piroshky?"

She never said anything about taking her home, so I drove back to the shop. Frank's upstairs light was out when I led her by the hand through the dark corridor into my studio. Switching on a small table lamp, I sat on the bed and pulled her down next to me. She looked around nervously, as if she wasn't sure it was safe to be there. While I found rock music on the radio and burned incense, she inspected posters hanging on the wall. "I like your little pad," she said finally and sat down looking more relaxed.

From a cabinet, I removed a half-filled bottle of red wine, and poured us each a glass. Reaching under the bed, I removed an old White Owl cigar box. Inside was a baggie filled with dried herb and a pack of Zigzag rolling papers. "Is that marijuana?" she asked.

I nodded. "It's Colombian. Have you ever smoked?"

"Only once, but I didn't get much out of it."

She sat close and watched intently as I dumped some of the weed into the box, separated the herb from the seeds and stems, and rolled a joint. Taking a deep hit, I passed it over. Her hand trembled when she toked and quickly exhaled. "Hold it in for as long as you can," I said. "It won't hurt you."

My senses quickly heightened from the effects of the herb, and I saw the light shining brighter and felt the rhythm of the music more intently. All evening, I was aware of her sensuality, but high on pot, sex oozed out of her every pore. We kissed passionately. When I reached up beneath her blouse and cupped her breasts, something I wanted to do all evening, there was no bra to stop me. She became a wildcat ripping at my clothes. Hugging and kissing on the bed, her skin like velvet, our minds and bodies merged into a divine sacrament of love.

CHAPTER 2

I WANTED TO BE GONE, BUT AFTER SIX MONTHS, I WAS STILL there. With only Frank remaining, the shop felt empty after Isabel left. When the house sold, the shop was our only connection, and working together only prolonged the pain and heartache of the divorce. She balked when I asked her to move her office to another location. To convince her it was in her best interest, I hid some type fonts she needed to finish a job. She called me every name in the book, but it persuaded her. On the day she moved, I helped carry her equipment into a rented truck. "The least I can do," I said, "is help you move your things."

"I can manage just fine," she snapped.

"While you're here, neither of us can start something new."

She hustled past me angrily and made a soft clicking sound with her tongue in disapproval. "It hasn't seemed to have stopped you so far."

"They were only flings," I said, to her back. Carrying a large box, she stopped, leaned it against the wall for support, and gave me a disgusted look. "I know you're angry," I continued. "What I did was crappy, but you wouldn't listen. You said you'd move when you were good and ready, and that might not be for a long time. For me to move presses, cutters, and a lot of heavy equipment didn't make sense. I'm really sorry. I didn't want it to end this way."

She looked at me for a long minute before answering. "Okay, you can help. Grab those boxes over there."

She came back inside when the truck was loaded. I saw pain when she took my hand and looked deeply into my eyes. "Goodbye, Jack, I hope all goes well for you."

I squeezed her hand and returned her gaze. "You too, Isabel."

She gave me a quick hug and walked out. After I heard the truck drive off, all the pain and sadness of the breakup exploded into my consciousness—along with the realization we would never be together again—and the weight of my feelings pushed me down to the floor where I sobbed uncontrollably.

———◦◦◦———

I MISSED THE VICTORIAN ISABEL AND I OWNED. IT WAS A BEAU-tiful old house, but I can't complain. I enjoyed it while I had it. When we separated, she moved in with her mother, and I occupied the house alone. I had my way with all the women I invited into that Victorian splendor. They couldn't resist me, but I never let myself forget it was mostly to the house they were responding and not necessarily to me. When escrow closed, I moved into the shop. It seemed important to spend time alone and consider what's next. I met Meg three months later. It felt good to be involved with a woman again, even if it was to be only temporary. She was perceptive, intelligent, and uninhibited in bed. But I was unable to shake the recurring feeling that to be with her would lead to disaster, and the more time we spent together, the more persistent the warnings became. Before ending the affair, I wanted friends to meet her and hear their opinions.

We visited Roy on a warm, Northern California afternoon. He lived with Marianna in Bolinas on the foggy Marin Coast. The town was located in a densely wooded area about two miles off Highway 1 adjacent to the newly created Point Reyes National Seashore, but unless you knew which road to take, it was hard to find. Bolinas was filled with hippies. It was where they moved when leaving the city. As quickly as the highway department put up signs, the refugees from the Haight-Ashbury removed them.

Marianna owned a trendy, hippie boutique, and Roy painted in oil, played guitar, and built distinctive furniture from junk lumber he reclaimed from the dump. Many of his customers were rock stars living in large houses along the coast. Isabel admired his work and purchased several pieces. I inherited one of them in our divorce settlement.

I thought of him as a modern, Renaissance man for his multidimensional creativities similar to Leonardo de Vinci. Although often praised for his distinctive furniture, chromatic, abstract oil paintings, and imaginative, innovative music, they were only a secondary focus. His greatest talent was as an actor. He spent several seasons working and living with a theatre ensemble. When the company was in production, the cast stayed in character twenty-four hours a day. They didn't act the part; they became the part.

We were expected for dinner. Roy answered the door, and the sneer on his face gave me an uneasy feeling. "It's good to see you, man," I said. "I don't see you much since you moved."

He immediately went into character. "All motion is relative. Perhaps it is you who has moved by standing still, and who is this young trollop you brought for our inspection? Apparently, someone's been feeding her too well."

I'm uncertain which characters Roy assumed, but with his dramatic acting skills, he hurled barbs at us all evening veiled in excerpts from different parts he played. He was short and stocky and reminded me of Charles Boyer, the old-time French actor. When he wanted, he could be as charming and debonair as the actor. At other times, he was coarse and overbearing as he was that evening, and it was a difficult side to handle. I never saw him quite as bad. He was quick-witted and scornful of anyone slow on the uptake and for most of the evening had Meg tongue-tied under his barrage. When she looked to Marianna for support, she threw her hands up in helplessness. His verbal torrent was a little much even for me, and I jabbed back calling him a groupie in reference to selling his furniture to rock stars. He became civil only once during the evening when we talked about the city. "Do you get in much?" I asked.

"Went to see my dad a couple of weeks ago."

"Did you notice all the remodeling going on in the Haight?"

"It's changing. It's all straight people moving in, and they're buying up all the Old Victorians. Next to the hippies, they look out of place."

"I call them the zombies."

"Good name, I talked with a few, and they're a bunch of carpetbaggers and totally bourgeois."

"Amen," I said.

As I drove home along the coast breathing cool, fresh ocean air, the sun hitting the horizon and the surf gentle at day's end, it felt good to be out of the hot seat. Meg sat silently huddled against the door. I wanted an opinion from Roy, but everything remained uncertain. Was he angry with me for my divorce from Isabel, or was he reacting to Meg? A second opinion came soon thereafter from an unexpected source.

Don Juan walked into the print shop several months earlier and quickly became a regular. He was a Yaqui Indian from Sonora in Northern Mexico, but I was unsure who he was. I believed he was Indian, because he looked Native American. We were totally different people from different cultures, but I felt a strange attachment to him. He possessed a keen wisdom, and life for him was full of joy and happiness. He loved to dance and sing, and I called him the Yaqui Bo Jangles. When he visited, he usually brought a joint to smoke and something to drink. "Hey, amigo! I bring you chuko-chuko," his name for marijuana, and from beneath his overcoat, he'd produce an expensive bottle of wine he probably lifted from the grocery store across the street. "I want to tell you about the beautiful witch I had last night. She screamed with pleasure."

He spoke good English with a Mexican accent. About a week later, Meg was at the shop during one of his visits. "Meet Don Juan," I said. The animosity between them was instant. Neither acknowledged the introduction, and Don Juan's natural exuberance quickly diminished. "And what do you do?" she asked, when it was apparent he was a street person, her tone and expression cold and judgmental.

"I'm a person of the world, " he replied. "Amigo, I just remembered, I need to see a friend. I see you tomorrow."

Because I was moving to the country and unhooking from society, I gave away all my business suits I hadn't worn in years, and Don Juan took one of them. The next day when he came in, he was wearing the blue suit with vest I gave him, and it looked tailor-made. I couldn't believe the transition. He could have been a prosperous businessman and even spoke differently. When I mentioned Meg, he shook his head negatively. His uncharacteristic seriousness told me what I needed to know. After witnessing Don Juan's reaction, I remembered Roy never relaxed all evening. Their responses reinforced the negative warnings I was receiving.

Although I planned to end the affair on Saturday night after dinner and a few drinks at a restaurant, I has some misgivings and was aware bringing it to closure would put a crimp in my plans. If I didn't move to the country after the print shop sold, I would have to find a job or start another business, and neither choice appealed to me.

While running a press in the back of the shop on Saturday morning, the doorbell rang. Strolling up to the front, I could see Meg's blonde hair through the translucent window next to the door and wondered why she came so early. We weren't supposed to be getting together until that evening. She was crying when I opened the door. "Come in," I said. "What's happening?"

"The miserable bitch I live with is moving her boyfriend in and kicking me out. I don't have money for a deposit on another apartment. I'm homeless, and I'm moving in with you." With that, she threw herself into my arms, clamped her lips against mine, and plunged her tongue down my throat. Brushing her hand across my crotch, she immediately knew my answer and led me into my studio. Stunned and overwhelmed by her nakedness in my arms pleasuring me, I couldn't think clearly. Was letting her move in the right decision? Had I become too good a salesmen, and was I getting more than I bargained for? But what the hell! What harm could it do! Although her moving in never felt quite right, with each passing day, I was less inclined to do anything about it.

Several weeks later, we took a weekend drive north along California's Coastal Highway 1. Once past the small town of Stinson Beach, the road follows the shoreline. Northern California is redwood country, and in the distance along the skyline were the giant trees and a hundred feet below the pounding Pacific. After exploring the towns of Mendocino and Fort Bragg, we stayed at a motel on the beach in West Port, the last town on the highway two hundred miles north of San Francisco in Mendocino County. Sand blew into our room under the door. Standing at the edge of the continent at day's end, the surf licking at our feet, we watched the sun disappear into the sea.

The area had few inhabitants and little traffic. Returning home the next day, we parked along a deserted beach a few miles south of town and watched waves crash against a rocky shore. A west wind pushed in occasional puffs of fog blocking out the sun but quickly burned off. Across the highway, the land shot up steeply for a half mile or more before reaching trees. I was feeling an unusual restlessness. "I'm going to climb the hill," I said. "Come with me."

"I'll stay in the car where it's nice and warm, thank you," she retorted.

It was steeper than I thought. The hill was empty, except for a few sheep grazing near the top. About half way up, I spotted two deer across a narrow gully where small trees grew. It seemed unusual because they usually ran when you came close. It was a doe and her fawn, and there was something unusual about them. I could hardly see them even though they were only a short distance across and somehow blended into the background. When I stopped and looked at them, the doe spoke to me. "She will give you children," she said.

She must have spoken telepathically because I didn't actually hear her words out loud. Nonetheless, I understood her clearly. I was unable to move until they wandered off and felt woozy and unsteady when returning to the car. "Did you enjoy the climb?" Meg asked. "You sure stayed up there a long time. What was going on?"

"Oh, nothing!" I replied. "Nothing!"

The talking deer had a profound effect on me. If she told me I'd win the lottery or some other such information, I would have shrugged off the incident as unimportant. But when she said Meg would give me children, I had to consider what was said more seriously. Isabel announced shortly after our wedding she didn't want kids, and I meekly acquiesced. How vital was it for me to have offspring? Until then, it seemed inconsequential. But more crucially, if she gave me progeny, as the deer prophesized, would it lay to rest any fears I might have that I made the wrong decision in choosing her, or rather, in letting her select me? While I accepted Meg hesitantly, we were now a couple, and the warnings I was receiving seemed irrelevant and blocked them from my consciousness.

———————

FRANK WAS THE LAST TENANT IN THE LARGE BUILDING ON COLE Street, and although he was the President of the San Francisco Chapter of the Sexual Freedom League, he was a very private person. At times, I wouldn't see him for days. If it weren't for the lights and soft music coming from his studio, I'd forget he was up there. I didn't tell him immediately the shop was for sale. A few days earlier, he related that his relationship with the cute redheaded chick he was seeing had ended, and he looked depressed.

A week later, we worked together in the darkroom. He was putting together the league newspaper. I was shooting halftones from photographs of people having sex taken at league parties that he would publish in the journal. After switching on the red photo lights, I perceived something unusual. Frank looked and sounded different, and his vibe felt discordant. I brushed it off as imagination and continued working as if everything was normal. A loud hissing sound from the suction board on the large camera holding the film in place interrupted our conversation, and a brilliant light flashed

John-Paul Cernak

inside when I tripped the shutter. He spoke after a long silence: "This is my last issue. I'm resigning from the league presidency and turning the chapter over to Steve."

I was shocked. "What will you do?"

"I took a job with a travel agency in their graphics department."

"Is it something good?"

He shrugged. "Not really."

Then I dropped the bomb. The timing was bad, but he had to know: "The shop's for sale. When it sells, you'll probably have to move."

He sat staring into space looking exhausted. The second the ceiling lights came on, he walked out. He became even more reclusive in the following weeks, and I rarely saw him. One day, I received a call from Isabel. It was the first time we talked since she moved. "Jack, I have bad news."

"What's happening?"

"Frank's dead. His body was found up in the Marin Hills where he shot himself."

WHEN THE PRINT SHOP SUDDENLY SOLD, WE DISCOVERED RENTS in the Bay Area spiked sharply. In better areas of Marin County and on the peninsula, our applications were flatly rejected when landlords saw my long hair and beard. They didn't want a hippie living in their apartments. It was the first time I experienced discrimination, and I didn't like it one bit. To save money, we rented a flat in an old, dilapidated Victorian on Castro Street about a mile south of the gay area in the Noe Valley district. The building dated back to the 1880s and was in such poor condition, I felt queasy merely looking at the peeling paint, rickety windows, and weeds growing out through cracked concrete everywhere. We managed to get the inside looking fairly good after a week of patching and painting walls. We lived on the second floor keeping us further away from the spiders, slugs, and other creepy crawlies. An occasional mouse found its way in, although the flat was free from *la cucarachas*.

We settled easily into domestic life. Meg went to work each day, and I—the house husband—provided a clean house and tasty meals. There was an old gas heater in the living room that we used as our bedroom, and there we slept, stayed warm, and made love in Meg's queen bed throughout the winter of 73/74. But beneath the surface, the intent of moving to the country continued to percolate. Still, I was in no hurry to make the change. After the intensity of the 1960s, the frenzied activity of the print shop, and the unsettling divorce, it felt good to kick back and enjoy the sensation of floating from day to day without concerns. With all of the old doors closed, it was one of the few times in my life when the world seemed in balance, while softly in the distance, I heard new doors opening.

After I introduced Meg to marijuana, she took to it totally. Wine was her favorite until the first night in my studio. After making love under its influence, she made sure we were never without it. I planted seeds in pots that spring, and after they grew about a foot high, I found the plants laying down and dying after forgetting to water them. Having resolved myself I wasn't supposed to grow, I emptied the soil into the backyard. Sometime later, I spotted a small plant growing where I deposited the soil. I was afraid it would be discovered and almost pulled it out until I saw it grew in an ideal location. It was concealed from the street and neighbors views by large bushes, and I let it grow. With minimal care, it grew over six feet high, was loaded with cream-colored flowers, and was, undoubtedly, the best marijuana I ever smoked. Several friends asked to buy some and offered to pay a premium. I declined. It was too good to sell. But from the experience, I learned how easy it was to grow something everyone wanted and for which they were all willing to pay a high price.

CHAPTER 3

"Hey, man! Get a move on. Remember, I have a job."

My friend Phil was giving me a ride across the bay. "Ok! Ok!" I said, and grabbing my backpack and sleeping bag, we were on our way.

The morning sun shined in our eyes, and the car shook when he floored the old Chevy and merged into traffic heading east on the lower deck of the Bay Bridge. With San Francisco's skyline fading fast and with water beneath, I felt the excitement of the road. He dropped me off in Berkeley on Interstate 80.

As heavy traffic whizzed past on a warm June morning, I stood hitchhiking on the shoulder of the freeway and remembering the sweet kisses Meg gave me before I left and already missing her. It would be six weeks before I'd see her again. I thought for sure she'd be pissed as hell when I told her my plans of thumbing across the country to see mom. I was surprised at how easily she accepted I would be gone that long. All she said was: "That's fine with me."

Our relationship was going so well that I almost canceled my trip. But mom was getting old, and this might be my last chance to see her before she left the planet. What I hadn't told her yet was that I intended to begin looking for land in the country when I returned. After only a few minutes, an older, Ford panel truck peeled off from the heavy traffic and stopped next to me. The window came down on the passenger side with two guys inside. "Where're you heading, man?" asked the driver from the other side of the cab.

"Chicago," I said loudly over the freeway noise.

"Get in; we're going to New York."

Wow! All the way in one ride. Throwing my backpack into the rear of the van, I tumbled in after.

Interstate 80 hugs the east shore of San Francisco Bay. At the north end near the town of Vallejo, the freeway swings east and winds its way through the Sacramento Valley, the agricultural heartland of California, and through the Sierra Nevada Mountains. It's a short hop into Reno, and from there, I-80 crosses the open plateau land of Nevada and into Salt Lake City. I took my turn driving the truck that had a steering problem and was all over the road.

My two companions were New Yorkers going home. We camped for the night at a rest stop somewhere in Utah, and I slept on the grass in my sleeping bag. We were back on the road at first light, and after a night of strange dreams, I awoke questioning where the adventure was in reaching my destination in one ride. As the sun peeked over the horizon on a fresh new day, I bid my companions farewell somewhere in southwestern Wyoming. That was where my trip really began.

After traveling at seventy-five miles an hour talking and laughing with my companions, without a house or car in sight, I walked in total silence down a sun-drenched, black-topped road that stretched in a straight line to purple mountains on the horizon called the Wind River Range. A lone hawk circled lazily in the clear blue sky above the desert. In a short time, a cowboy gave me a lift.

Up close, there was something majestically beautiful about those jagged peaks that affected me in a deep, spiritual way. While hitchhiking along a highway that ran parallel and up to the Shoshone Indian Reservation, I saw bright points of light flashing off the rocks that hypnotized me. While sitting across in a deep altered state, I experienced a vision of riding horses, having a wife and infant daughter, and spending time alone in the wilderness on a vision quest. It was winter in my revelation, and I was worried. Deep snow covered the ground preventing me from hunting, and I feared starvation. What I experienced was a past life. As my con-

John-Paul Cernak

sciousness returned to my present reality, my mind was suddenly filled with images after I remembered having a similar incident years earlier, while visiting a small community not that far from where I hitchhiked.

The memory took me back to when I was a kid just out of high school, and I was in Sheridan, Wyoming, an isolated town in the central part of the state on the Montana Border in the heart of the Great Plains. I was there to help open a new store for the company I worked for. At first, I was hesitant to go. What does a sophisticated big city kid like me have in common with country hicks? Little did I know what lay ahead.

After boarding the redeye at LAX, I flew all night. On the plane's final approach to Sheridan's Airport, from 20,000 feet above the Earth, catching reds and golds reflecting off the Big-horn Mountains to the west, the rising sun staged an amazing lightshow and sent me and the other passengers into delight. The colors and images displayed inside on the cabin walls awakened some long forgotten memories and began the transformation of my consciousness. "Thank you for flying Western Airlines," said the captain, his voice coming over the intercom. "The temperature in Sheridan is thirty degrees."

Wearing only a light jacket, I didn't feel cold in the crisp, dry air of the Great Plains. What I felt was an exquisite tranquility and a deep, subconscious recognition that this was where I was from and that I had come home. On a walk through the town that first morning, I discovered Sheridan's architecture looked as if it came from a Hollywood movie set of an old 'Wild West' town and gave the impression I somehow time-traveled into the past. Wearing buckskin and large-brimmed circular hats, angry-looking Indians lurking in dark doorways and in the shadows of buildings seemed to lunge out at me as I passed. Their hostile vibe and attitude seemed to say: "We are still at war with you."

I stayed at the Old Sheridan Inn built in the 1890s. The hotel was a large multi-storied wooden structure with numerous tiny dormers built in a straight line atop a long gabled roof. It was reputed to be haunted. Although I stayed there for three months, I never heard any strange noises. Having a drink at the bar one evening while still under age, I experienced flashes of cowboys drinking whisky and wearing six guns. I gave the vision little credence after having several beers. I then learned it was the same bar where Buffalo Bill Cody did his drinking, and it increased the uncanny feeling of familiarity I experienced since arriving.

The new store was still under construction and filled with carpenters, painters, and electricians putting on the finishing touches. I quickly made friends with a bunch of local people. Taking me under their wing, the older guys showed the young city kid around and introduced me to their Western Culture. With everyone outside in the sunshine eating sandwiches out of lunch pails, a carpenter named Vincent talked about living on the plains. "We're all fishermen," he said, "but we don't hunt."

"Why not?" I asked.

I remembered his name only because he looked like Vincent van Gogh, and even had red hair and a goatee. "It's too easy." He pointed towards the rolling hills surrounding us. "See those black dots on that hillside?"

I could just make out tiny dots far in the distance. "I see them."

"That's an elk herd, and I can have one in a half hour."

On the weekend, they took me into the mountains. What memories remained from that time were mostly feelings and impressions. Everything else was a blur. I remembered standing at the bottom of a canyon more beautiful and more grand than Grand Canyon, a fast, flowing river at my feet, and the sun's rays triggering prisms of spellbinding, rainbow-colored lights all around me.

After their work at the store was finished, the trade people moved on to other jobs, and I never saw them again. My encounters with them and everything I experienced since arriving blurred the distinction between past and present, and began to dislodge my perception of reality. Everything coalesced on a visit to the battlefield of Custer's Last Stand near Sheridan several weeks later. As I walked uphill on the battlefield feeling the spirituality so strongly that tears streamed down my face, it seemed I hit a wall and could go no further. When I sat on the ground, it was as if someone turned on a movie projector, and I watched the Battle of the Little Bighorn projected on my mind screen as it occurred almost a century earlier. I had returned, and the spot on which I sat was precisely where I fell that day in 1876 when shot off my horse.

My vision revealed I was an Indian warrior and medicine man and belonged to the coyote clan. I saw myself preparing for battle applying war paint and hearing the battle-whoops of my warrior brothers. Wearing a headdress containing many eagle feathers I earned counting coup, I was offered a gun before going into battle. It belonged to a dead soldier. I refused to touch it. I chose to fight in close, hand-to-hand combat. I wanted to see the agony on my enemy's face when I killed him. Riding my palomino I was one with and holding the carved handle of my tomahawk, I led a charge uphill seeking revenge against Long Hair for killing my wife and child and massacring the people of my village. I felt contempt and anger for the white soldiers, their leader, and the system they represented for all the lies and broken promises.

The battlefield was in disarray without defined battle lines. Scattered around were small groups of soldiers who were quickly surrounded and easily annihilated. Firing came from near the top where soldiers killed their horses and used the dead animals for cover. I loathed anyone who would kill his horse. Dismounting a short distance off, I worked my way towards a small group and learned only one soldier remained alive. He quickly fired his rifle when he saw me. The bullet missed grazing my shoulder. I charged at him screaming a war whoop. He fired a second time. For a moment, I thought I was dead, but his gun misfired. We looked into each other's eyes. It was only for a brief instant, but it felt like a lifetime. I saw fear on his face. He was a big man with a handlebar moustache. I saw soldiers with them at Fort Laramie.

He charged at me using his empty rifle as a club. I easily avoided him and buried my tomahawk into his skull and killed him.

As I rode towards another group of soldiers exhilarated by the joys of killing my enemies, my thirst for the blood of those stealing Indian land had reached a frenzy. The impact of the bullet knocked me off my horse. Feeling a searing pain in my chest and struggling to breath, I lay on the ground looking up at the sky. Although the battle raged around me, all sound was mute, my pony next to me with his head hanging down. I reached up to touch him. Feeling peaceful, I said a prayer to the Great Spirit and hitched a ride on a fluffy cloud floating past as the world faded away.

I didn't understand what I had experienced, and I told no one afraid I was going crazy. It took several days before my consciousness fully reintegrated into my present reality, and I experienced flashbacks for months. The day of my visit to the battlefield was June twenty-fifth, and I learned it was the same day as the battle.

The past life I experienced while hitchhiking merged with the one I remembered on my visit to the battlefield. They were two chapters of the same story of an Indian living on the plains who died defending his people and to preserve a way of live his ancestors lived for thousands of years. Although I remembered visiting Sheridan, the memory of my vision on the battlefield vanished until the day hitchhiking when it returned as clear as if I experienced it the day before. The trades people at the store must have been Indians in their past lives as I was. They took me to a sacred place to help me reconnect with the person I was in my previous incarnation. Learning I lived as an Indian solved the mystery of why I experienced joy each time I heard the Indians defeated Custer at the Battle of the Little Bighorn.

———※———

WHEN A VEHICLE STOPPED TO PICK ME UP, I WAS STILL IN A DREAM state and reluctant to come out, suddenly remembering I was far from home and hitchhiking somewhere in Wyoming. The driver must have noticed my backpack, because I didn't have my thumb out when he stopped. Contrary to popular belief and propaganda spread by the government and supported by the media, hitchhiking was a safe and interesting way to travel. It brought people together, and the establishment saw that as dangerous. Of all the times I thumbed, I encountered few problems, and those times that I did were usually with the police.

There are hazards associated with soliciting rides from strangers as there are with all forms of travel. Hitchhiking could prove dangerous for anyone not fully aware of his or her surroundings, and because of that, I never smoked marijuana when on the road. Similarly, unless you trusted your intuition, it was safer if you adopted a more conventional mode of travel. I never accepted rides from anyone until I could feel their vibe and refused rides after detecting hostility or anger. I could usually read the vibe from a vehicle as it approached and knew if it was safe before it stopped. So, when a shiny, new, red Ford pickup stopped next to me, I quickly shook myself out of my altered state and listened to what my intuition was telling me about the driver.

He was an oil worker with a few days off and out for some R and R. Dressed simply in jeans and T-shirt, he was in good physical shape, and in contrast to my shoulder-length hair and full beard, he was clean shaven and wore his hair cut short. As we started rolling, he extended his hand. "I'm Bill," he said.

I didn't pick up anything dangerous about him, except he was a bit of a hotrod and took unnecessary chances when passing. I casually reached behind me looking for the seatbelt. After driving some miles, we stopped and had lunch at an A&W. I was still a little spacey and paid little attention to what town we were in or how far we traveled. The restaurant was an old-fashioned drive-in where waitresses came out to cars parked under a long, roofed walkway. We choose to stretch our legs and went inside. He walked close to the counter to get the attention of the cashier. "Hi sugar," he said.

We sat in a booth next to the windows to keep an eye on my backpack in the bed of his truck. I looked over the menu for the least expensive item. While hitchhiking, I carried little cash, and if alone, I would have gone to a grocery store and purchased something inexpensive. "Listen man," he said, "I was just paid, and lunch is on me."

I was ready to protest, but changed my mind after realizing how hungry I was. Since last evening, all I ate was a couple of candy bars from a vending machine. "Mighty nice of you, friend."

"Yeah! Just order anything you want."

The bacon and eggs breakfast they served all day sounded good to me. The waitress taking our order was young and pretty and wearing a short skirt. "You sure look good, baby," he said. "How about us getting together?"

On the way out, he teased the cashier and got her to smile. Two women sat eating lunch in their car parked next to his truck. He opened the rear door of their car and started getting in. "Will you please get out." said the driver.

"Oh! Come on, baby. We're meant to be together."

He came on to women a little strong, but what did I know about what was right for small towns in Wyoming? Feeling full and satisfied, I hadn't completely reoccupied my body, and his un-cool behavior seemed unimportant. As we drove out of town, I could see someone in the distance hitchhiking on the shoulder of the road. Everything suddenly became more interesting. As we approached, I saw the hitchhiker was a woman, an Indian Woman. "Do you see what I see?" he exclaimed, loudly. "What a beautiful savage. We've got ourselves a victim!"

Instead of driving up slowly, he drove in fast and hit the brakes hard at the last second and slid in next to her, the expression on his face almost sinister. Now more alert, I watched him with interest, but the Indian woman standing next to the truck quickly grabbed my attention.

Strikingly beautiful, she was tall and slender with soft dark eyes and displayed an unusual shyness that reminded me of a gazelle. I

John-Paul Cernak

could feel her desire to flee. She wore a dress made from buckskin with fringes that hung below her knees. Her skin was the color of coffee and cream, and she tied her long, black hair into a single braid that hung down her back. I couldn't stop looking at her. She reminded of a Creole woman I once saw while eating breakfast at the coffee shop in the Walgreens drugstore on Canal Street in New Orleans. I couldn't take my eyes off of her either. I held the door open, and when she slid in between Bill and me, I could feel her distress. Bill apparently found what he was looking for. "Where're you headed?" he asked.

"South Dakota," she answered. She sat quietly and didn't say much, and when she spoke, her voice was soft and low. "My name's Willow."

When we stopped for coffee later, all eyes followed her as we took our booth. I wondered why a woman as beautiful as she was hitchhiked alone but quickly understood. Indians are poor and have no other way to travel. Most of the beautiful women I knew desired the limelight. Look at me, look at me, they advertised, wanting everyone to notice them—see how beautiful I am. Willow hid her beauty. She didn't want people to notice her and had a knack of somehow blending into the surroundings. I didn't know how she accomplished it. It must have been a way she learned to protect herself, especially while hitchhiking on the road alone. Bill again insisted on paying the check. We were quiet with each of us into our own thoughts as he drove north through the countryside for what remained of the afternoon.

As evening approached and twilight settled in over the hills and towns of Wyoming, neon signs of taverns and honky-tonks stood out against the darkening sky and beckoned us to stop. Bill seemed to know the area and pulled into the parking lot of a tavern with a large twenty-foot sign of a cowboy twirling a lasso. After a mostly quiet day, the noise and commotion of the crowded saloon hit me like a ton of bricks. We picked our way around the circular bar looking for three empty stools together in a tavern filled with cowboys and everything in a western theme. Painted on a wall was a large mural glowing in black light of a wrangler hogtying a steer.

Willow sat between Bill and me, and as I was getting myself comfortable, everything suddenly quieted. When I looked up, what I saw almost knocked me off my stool. All the cowboys at the bar were looking at us. They must have wondered who the weird trio were. How often did a straight guy, an Indian Woman, and a hippie walk in together, and most were staring at me, the long-haired hippie. Feeling suddenly warm, I quickly checked where the nearest exit was in case I had to make a dash for it. It was in the front door all the way around the bar making escape unlikely. My two companions were no help and sat quietly watching me struggle. Stay cool, man, I said to myself.

On my other side sat a slim, lanky cowboy with his back turned. He was talking with a woman wearing a very low cut blouse. Turning slowly, he looked at me with an amused smirk and an unlighted cigarette dangling from his lips. "How're you doing, hippie?" he said.

"Not bad, man," I responded.

Feeling his remark friendly, I greeted everyone at the bar with a wave and extended the good feelings all around. "How's everyone doing?"

My cordiality worked, and everyone went back to drinking and enjoying themselves. In a few minutes, they forgot about us, and we were accepted. All in a day's work I said, quietly congratulating myself.

When the bartender came around, I ordered beer. "This night's on me," Bill said, and before I could dig out any money, he threw a hundred-dollar bill on the bar and ordered a drink for Willow. The three-piece band started their first set with a familiar, danceable cowboy tune, and Bill and our Native American princess did a swing out on the dance floor. This is how it went most of the evening. I danced with her once or twice, and although he made it clear she was his woman, I wasn't excluded. We talked and laughed together, and whenever I ordered beer or food, he was there with a twenty-dollar bill. What a generous guy; he wouldn't let me pay for anything, but now, each time he paid, an uneasy feeling rose up in me. Although it bothered me, I was having fun, and with each beer, my disquiet was easier to disregard.

I watched our beautiful Indian maiden throughout the evening, as did every cowboy in the bar. Each time she got up to dance, all eyes followed her. She was modest up-close but expressed herself with creative abandon on the dance floor leaving everyone longing for more. Her beauty turned everyone on even the women. All evening, Bill had her to himself and kept his arm around her waist, and nobody had the nerve to ask her to dance.

Later, during a break in the music, I heard the roar of motorcycles out in the parking lot. The door swung open, and three big guys swaggered in, a Jolly Roger skull and cross bones painted on the backs of their leather jackets. They seemed already intoxicated, and the mood quickly became tense. It didn't take long before they spotted Willow. Nudging Bill, I let him know they were going to ask her to dance. "Do you think it's time to get out of here?" he asked.

"It might be." I glanced at the clock, and it was close to midnight.

"Look, you guys," he said, "let's find a motel and crash for the night." I must have looked at him skeptically, because he quickly added: "Hey! Don't worry about a thing. I'll pick up the tab."

As a biker dude walked towards us, Bill on one side of Willow and I on the other steered her out of the tavern, and we roared down the highway feeling smug with ourselves for avoiding what could have been a nasty situation. At the end of town, he pulled into a motel and rented a room with two beds, a queen and a single. It was clear I would take the single and they the queen. The arrangement, however, wasn't necessarily to Willow's liking. I was too tired and drunk to worry much about it. After the lights went out and I was drifting off, I heard them struggling.

I was suddenly wide-awake and straining to hear what was happening. Was he forcing himself on her? Everything was silent.

Although she initially objected, she seemed okay with the arrangement and got into bed with him. I listened intently. If she called out for help, I would have jumped out of bed like a jackrabbit and stopped him. I lay there uncertain of what to do and remembered an incident when I intervened believing a woman was being raped. They both hurtled insults at me and told me to mind my own business. I'm not sure if his paying for everything all day influenced me. It probably did, but how much I'm not sure. I then remembered they were as drunk as I was and must have fallen asleep.

In the morning, I dressed quickly and went to the diner across the road for coffee, still a little unsettled about the previous night. Willow and Bill quickly joined me. In daylight, there was no pretense of togetherness between them, but I saw no hostility. It was time for me to move on, so I'm not sure why I agreed to go with them when Bill suggested we go for a swim at a nearby pond.

The water was a lush ten-acre lake fed by springs. A flock of ducks landed on the opposite side. As I undressed, I became aware I'd be swimming alone. Afterwards, while dressing, Willow came around and stood next to me. "Are you heading east?" she asked.

"As soon as I get myself ready, I'm boogying out of here."

"Take me with you!" she said, and in her subtle way implied she would give me sex if we traveled together, and I protected her.

I had a love waiting back in San Francisco and intended to stay true, but Willow was such a beautiful woman, I wouldn't be able to resist her if we traveled together. But something changed after experiencing the past life, and I knew everything would work out. We walked out onto the highway together, and the first car that came by picked us up. The occupants were a middle-aged couple. "Where're you folks headed?" I asked

"We're on a driving holiday and heading home," replied the driver, "and we live in Sioux Falls, South Dakota."

I wasn't surprised. Leaving Willow with the couple, I exited a few towns later. I traveled alone, and she would only slow me down.

SEVERAL DAYS LATER WHEN COMING OUT OF THE BLACK HILLS of South Dakota, I hitched north to a road that would take me into Minneapolis and St Paul. I was going to the Twin Cities to visit an old girlfriend who went to school there.

With the sun blazing down from a cloudless blue sky, I walked for over an hour along an empty but well-maintained road without seeing any houses and without any cars passing. Taking occasional glances at the beautiful rolling hills of the Great Plains that surrounded me, I noticed a dust cloud rising on the horizon. Stopping to watch, I should have been surprised when a huge herd of buffalo emerged, but I wasn't. There were thousands of them—as many as there were blades of grass. I experienced confusion for only a moment. I was back in my past life and riding my palomino. Feeling excitement and an exquisite joy in anticipation of the hunt, I urged my horse forward. As the many ponies of the large hunting party merged with the herd, there was chaos and choking dust. Riding alongside a large bull, I strung an arrow into my bow and sent it straight into his ribs. He fell to his knees and tumbled rolling over two or three times before stopping. The dust settling revealed many dead animals. The hunt was successful, and the tribe would have enough meat for the winter.

As my awareness reintegrated into my present consciousness, I again walked along the empty road as little worry beads crept into my thoughts. The flow of air currents surrounding me changed from a soft breeze into a stiff gale. Listening to the gusts whistling through the uprights of my backpack changing pitch and tone, I became aware the wind was talking to me. Somewhere out on the plains of South Dakota, we held a conversation. It told me many secrets and explained everything was fine and not to worry. Soon thereafter, I heard the chug, chug, chugging of an ancient prewar pickup driven by an old farmer. He stopped and hailed me. "Where 'ya headed, young fella? Need a ride?"

"I'm heading that way," I said, pointing east.

"Hop in and sit for a spell. I'll drive you as far as my place."

He was more than friendly and at his farm introduced me to his wife. She brought out a large pitcher of lemonade, and I sat in the shade resting before moving on. They were old timers, and after the farmer's wife offered to fix me some food, with all the hippies hitchhiking, I wondered if the times reminded them of the depression years. Travelers during those troubled times probably hadn't eaten for a while. The farmer and his wife learned the old tradition of sharing what they had with the less fortunate.

Later that afternoon when I passed through the Cheyenne River Indian Reservation in the central part of the state, groups of Indian kids walked along with me on the side of the road as I hitch-hiked. I could feel their friendliness and cooperative spirit. They smiled wondering who I was. I felt at home with them. Although I hadn't received any information from my past life experiences to identify my tribal ancestry, something told me I was Cheyenne.

Two Indian men soon picked me up. I believed they were Sioux. It was hot, and I sat in the back of their pickup baking in the ninety-degree heat. When one of them came out of a grocery store carrying a six-pack of beer and saw me withering away, he pulled off a can and threw it to me. It was hot, but I was just a stranger they picked up. My take was he recognized me as an Indian as had Willow.

As I traveled, I connected with folks whenever possible looking for a place to sleep for the night and a shower in the morning. There were safe houses throughout the country where hitchhikers were welcomed to spend the night. The information as to where they were located, as well as what problem towns to avoid, was passed along between hitchhikers. On those nights when I was unable to connect with anyone and there were no safe houses around, I walked out into the countryside until finding an open field and there bedded down for the night after making sure no one saw me. Of all the times I hitchhiked and slept outside, I always slept well and was never bothered by bugs, humans, or any other creatures and amazingly never rained on, although I came close a few times.

Hitchhiking is more than standing on the shoulder of the road with your thumb out. It requires large amounts of energy. When I entered Minnesota, for some reason, my energy ran out, and when I stuck out my thumb, it wasn't with much enthusiasm. People feel your lack of motivation and don't stop. I wasn't able to move very far that day. With daylight fading, I was out in the open without even a farmhouse in sight and a nasty storm moving in fast. The sky to the west glowed with lightning flashes and loud thunder, and not one car passed in the last fifteen minutes. Without a place to shelter myself, it looked as if my luck was about to run out, and I would spend the night out in the storm, cold and wet.

Just as I gave up hope, a car approached. Petitioning the spirits, I said a quick prayer. Regardless, it zoomed past and shattered any hope I might have had. The only thing that would save me now was a miracle. Wait a minute! Maybe the gods did hear my plea. After traveling the length of a football field, the car unexpectedly pulled over onto the shoulder of the road and stopped. Breathlessly, I watched feeling the cold, damp wind of the approaching storm on the back of my neck, as they slowly backed up to where I stood. "Nasty evening," said the woman driver. "Need a ride?"

My rescuers were a couple in their early thirties, and my phenomenal luck held when they offered me a place to stay for the night. The storm hit seconds later in a fury of lightning and thunder, with huge raindrops splashing against the windshield of their vehicle.

They lived with another couple and were urban people in a rural lifestyle. Their living arrangement was more like a group marriage than a commune. I'm unsure how they related sexually but believed it was like an open marriage, because they each had separate bedrooms. The woman who picked me up was friendly and came around to talk. She might have been looking for more than conversation, and although she was attractive, I pretended not to notice and avoided complications. During the sixties and seventies, there were many experimental group living situations such as the one they were in.

Once on the road again, I picked up rides effortlessly and reached Minneapolis-St. Paul the following day. I immediately went to the school where my old girlfriend, Jane studied, although, I wasn't totally sure why I wanted to visit her. I had her paged. She was in class and wouldn't be available for an hour. As I waited sitting comfortably in front of large windows watching traffic, my mind drifted back to when we first met.

Isabel and I recently separated, and I was lonely. I must have been looking for someone to help me through a difficult time, and Jane was the perfect woman. She came into the print shop in the Haight-Ashbury to have her art printed into calendars. In my office, we stood looking deeply into each other's eyes without speaking, and I was in love at first sight. From her enthralling smile that communicated delight and surprise—the way a woman looks when something nice is happening to her—I knew instantly we would be lovers.

Jane wasn't hippie nor was she straight but that in-between place people of that era often adopted. She was tall and slender with long legs, big boobs, and big trusting blue eyes. She was dressed in bell-bottoms and peasant blouse, her long, blonde hair spilling down her back from beneath a Barnaby Street Cap. She was everything I wished for. We knew it wasn't a forever kind of affair. After six months, the relationship went into decline. Even though it was over, we continued to see each for several more months but usually only for sex. She'd drop over unannounced. Somehow, her timing was always perfect, and after some of the most uninhibited and torrid lovemaking I ever experienced, she'd leave. One day after an extraordinarily passionate session, she announced: "Jack! I won't be coming around anymore. I'm afraid this is goodbye."

Although I knew the end was near, I was shocked and saddened nonetheless. "Have you found someone new?" I asked.

"No! No! It's nothing like that." She kissed me gently with tears in her eyes. "I'm leaving San. Francisco and moving back east. I'm

John-Paul Cernak

entering a seminary to become a minister. I'll miss you, baby."

It was fun remembering. As I slowly drifted back from my reverie, an hour had pass, and she was on her way down. With butterflies in my stomach, I watched the elevator doors open. Two women exited, but neither was Jane. As the door began closing, someone inside stopped it. A dowdy-looking woman stumbled out wearing an ill-fitting dress and ridiculous shoes. I almost laughed until I realized it was her. Without makeup and her hair chopped short and noticeably darker, she had little resemblance to the beautiful woman I knew in San Francisco. It wasn't her physical appearance as much as her depressed body language and gray aura that startled me. My heart dropped when I saw there was nothing left of the gorgeous woman I loved or of the unforgettable passion we shared. I was certain my visit was a mistake.

I was more than surprised by her warm hugs and welcoming attitude. As we talked over dinner at a local restaurant, her energy and old vivaciousness slowly returned. "Are you in a hurry to get to Chicago?" she asked.

"Not really. What do you have in mind?"

"I'm heading up to North Dakota to visit my cousin's farm over the July 4th weekend. Want to come along?"

Since I was never up there, at least not in this life, it didn't take long to decide. She snuck me into an empty dorm room where I spent the night, and the next day, I was amazed at how her energy and aura improved. We talked nonstop throughout the drive. I was only vaguely aware of the rolling hills and farms of the Minnesota and North Dakota countryside. We arrived in late afternoon.

Work on a farm never stops, and even on holidays, everyone had their tasks and didn't have time to socialize. Throughout the weekend, I didn't see Jane much. I spent time horseback riding with a ten-year-old cousin but mostly explored alone. The men in the family worked out on the land most of the day. Their farm was large and miles from town: yet I saw no wild animals and not many birds. There wasn't any place for them to hide or build nests. The two brothers who ran the farm talked about trashing the ditch, which I learned was cutting the grasses along the road and removing all the cover from that treeless plain. I vowed that if I ever owned a place of my own, I would keep things as natural as possible and give shelter to the wild things.

On the Fourth under a featureless sky, the local farm families gathered in a park for a picnic that included a cornucopia of delicious food. The day reminded me of a scene from the movie, Bonnie and Clyde, in which everything was scripted and everyone moved in slow motion like in a dream. Kids with fireworks brought the day back to reality, putting cherry bombs under beer cans and sending them high into the air. The next day in Jane's Buick, we drove back to Minneapolis. We didn't speak much on the return trip. I guess there wasn't much left to say. With my backpack on and ready to travel, we embraced and looked deeply into each other's eyes similar to the first time we met in my office at the print shop in the Haight-Ashbury. "Farewell, Jack," she said. I turned and walked out the door.

—⟵∅∅∅⟶—

AFTER THREE WEEKS ON THE ROAD, I REACHED THE WINDY CITY, and some inner volition moved me towards where my mother lived and to the house I inhabited the first years of my life. I arrived in the city on the far north side, and my trip across town to the distant, south side was a long one. The fastest way was the elevated. The train took me through the downtown and many different districts. Going through the Loop, it went underground and became a subway. In some districts, it passed only a few feet from apartment buildings. I saw flashes of people in their kitchens eating lunch and in their bedrooms having sex.

With my backpack on the floor in front of me and my elbow resting on the sill of an open window, I must have looked fierce with my long hair, full beard, and my knife in its sheath strapped to my belt. No one sat next to me for the entire trip which took two and a half hours. A group of kids boarded when I went through a black area on the south side. After spotting me, they must have wondered who the dangerous looking white guy was. None of them would come close. They exited at the next stop. While the train paused discharging passengers, the bravest of them rushed past my open window and tapped me on the elbow. He stood at a distance looking at me and smiling. Because of my Indian awareness, I knew he counted coup and would have earned an eagle feather for his headdress. I gave him a thumbs-up, and they all cheered.

In late afternoon on a warm sunny day, I arrived in a quiet, well maintained, working class neighborhood on Chicago's South Side. When I walked up the block from the busy streetcar line, neighbors I had known looked at me with suspicion wondering who the longhaired hippie was and why he was on their street. The red brick Cape Cod-style house looked about the same as I remembered it. The lawn was well tended with multi-colored zinnias blooming along the borders where they always had. Not much changed on the block either, except houses filled all the vacant lots where I played as a kid.

I pushed the doorbell hard next to the front door. There was no answer. I didn't let her know I was coming. I should have, but she was such a homebody, I was sure she'd be there when I arrived. I felt a moment of panic when the second ring went unanswered. After a third, I sensed a stirring from somewhere deep inside the house. Slowly, the large heavy inner door swung open, and a wrinkled old face appeared in the window. She peered at me through the glass. Then a flicker of recognition flashed across her face seeing through the beard and long hair to the person beneath. Holding the door open, she smiled warmly. "Welcome, stranger," she said.

I quickly removed my backpack and turned to face her. "Hi, Mom. How are you?

She must have been really glad to see me, because she hugged me. I could count on one hand the times she embraced me throughout my childhood. Although she had trouble showing affection, she wasn't an uncaring person, She demonstrated her love by preparing superlative meals and baking delectable old world pastries. It was her need to control and her mania for keeping everything neat and clean that were a constant source of conflict. What I needed was love and understanding, as all children do, instead of her need to bend my will, and I wasn't back fifteen minutes when I learned she hadn't changed. "Where are you living," she asked, "now that you sold that old house you called the Victorian?"

"I still live in the city but in a different neighborhood."

"You live alone?"

"No, I live with a woman."

"Are you married?"

"I would have written had I remarried."

"I don't like that! I will not allow my son to live with a woman if he's not married!"

Her attempt to coerce me into accepting her values was how she operated throughout the years I lived with her, and I mostly gave in to her demands. Only when they became unreasonable did I rebel. To avoid another similar incident, I was ready to ignore her remarks. But after living on my own for years and hitchhiking two thousand miles, I wasn't willing to fall back into an old pattern. "I'm an adult now mother, and I'll do as I please."

She glared at me intractably but never mentioned it again. The encounter triggered an awareness that my first divorce wasn't from Isabel. It was from my mother.

During the week of my stay, I visited sisters, nieces and nephews. There hadn't been much communication between us in the years I was gone, and although they were friendly, I sensed a distancing. I believe it was mostly because of my long hair and hippie looks. All the old memories they had of me no longer applied. I was a stranger. I didn't call any Chicago friends for the same reason and would have difficulty explaining why I hitchhiked across the country. I called Meg. She said she was doing fine. On a clear, hot day in the middle of July, I began my return journey west taking Route 66. It was the same road I took when moving to California the first time. By then, freeways were built, and the old road was mostly unused

After traveling for seven days through Illinois, Missouri, Oklahoma and Texas, I arrived in New Mexico where the old highway was still traveled. In the middle of sagebrush and tumbleweed just outside Tucumcari, I hitchhiked in the heat since early morning without anyone stopping to pick me up. Besides not getting any rides, I felt nervous and agitated and was unable to identify the cause of my apprehension. All morning, cars whizzed past filled with local folks going shopping. What grabbed my attention was that most of the women wore similar hairdos. After experiencing the individuality of San Francisco's women, I thought it unusual to see so many looking the same.

Around noon, a county sheriff's vehicle darted past and quickly parked to let me know he was going to confront me. The deputy approached walking fast and looking stern. His body language said he was going to arrest me. Dressed in cowboy boots, jeans, a striped western shirt, and a gigantic ten-gallon hat that covered most of his forehead down to his eyes, he looked like a cartoon character. I almost laughed. "Hi sheriff," I said, holding back a giggle.

"May I see some ID."

His voice was gruff and threatening. "Nice day!" I handed him my driver's license.

"Where're you from? We don't allow hitchhiking around here."

"I live in San Francisco where I have a printing company."

When I said I have a business, he instantly calmed and became less aggressive. He looked at me questioningly. I still looked hippie but having a print shop tapped into his values. Suddenly, I was more mainstream than counterculture. It also let him know I wasn't without money. "If you have a business, why do you hitchhike?"

"I enjoy traveling this way. Doesn't everyone? "

To impress upon him I wasn't breaking the law and that he didn't intimidate me, I continued hitchhiking as we talked. He looked at me curiously and seemed perplexed by my actions. Just then, a car drove past with a woman passenger who again wore the same hairdo I saw all morning. "Do all the women around here look the same?" I said. He looked at me as if I were crazy. "Look! Look!" I said, pointing excitedly, as a second car passed. "They all have the same hairdo."

My strange behavior and unperturbed manner threw him into confusion. I must not have fit the profile of the other hitchhikers he confronted. Several times, he took a step forward, as if to arrest me, but each time stepped back. Finally, with an air of resignation, he walked back to his vehicle and drove off.

While I succeeded with the sheriff, cars continued to speed past without anyone stopping. Wearily, around four that afternoon, I gave up and decided to take a motel room for the night. It would be the first after traveling over three thousand miles. Perhaps sleeping in a bed and watching TV would help dispel whatever was bugging me

I entered the lobby of a small motel at the edge of town and rang the bell. A middle-aged man entered and sat himself on a stool behind the counter. I tried to assess if he was someone I could talk into giving me a discount on my room. "How much do you charge for a single?" I asked. Slipping off my backpack, I leaned it against the wall

"Where're you from?" he shot back without answering my question.

His face was expressionless and gave no clue as to what he was thinking or feeling. He looked me over slowly from head to toe and then my backpack. "I'm from San Francisco and heading home."

"Have you been on the road long?"

"It's been over five weeks now. Went to see my mom in Chicago."

When I told him how long, he sat back on his stool with a dreamy look. "My father spent three years roaming around during the Great Depression years of the 1930s. As a kid, I loved listening to his stories of hopping freights, hitchhiking, and moving easily about the country. One day he'd be in New York and a few days

John-Paul Cernak

later in California. In the depression, the people on the road were called hobos; it was like a brotherhood. I've never traveled much. Always had the desire, but now I'm stuck in this motel. Can't trek around when you own a hotel."

"I guess not," I concurred.

"I can't give you a room," he said, coming back to the present. "My policy is to never rent rooms to anyone without a car, but I have a storeroom in the back where you can stay. There's a cot back there and even a shower. I won't charge you anything, but you need to be out by eight in the morning. The help comes in around that time, and it's where the washer and dryer and all the linens are stored. You need to be gone before they come in."

"That's mighty kind of you."

Before dark, I walked back to town and grabbed a burger at an A&W and was asleep before nine.

In the morning, I left Route 66 and hitched north towards the town of Taos. As I stuck out my thumb, another hitchhiker joined me. His name was Jimmy. It felt good to have someone to talk with. He was a big guy, around six-three or four, and I felt comfortable with him immediately. I could tell he was a mellow guy from his friendliness and from the softness in his eyes, but he seemed stressed. He carried something heavy in his backpack. "My truck broke down a couple of days ago, and I left my family back at a trailer park in Taos. Small towns don't have parts for older vehicles. I came into Tucumcari for this replacement."

"Where are you folks from?" I asked.

"We're from Montana, and we're moving down here to New Mexico. I heard there are jobs here."

No one stopped after hitchhiking over an hour. It was disheartening to watch cars rocket past carrying only the driver. Jimmy looked a little downhearted. He wanted to be back with his family.

"As much as I enjoy having company," I said, "my gut feeling is folks are hesitant to pick up two guys. We'd have a better chance splitting up. I'll walk up the road, and if someone picks you up have them stop for me."

After twenty minutes, I walked a long way, and when I looked back, Jimmy was just a blur in the distance. Several vehicles whizzed past kicking up dust that burned my eyes but didn't stop. When I looked back a second time, a vehicle finally paused where he stood. I watched as it approached. When it was still at a distance, I recognized it as a converted van. But something felt odd. I was receiving strange vibes that put me on edge and wasn't even sure Jimmy was on board. My anxiety increased the closer it came. When it stopped in front of me, my heart raced, flags waved, and red lights flashed in my head. Slowly, the sliding door opened. Everything inside was dark. I hesitated not knowing what to do. Jimmy stuck his head out the door. "Get in, Jack! It's OK! They're deaf mutes and really nice people."

Still in shock, I climbed aboard and sat on the floor calming myself. The occupants were two couples in their late thirties. They smiled and welcomed me. It was their unusual vibe that confused me. When I finally tuned into it, I discovered there was something pure and beautiful about them. They seemed almost to glow. I communicated my thanks for picking us up and watched as they talked among themselves using sign language. Several young children in the rear of the van talked together and listened to a radio and seemed to have normal hearing

Jimmy invited me to spend a few days with him and his family at the trailer court in Taos. He was a person I wanted as a friend. It would have been a pleasurable visit with him and his family. I was feeling an inner turmoil that pushed me onward and wouldn't let me rest.

Later that morning, as I walked along a street in downtown Taos, I noticed two Indian Women watching me. They wore plain dresses, were without makeup, and tied their long, black hair into ponytails similar to the other native women I encountered in my travels. The shorter of the two smiled and spoke as I passed: "Hi, hitchhiker! We have a place where you could spend a few hours to rest and refresh yourself."

It would have helped to stop and catch my breath, but I declined and casually said, "I'll see you later." The taller of the two, who hadn't spoken, retorted sharply: "Why do you say see you later when you don't mean it?"

The negative exchange made me aware how uptight I was, and feeling agitated and pressured, I pushed westward wanting to be with Meg back in San Francisco.

When leaving Taos, I caught a ride with a young Navaho Indian student. I was connecting easily with the Indians. They must have recognized me as one of them, but with my troubled mind, I was unable to appreciate the significance. My next ride was with a Navaho Indian family. I rode in the back of their pickup with the grandfather and the groceries. The old man had a soothing and gentle vibe. Although we didn't speak much, as we drove through a wheat field in a beautiful valley, he suddenly pointed. "That's Apache land," he said in an ominous voice.

I was moving fast now, and at the town of Farmington in the northwestern part of the state, near the four corners, I caught a ride with a college student working a summer job delivering janitorial supplies to the intermountain west. Taking turns, we drove all night and reached Salt Lake City and Interstate-80 at dawn. After a few hours of sleep, I was back on the road for the last leg of my journey and was quickly picked up by three guys heading into San Francisco. To get a ride all the way home, I invited them to crash for the night at the flat. Within minutes, Meg arrived carrying a bag of groceries. I hugged and kissed her enthusiastically if not passionately and felt joy to be home. As we embraced, I experienced an unsettling, discordant feeling. It was similar to hearing a musical note off key, except I felt it instead of hearing it. But because it came and went so quickly, in the excitement of the moment, I ignored it.

We sat together on the couch across from the three guys. Bruce was the leader, and when he spoke, his two buddies listened. He talked about his adventures which seemed to intrigue Meg, and in a short time, she was paying more attention to him than she was to me. A conversation developed between them that excluded everyone else. Although I saw what was happening, I was exhausted after traveling two thousand miles, and my head wouldn't allow me to fully comprehend the situation. After I was gone six weeks and within a few hours of my return, Meg left with Bruce and the two other guys.

I sat staring at the door unable to believe she walked out on me as if I meant nothing to her. I desperately wanted to believe she'd walk back in at any moment and announce it was a joke. As reality set in, disbelief turned into anger. Beating my fist into a pillow, I screamed: "DIE, YOU BITCH." Walking around the agonizingly empty flat feeling excruciating pain, I tried keeping myself together. The torment eating away at my insides was telling me I was worthless. In a flash, it demolished the years of work I did on myself to gain confidence, and I was a shattered and bewildered child again. At the bed where we experienced such ecstasy, I fell in and wailed. Suddenly, I stopped and sat up remembering something. Now the warnings that I received about her and chose to ignore came slamming home

During a sleepless night, distress came in waves. After short periods of relief, the next surge overwhelmed and dumped me into spasms of emotional turmoil and inconsolable anguish. Throughout the night, I relived every betrayal I ever suffered, and with each incident remembered, another nail was hammered into my bleeding emotions. Near dawn planning revenge, I would pile all her belongings next to the door and at her return throw them piece by piece into the street and end the relationship in dramatic fashion. No! I screamed. Feeling intense frustration, I put my plan on hold. I was caught in a dilemma. By ending the relationship, I would also end my dream of moving to the country.

Without unpacking, I was back on the road early in the morning and was quickly picked up by a couple heading north into Oregon.

I rode all day in the back of their pickup with another hitchhiker. The day was dark and cloudy like my mood, but with every passing mile, I was regaining strength. As evening approached, we camped under a large old-growth forest in a deserted campground high in the Trinity Alp Mountains of Northern California, the nearest town twenty miles down the mountain. As daylight faded, a deep hush fell over the forest. After a quick dinner of cheese and crackers, I crawled into my sleeping bag and fell into an exhausted sleep.

Sometime later, two carloads of people invaded the campsite next to ours and awakened me playing loud music on their radio. Sitting in a semicircle around a campfire, they passed around a bottle of whisky, except for a stout fellow chopping wood. Walking resolutely out of the darkness and into the light of their fire, I heard gasps of shock and surprise, except for the woodchopper who had his back turned. "I can't sleep with all the noise," I said, and put my hand on his shoulder. Stunned, he tottered backwards. I turned and disappeared into the night as if I never existed. A bewildered silence fell over the group, and after quickly extinguishing their fire, they were gone within minutes. The next morning, I wasn't sure if the incident was real or a dream until I noticed strange looks from my traveling companions.

Later that morning, as I walked along the main street of Cave Junction, a small town across the border in Oregon, I chuckled after reading a sign on the door of a tavern that read: "No dogs or hippies allowed." At a real-estate office in the next block, a well-groomed agent welcomed me and for the remainder of the afternoon drove me around looking at parcels of land for sale. I made a low offer on a twelve-acre parcel that bordered the middle fork of the Illinois River near O'Brian, a hamlet with two houses and general store ten miles south of Cave Junction on Highway 199.

The Castro Street flat was empty when I returned on Wednesday afternoon. I didn't know if Meg was at work or even returned from her outing with Bruce. I felt calm but was uncertain how I would react when I saw her. I was excited about making the offer on buying the land. She arrived a short time later. When she saw me, she casually put her arms around my neck and kissed me as if nothing happened. I kissed her back. I guess I made my decision and would never let her know she hurt me. Moreover, my focus changed, and I couldn't think about her infidelity. I didn't want anything messing up my plans of moving to the country.

Although I had difficulty admitting it even to myself, her betrayal affected me deeply. If I viewed myself in a mirror, I looked the same, but I wasn't the same person inside. It was a life-changing event catching me totally off guard. I had to fight to stay sane. From my past life, I remembered I was a warrior. Somehow, I tapped into hidden powers, and, like the Phoenix rising out of the ashes, I went through a transformation. I would bide my time and let circumstances dictate how it would play out but aware that the bond of trust between us was forever severed by her treacherous unfaithfulness

The following week, I purchased a Datsun pickup from a dealership in the Mission. The truck had no radio. I was unhooking from society and was finished listening to commercials, news about the war, and inflation. My hitchhiking days were over.

John-Paul Cernak

CHAPTER 4

THE OWNERS OF THE LAND ON THE ILLINOIS RIVER REJECTED MY low offer and sent a counter offer. In the second week of August, 1974, We drove up to Oregon and on a warm day after inspecting the twelve acres sat talking in the truck on the shoulder of the road. No dwellings were visible. "What do you think?" I asked.

"It's nice, but it isn't what I expected."

"Really!" I was taken aback by her tepid response.

"The land doesn't have any trees, and where would we live?"

"I'd have to build a house or move in a mobile after building a road and installing a septic system."

"You forgot a well. I wouldn't want to drink water out of the river."

"OK! And a well."

"How long would it take to do all that?"

"I don't know, maybe six months to a year."

"A year! And it's not remote enough. There are too many houses around."

"You want to be more isolated than this?" From where we sat, I could see only distant mountains, forest, and river for about fifty miles. "This is remote enough for me, and since we both lived in the city all our lives, it'll take considerable adjusting even this far out. I'm not moving to the country for it to become a hardship."

"Where's your sense of adventure, Jack? If we're going to live in the country, let's live in the country!"

"OK! If that's what you want, let's go exploring."

After having lunch in Grants Pass, we drove north on Interstate-5 through densely forested mountains passing only isolated farms and an occasional small community buried in the woods. Traffic was light, except for large trucks. After driving many miles and up and down numerous hills, a sign on a long downgrade announced the town of Centerville as the next exit, along with a connecting highway east towards the Cascade Mountains and Crater Lake. "Let's checkout this town," she suggested.

Centerville was a western looking town built on hills and was larger than I expected. There were no horses or cowboys, but everyone drove pickups. I pulled into the parking lot of a small, "A" frame real-estate office along the main drag with a sign across the front that read: "Western Ranches." A tall, middle-aged saleslady welcomed us. "Do you have any land for sale that's a little remote?" I asked.

"All the land around here is a little remote. How secluded do you want?"

"I'm not sure. What's for sale?"

"There're a few parcels up in the national forest owned by a local merchant, and they might be exactly what you're looking for.

"What kind of land is it?"

"In all honesty, I've never been there. It's just too far up for me, but I understand it's beautiful. Hughie Hodges owns the land, and he owns the feed store in town. You'll probably find him up there. He spends most of his time in the woods."

After spending the night in a motel and an early start, with the rising sun in our eyes, we drove east on a road that followed the fast flowing South Umpqua River taking us through forest-covered foothills and pastures filled with grazing cows. After passing a few large, stately older homes on large acreages, I received images that the houses belonged to judges and other officials. I stopped at a small community and photographed a white, covered bridge shining in the morning sun. A few miles later, we entered Tiller. It was only slightly larger than O'Brian, but at the end of town next to the river was the Tiller Ranger Station. I parked in front of the large, modern building. Meg reviewed the real estate lady's instructions. "She wrote to continue up river into the national forest for another twenty-five miles."

"Wow!" I said, "That's a long way into nothing." I spread the Oregon roadmap over the steering wheel and pinpointed our location. "From here, there's only national forest for what looks like hundreds of miles. This town is already the end of the world. Let's stop in. Maybe they can give us more information."

Wearing a yellow feather in his green cap, a poster of Woodsy Owl hung on the door. He admonished us to: "Give a Hoot and Wipe Your Boot." Inside hung an almost life-size picture of Smoky Bear pointing at us and saying: "Only You Can Prevent Forest Fires." The office was vacant, but in a short time, a friendly woman in civilian dress loaded us down with maps, charts, and directions. Everything had a deep woodsy feel that reminded me of my Boy Scout days, but this wasn't for a weekend camping trip, it was for real. I felt excited but also apprehensive. To go hunting for land in the wilds of the national forest was not on my agenda when I left the city two days ago.

At the time I first began thinking about moving to the country, my idea was to have a place close to town where I could drive in easily on Friday evening, have dinner in a nice restaurant, and see a movie. Without planning it, I was about to drive into a wilderness miles from anywhere. Even the land at O'Brian was a stretch. I made a hasty decision distressed over Meg's infidelity, and I'm not sure I would have made the same decision in a calmer moment. When I realized where I was, I thought I lost my mind. On the other hand, I felt more excited and more free than I ever felt before and was ready to unshackle myself from everything ordinary, boring, and routine. A mile out of town, a large sign welcomed us to the Umpqua National Forest. I relaxed; my thinking diminished, and I gave myself over to the adventure I was on eager to experience everything to its fullest.

As we drove east deeper into the mountains, we passed a few isolated houses built along the river and a small community with a general store. The road took us past several deserted campgrounds lost in the shade of tall conifers growing thick along the river. At an abandoned sawmill, we came upon a rusting metal cone-like structure called a teepee burner. It was where they once burned sawdust. When passing occasional breaks in the trees, vistas of snow-capped mountain peaks opened before us—or what snow remained after a long, hot summer. The road was paved and in good condition and with little traffic, except for an occasional log truck that rumbled past coming out of the mountains loaded with huge old-growth timber but for mile after mile only forest, mountains, and river. When a little, green sign suddenly appeared along the side of the road, Meg reacted: "There it is! That's the road we're looking for. I knew we were getting close."

I quickly turned onto a gravel road kicking up a cloud of dust and climbed steeply for a mile or more under a thick forest canopy. As the road leveled off under open sky, a small sign appeared before a cattle guard: "Private land on both sides of the road for the next two miles." After driving around a large rock, the road curved, and a valley suddenly materialized out of the surrounding forest. I sat staring. Its beauty and majesty rendered me speechless and awakened some long forgotten memories that transported me into a past life, perhaps to Atlantis the lost continent, or to Ancient Egypt, or to a forgotten Mayan City buried deep in the jungles of Mexico's Yucatan Peninsula.

It was long and narrow, and although clear of trees, huge old-growth forest covered the slopes that shot up steeply from the valley floor. Several small clear-cuts were visible, but they hardly diminished its rugged beauty. A building with the sun reflecting off its metal roof far up the valley and a log barn a short distance ahead were the only structures visible. Next to an old antique bulldozer was a road to the left leading to a red pickup parked in front of a small house trailer. Working in a large garden, a burly man leaned on his hoe and watched as we pulled in. "Hello!" I shouted.

He stood unresponsive for a long moment before slowly moving towards us pushing his hair to the side as he came. He was short, possibly only five one or two but with a huge barrel chest and arms as large as my thighs bulging out from beneath his T-shirt. He was built like a tank. His round head seemed small sitting atop his massive shoulders. I would have guessed him to be in his late forties to early fifties. "That's a man to be reckoned with," I whispered quietly to Meg.

"Howdy," he said, in a high, booming voice, "beautiful summer day," He stopped short of the truck and peered at us through half-closed eyes, as if he wasn't sure about us.

"Nice place you have here," I responded. "I hear you have some land for sale."

He bounced as he spoke and waived his arm in a circular motion. "Whole valley's fur sale. All exceptin' this front twenty acres I'm keeping fur myself. I'm Hughie Hodges. Howdiya find out about this place?"

"Nice to meet you," I said. "We stopped in a real estate office in Centerville. I'm Jack Cernak, and this is Meg." I reached my hand out the window. He moved closer to shake hands. I could feel the power in his large, callused hand. "We're looking to buy some land in the country."

"This is as country as it gets," he responded gesturing to the spot where he stood. "We're smack dab in the middle of the national forest."

"What about those clear cuts?" I asked. "Are the forestry people planning to cut more?"

"Couldn't rightly tell you, cause I don't really know. They was taken to court on this last cut a few years back, but the judge came down in their favor. You never know from year to year tho. Wouldya like to take a look at the valley?"

"We'd love to," said Meg.

Hughie's red pickup led the way, and the first stop was where the valley widened in front of a white-framed house. A young calf grazed on a large, fenced lawn filled with half a dozen large apple trees. Alongside was a cattle-loading ramp built from logs and a

The Odyssey of a Hippie Marijuana Grower 61

one-room log cabin across the road. We gathered at the front gate. "This is the original homestead," he said. "It's a log house beneath the board and batten."

"How did this become private land so deep in the national forest?" I asked.

"Folks from Germany settled here back in 1914, when you could move into the national forest, make improvements, and claim the land. The government won't let you do that anymore, but this homestead remains private. The legal title is the Erlebach Ranch, but everyone calls it Ash Valley."

"How did they earn money so far from civilization?" I asked.

"They raised cattle and grew potatoes and brought out their crops in covered wagons on paths along the river. I understand it took three days to reach Centerville."

"They must have been hardy folks from old pioneer stock," Meg remarked.

"They're still alive and in their nineties livin' somewhere on the coast."

I walked up the road a few steps to be alone with my thoughts and to get a feel of the place. A cooling breeze kept me comfortable on a hot summer day. The valley was beautiful and would be a great place to live, but was it the right place? How could I make a decision when I knew nothing about living in the country? Another problem was that after Meg rejected the land at O'Brian, I was skeptical we'd find a place we would both agree upon. Now that everything I hoped for was near, I was having doubts, and the remoteness added uncertainty. "When I bought the place in the early fifties," he said, "the creek meandered throughout the valley, and when you get fifty to sixty inches of rain a year, there's water everywhere. With that big old cat you saw coming in, I worked the creek into a main channel at the back of the valley. Let's take a walk."

As we passed the house, an attractive woman in her mid-twenties stepped out onto the porch and smiled. Two little blonde girls hid behind her legs. "That's Cancer Nancy," he said when out of earshot. "Sweet gal and takes real good care of those kids, too."

"Does she live there by herself?" Meg asked.

"At the moment she does. The father lives in California."

We zigzagged around cow patties littering the pasture. I could see a large herd grazing in the distance under a tree. "What's that building?" I asked, pointing to the structure with the metal roof that was visible when we entered, as were now two small, one-room cabins.

"That's the hog barn. A couple of young fellows live there. I built it for a hog operation but shut it down a while back when the price of pork dropped. Had half dozen breeding sows for a while."

Walking the remainder of the way to the creek in silence, my insides tingling, we came upon a huge buck deer down in the creek bed. He raced off splashing water with each step. He was a magnificent stag with a huge rack. We walked up on him only because the creek was fifteen feet below the surface of the valley, and he couldn't see or hear us approach. As he ran, his muscles flexed like a racehorse straining at the finish of a race. He seemed almost to glow. He looked in our direction and quickly disappeared around a bend in the creek.

How fortunate to have walked up on such a splendid animal. Then something clicked in my head. What were the odds of accidentally stumbling upon him? When I looked at Meg and Hughie, they looked frozen. Time stopped for them, and only I saw him. It was me he was looking at when he looked in our direction. His gaze was an invitation to purchase land in the valley. He was an omen and the sign I was looking for. The spell lifted and the world resumed when Hughie pointed down into the creek. "The water's dug a deep channel," he said, "and I don't know how much deeper she'll get. When the rains settle in, the creek sometimes overflows. You'll find native brown trout in the deeper pools and plenty of crawdads and frogs."

"Are there people living in the cabins?" I asked, pointing to the one across the creek

"They have families living in them that belong to a hippie commune. They call themselves the Whole Earth."

"Are they from San Francisco's Haight-Ashbury?"

"You know them?"

"It's a large community, and I know a few members. What are they doing here?"

"They want to buy the whole valley. In fact, they did purchase it and gave me a large down payment last fall."

Suddenly, I was aware this was where I belonged and where I wanted to live, and his statement sent a shock through me. "I don't understand," I said. "If they bought the whole place, how are you going to sell any of it to me?"

"When they gave me their deposit, it was with an agreement they'd pay the balance this July. Even the ladies worked all winter and spring in the rain cutting firewood they sent down to Frisco for the city branch to sell. Don't know how many large truckloads they sent down but plenty. I understand firewood fetches a pretty penny down there. By early summer, they'd earned enough to pay me what they owed, but whoever was in charge of the money went on a cocaine binge and snorted all the profits up his nose before they could pay me. I took the valley back last month. Now it's fur sale again. I'm letting 'em live here free until they decide what they wanna do."

After hearing the Whole Earth's difficulties, it seemed to substantiate I read the omen correctly. I was the one who was supposed to purchase land.

The barn with the metal roof was our next stop up the valley. Unlike the main house, the surrounding area felt wild and unsettled and was more what I was looking for. The structure was built on a knoll that kept it high and dry in wet weather, and it could be converted into living space. There was no fencing, except huge logs placed in a box pattern along the side, like a corral, keeping in the pigs. I disliked that the barn was built close to the road. I did like that the forest started only fifty feet from the front door. Two longhaired guys stuck their heads out and greeted Hughie. After looking us over, they disappeared inside.

"Let's take a walk," he said.

After crossing a small creek on a narrow bridge, we startled a blue jay. He flew up to a branch of a maple tree and squawked at us loudly. Hughie led us through a jungle of shrubs, ferns, and sapling trees up to the ancient forest. Stopping next to a huge cedar tree, he pointed to water bubbling out of the ground. "This spring," he said, "will give you four to five gallons a minute in summer. It's enough for a large garden and some crops, and its high enough to give you good pressure."

The next stop on our tour was to a house covered in weathered plywood tucked into the side of a hill. A road ran up alongside. Down in the valley, the sun reflected off a large pond. I could hear the purr of a small gas engine powering a sprinkler that sent water in a long arc across a large garden. "This is the Whole Earth's Communal House," he said. "Nobody lives here, but it's where they meet and have their meals."

"Where does this side road go?" I asked.

"It goes nowhere and dead ends a short way up. None of them go anywhere. Even this main one ends in a couple of miles." He pointed to a large mountain with a clear cut at the back of the valley. "The only way out is down to the river. I've logged up here twenty-five years and know the area as well as anyone. The forest is full of coyotes and large cats. Saw a bear the other day so large thought it was a grizzly. Need to be careful when walking in these mountains. Plenty of ways to get into trouble."

The valley narrowed and the forest closed in around us when we continued our tour. The sun shining through low overhanging foliage created a mosaic of shapes, textures, and colors with a hypnotic effect. Meg's face displayed a combination of peacefulness and excitement. "What did you think of the area around the hog barn?" I asked.

"I loved it, but it's so close to the road."

"That's a drawback, but you heard the man say none of them go anywhere. How much traffic can there be?"

"I love it back here," she added, "but it's too narrow. I'd get claustrophobic. We wouldn't get sun until late morning and lose it in early afternoon."

After crossing another cattle guard, we entered the national forest on the backend and drove to the base of the mountain with the clear-cut. Strewn about were pieces of cable and other remnants of a logging operation. "Let's take another look at the hog barn," I suggested.

The two hippies living there were gone. It was one large room with an open ceiling fifteen to eighteen feet high. The light inside was almost as bright as outside from eight skylights built into the roof. Aesthetically pleasing roughhewn timbers holding up the roof looked like crosses lying on their sides. The hippies created a sleeping loft at the rear by laying boards across the beams, and a wood-burning stove made from a fifty-five gallon metal drum sat in the center of the room. Its chimney stretched straight up through the roof. "Why is the floor high in the middle and sloped down to each side?" I asked.

His response was that he "built the barn from the wood of an old sawmill over two concrete bunkers. With a slanted floor, it was easy to shovel the pig manure into them. By now, it should have composted into good soil and would help a garden grow real good if someone hauls it out."

Out in the sunshine once again, a breathtaking view to the southeast grabbed my attention. The distant mountains framed the closer hills and gave it an added dimension. Meg quickly gave her approval when I suggested we purchase the barn and twenty acres. I was surprised how little Hughie asked. He must have felt guilty after taking the Whole Earth's money. We shook hands, and he pointed out his approximation of the boundaries. I wondered what I would do with all the land.

On the drive back, we grew quiet and contemplative until past Tiller. "Are you having second thoughts?" she asked.

John-Paul Cernak

"No! No! I love the place. I'm just feeling overwhelmed. I don't usually make decisions this quickly, especially one that will change my life so drastically. By the way, there's electricity up in the valley isn't there?"

She hesitated before answering. "I'm sure there is. I'm sure I saw power lines, didn't you?"

"Now that you mentioned it, I believe I did."

CHAPTER 5

A FRIEND FROM THE PRINT SHOP DAYS VISITED A FEW DAYS AFTER we returned from Oregon. After Steve made a lot of money as a stockbroker, he took Timothy Leary's advice and tuned in, turned on, and dropped out. When I first knew him, he looked dapper dressed in the latest styles, lived in an expensive apartment in the marina, and went to the best restaurants accompanied by the prettiest hippie chicks. Recently, he moved to a cheaper apartment and looked scruffy dressed in worn bell-bottoms, faded wide-lapel shirts, and his perfectly groomed and styled long hair of the past a tangled mess. Steve lived life spontaneously and held nothing back. If he had it, he spent it. His lifestyle change suggested he was running out of money.

We sat in the living room on a warm, sunny day sharing a joint and listening to music. He knew I talked about moving to Oregon but was surprised I was actually going to do it. "What was it I said, Steve that made you think I wasn't serious?"

"Do you know anything about Oregon?" Looking at me skeptically, he took a hit and passed it back.

"I know it's a large state with a small population and with most of the people living around the city of Portland. And they grow a lot of trees."

"As a kid, I visited an uncle who owned a farm in the Applegate Valley near Grants Pass. My visits were really fun, and I loved the area. Listen to what he told me about Oregon that most people don't know."

"I'm moving to Oregon, Steve. It's the next state north not some backward country deep in the heart of Africa. How much different can Oregon be from California?"

"Don't kid yourself, Jack. Are you aware Southern Oregon's called, 'Appalachia of the West,' because it's so poor? The people live isolated in the mountains and suspicious of outsiders, and for that matter, of each other."

"I'm like the mountain man, Jeremiah Johnson. I just want to live in the mountains and be left alone."

"Dig this man!" he said. "The first three towns of Medford, Grants Pass, and Roseburg had the largest membership in the Ku Klux Klan outside the South, and incest was rampant. Roseburg is full of John Birch Society people that want us out of the UN, and they believe there's a communist under every bed. You're a progressive, Jack. They're not your kind of people."

After Steve left, I pondered his warning and remembered a conversation with a couple of thirty-something athletic guys on the return trip after buying the land. We spent the night in a motel in Mt. Shasta, a trendy town at the base of the fourteen-thousand-foot peak about a hundred miles inside California and had breakfast in a restaurant. They were sitting at the next table. "How are you guys doing?" I asked, after one of them nodded. Wearing a bright red shirt, he looked Nordic with blonde hair and blue eyes.

"We're great, but we'll be doing better when ski season opens."

"Are you guys local?"

"Yeah, I lived in Shasta most of my life, and he," pointing to his friend, "is from Southern California. Where're you folks from?"

"We're from San Francisco," piped in Meg already sitting at the table. "We were up in Oregon looking at land in the mountains we're gonna buy."

"Really! What kind of land?"

After she gave them a quick rundown of the last few days, there was a long silence. "Well!" he said, finally, "I wish you folks a lot of luck. We don't go to Oregon much."

"Why not?" I asked.

The Odyssey of a Hippie Marijuana Grower   69

"I'm not sure how to explain it, but something happens when you cross the border. The people are different somehow. It doesn't feel good. We don't like the vibes."

I thought I already made up my mind, and I didn't want to hear the kind of stuff Steve and the skiers talked about. All it did was create doubt, and I hated the feeling of indecision. I paced throughout the flat for most of the afternoon struggling with my dilemma. On the plus side, my enthusiasm for living in that beautiful valley hadn't waned, and I determined I would have difficulties wherever I moved. In thinking back, I remembered feeling the difference in vibes the Skiers talked about, and it concerned me. Communication would be difficult with people who saw the world vastly different. When hitchhiking up and down Interstate-5, I remembered large billboards outside Roseburg urging the US to get out of the UN. I always avoided the town, as did all hitchhikers, and never accepted rides that would end there. The place was filled with hate from right-wing and religious groups and the cops worse than the Gestapo.

After counting up the pros and cons of purchasing the land, the cons were far ahead. However, when Meg returned from her job that evening, I resolved the issue in favor of buying the property. What turned the tide was a poignant, unstated reason that far outweighed any doubts or objections I might have against purchasing it.

For a long time, I held the belief that civilization was doomed. Any day everything would collapse and descend into chaos, and I along with it. I didn't think the world would end, but it would be a time of revolution, upheaval, and great change. I'm not sure how long I held the belief or where it originated, as no one I knew thought as I did.

I remembered the first time I became aware of its existence. It was Friday, and I was in class working intently on an art project. When the girl next to me began to cry, it broke my concentration. Looking around, I saw all the women were in tears. "What's happening?" I asked. "Why is everyone bawling?"

"They killed him," she said

"Who?" I asked.

"They killed President Kennedy."

It was November 22, 1963, and on that day in Dallas, Texas, the president was assassinated. To add to my belief that civilization was headed for destruction, his death came shortly after the Cuban Missile Crisis, when the world narrowly escaped nuclear holocaust. Afterward, came the Viet Nam War, the assassinations of Bobby Kennedy and Martin Luther King, the Watts Riots, Kent State, and a host of other thorny issues, and each brought judgment day closer.

Reluctant to acknowledge I wanted it to fail, I always believed society was immoral. The genesis of my thinking must have come from remembering how society was structured when I lived as an Indian on the plains. Status came from achievement and not from the acquisition of material wealth. It was considered an aberration, a sickness, to accumulate wealth and not give it away. There was no private ownership of land; it belonged to everyone, and no one was left out. You could own a knife or a horse, but you couldn't own ground any more than you could own the sun or the wind. The Earth was their mother and part of the cosmos given to all creatures by the Great Spirit.

After the civil rights movement, the mass demonstrations against the war, and a thousand other revolutions in progress, civilization teetered on the brink. Only a small push would topple it, and apocalypse would descend upon the land. Without any way to protect myself against the coming pandemonium, I felt vulnerable until Meg rejected the land at O'Brian. Above all else, a feeling of security came over me when I entered that valley deep in the mountains, and I saw that living in the middle of a national forest far from civilization as the key to survival. That evening over dinner, we shared a bottle of wine and toasted to our future.

"My plan," I said, "is to go up to Oregon in two-week intervals and work on the barn. I hope you stay at your job until we move. It's the only money coming in."

September, 1974

WHEN I DROVE MEG DOWN TO CHURCH STREET TO CATCH HER streetcar on the morning I left, I was aware of the glaring contrast of our destinations. She was headed into the middle of San Francisco's Financial District and I into a national forest. I stayed the night in a motel in Centerville and was back on the road before dawn. The leaves of trees along the river turned reds and yellows, and with a cool nip in the air, I was reminded of autumns in the Midwest where I lived as a boy. Leaves rarely turned color in San Francisco where there was little change of season.

Everything was still in shade when I entered the valley. A woman in a long nightdress stood in the doorway of the one-room log cabin across from the main house and looked at me impassively as I drove by. The two hippies living in the barn were gone, and as I feared, there was no electricity. Lines came to an abrupt halt a few miles outside Tiller, and my power tools were useless. I never lived without current before, and I wasn't sure I was looking forward to the experience. When it took all afternoon to build a simple lean-to for firewood using hand tools, I became aware how ill-prepared I was for what I was about to experience.

The barn had a sink with running water, but there was no bathroom. The outhouse was down the road a few paces and up the hill about fifty feet. Embarrassingly, it was open and faced the road. While sitting on the throne that afternoon and enjoying a great view of the valley, I nervously watched the road in fear someone would drive by and see me. When no vehicles passed the whole day, it left me with a tense, uneasy feeling. I was suddenly alone in the mountains without TV or radio and without a way to communicate with the outside world. Although the valley was beautiful and I loved being there, I would have liked it if someone came by and talked with me. With only myself for company, I wondered if I liked myself well enough to spend that much time alone?

The barn received full sun on its day-long journey across the sky. At what I determined was five o'clock, its rays caught the tall sugar pines on the hill, and a narrow shadow appeared on the road and front of the barn. Slowly, like a flood, the shade advanced across the valley and up the mountainside until only the pinnacle received sunlight. After feeling positive all day, as daylight faded, scary thoughts maliciously crept into my thinking and eroded my confidence. Everything looked different in the dark, and the large barn lost its familiarity. I made friends with the night many year ago, and it wasn't darkness I feared. Although there were a few scary moments, it was vulnerability and insignificance I felt surrounded by millions of acres of forest and mountains stretching north for hundreds of miles into Canada and south into California almost to the Mexican Border. My scariest fright occurred when my camping lantern projected my shadow into ghostly phantoms on the wall across the large, empty room. But even worse was the unnerving silence. When in the city, even on quiet nights, I heard the hum of the refrigerator from the kitchen or the mournful cry of a distant train speeding through the night but now only deathly silence that left me feeling disconnected and a little scared.

I felt more together after eating cold chicken and drinking wine Meg packed for me. After I rinsed my plate in cold water at the sink, I opened the side door. Unsurprisingly, it was a black hole. For a moment, I studied the darkness that seemed to have viscosity like oil. Jokingly, I speculated it was a doorway into another dimension, and if I tried walking through it, I would get stuck between the two worlds. It was a fantasy that proved to have substance, because in the next instant, I slammed the door shut and locked it. As the floor swayed beneath me, I leaned against the wall to keep from passing out, my thought and emotions running rampant.

"Oh God!" I said aloud. "What have I done to myself? Why did I come here?"

When I attempted to understand what sent me reeling, there was no rational answer. It was dark, and I saw nothing. Yet my body perceived something out in the night so terrifying I almost crumpled. What made it the most frightening event in my life was that I didn't understand how I perceived it, only that something horrific was out there. Until then, my fear was always of the known. This was terror of the incomprehensible.

Confused and trembling, I questioned how I could remain there if something ghastly was stalking me out in the night. My first panic-stricken solution was that I wouldn't go outside at night. Quickly recognizing the absurdity of my thinking, I determined I had two choices. The first was to leave in the morning and never return. The other was to go outside, face the night, and confront what was out there. To leave was unacceptable. It was my place, and I had to claim my right to be there.

Before I could change my mind, I stepped out into the night clutching a flashlight. Darkness engulfed me. I saw nothing. Fighting a desire to shine the light, I stood pressed up against the barn listening, the night air cool on my hot skin. "Trust your feelings" said a voice in my head. After a few minutes, a silhouette of the sugar pines on the hill and an outline of the road became visible from an incredible display of stars. Cautiously edging away from the protection of the barn, I stood out on the road facing the forest. Without warning, a blast of wind hit me in the face, although the night was perfectly still. As tears ran down my face and feeling I was about to die, I struggled to contain my consciousness being torn from me and everything a confusing jumble of thoughts, feelings, and emotions.

There must have been a lapse of time, because suddenly it was over, and I came back to awareness unsure how long I was there. I felt calm and heard crickets chirping. Although I didn't feel different, something changed. When I stopped to pee before going inside, I became aware I was marking territory with my urine.

Exhausted, I snuggled into my sleeping bag up on the deck. As sleep was about to claim me, a howl exploded from out of the darkness and jolted me awake. The valley was suddenly alive with a chorus of barks, whoops, and yelps that echoed and reverberated between the hills of the narrow valley and triggered a primordial remembering of running with the pack and the joy of the kill. Then silence that left me wanting more but thankful coyote was free and uncorrupted by man and his civilization.

———◦◦◦———

THE SUN MADE A RECTANGULAR BRIGHT SPOT ON THE FLOOR OF the barn beneath the rear window on a clear morning. Through a side window, I watched a red pickup slowly drive up, followed by a sharp rapping on the door and Hughie's booming high-pitched voice. "Anybody home?"

"Morning," I said, holding it open.

"I see you made it back."

"Good to be back. How are things in the valley?"

We moved toward the rear of the barn where the kitchen would be. "Good, as long as the weather holds. Had a good rain last week, but she's not ready to settle in yet."

"It's only September. Do the rains begin this early?"

"Some years. In others, we get lucky and not until November."

"Coffee?"

"Nope, can't stay. Hauling a load of hay to Medford this mornin'."

"What's your feeling about this year?"

"Hard to say. It's an early fall, with the leaves already turnin'. I see you made yourself a lean-to for firewood. Gonna need more firewood than that, a lot more, and you're gonna need a good chain saw. You own one?"

"No. You sell them at your feed store?"

"Yep! Can fix you up with one easy. Come in when I'm there and try a few."

Turning, he headed out the door. I listened to the sound of his truck tires against the gravel road until it faded into the distance. Hughie was the first person I spoke with in almost three days, and his words echoed in my head for hours. My job that day was to finish cleaning out the barn and write a shopping list. Tomorrow, I would make my first trip into town.

The next morning, with an Oregon Road map spread open on the floor, I understood the great distances I would need to travel that day. My first stop was over eighty miles to Medford, and I reminded myself not to forget anything needed for the next two weeks, because trucking back to town was a whole day's affair.

I returned after sunset and quickly unloaded the small propane stove and canisters purchased at a second hand store. I dumped the long 2x6 tongue-and-groove lumber for the new floor outside in front of the door and crawled exhausted into my sleeping bag.

Struggling to balance one of the long boards the next morning, I felt someone behind me grab it. Spinning around, I was surprised to see it was a young hippie chick holding the other end. "Who are you?" I asked.

"I'm Carolyn. Let me help."

The weather turned hot and sunny, and after the boards were inside, we stood in the shade of the maple tree across the road drinking water. "You live in the valley?" I asked.

She was younger than I first thought, possibly under eighteen, her hair in pigtails. My first impression was that she didn't look well. Without makeup or lipstick that would have helped outline her barely visible lips, she looked undernourished, and her skin was white and pasty. I wondered if she was getting enough food. Her high boots disappeared under a long, buckskin leather skirt, and tiny, yellow flowers dotted her not so clean white blouse. She seemed shy in the way she avoided looking at me, but I somehow knew otherwise. "We're living in the back of the valley," she said, "and making payments to Hughie. I have an old man. His name's Larry. I'm a Cancer, and he's a Taurus. We've been together since he fucked me in the back of his pickup two years ago. Do you have an old lady?"

"I do, but she can't be here until spring. Are you members of the Whole Earth?"

"Not exactly, but Larry's real close with the other guys. They all lived together in the Haight. Will you be here tomorrow?"

"I'll be here for the next two weeks."

"I'll come by."

Carolyn visited each day during my first two weeks and helped with my work. I wondered why she came when she had an old man at home, and after she'd leave, I'd have an uneasy feeling about her.

The two weeks went by fast. As I worked outside in front of the barn learning to saw lumber straight with a hand saw on my last day in the valley before returning to the city, an older, dark pickup approached. It slowed and stopped next to me. The window came down on the passenger side revealing a scruffy, bearded face. His hand darted out to shake hands. "How you doing, man?" he said. "I'm Cecil. I live down at Crooked Creek. That's eighteen miles downriver as the crow flies. Are you the new guy everyone's talking about?"

"I'm the new guy, but I didn't know I was being talked about. Are you a member of the Whole Earth?"

"I'm just a friend who hangs out, but you sure caused a stir among the folks living here in the valley."

"Really!"

"Oh! They'll get over it."

"Get over what?"

"You know, man! They're all riled up. They had the whole valley bought, and you come along and buy a section in the middle splitting it in two and killing their dream."

MEG GREETED ME BACK WITH WARM HUGS AND KISSES, AND WE made love with renewed passion. The good news was that she struck a deal with her boss at the travel agency where she worked. If she stayed with the company until March, which was exactly what she intended to do, he would lay her off, and she would be able to collect unemployment insurance.

I felt radiant on a warm, Saturday afternoon, but the noise and commotion of the city seemed harsh after spending two weeks in the quiet and tranquil mountains. Meg returned from shopping with dried foods like beans and rice that needed no refrigeration. We funneled everything into gallon wine bottles in the kitchen. As we finished, I held one up filled with beans. "Win a prize," I said, "if you guess how many are in this jug."

"What's the prize?"

"Me! You lucky lady."

"What makes you think I want you?"

She removed our marijuana pipe from her pocket already filled. The organic matter turned an angry red when I sucked in the pungent smoke. Taking her turn, she held in the smoke and kissing me deeply blew the smoke into my mouth. I was high instantly. Reaching up beneath her blouse, my hands on her bare breasts, I held her up against the wall as my tongue probed deeply.

Kissing, hugging, and probing each other, we moved toward the bed in the living room leaving a trail of clothing behind on the floor. Sunlight streaming in through the windows took on subtle tones of reds, yellows, and violets. I heard clearly every guitar note from an album playing on the stereo, her passions a workshop of emotions and lustful desires. *You can't always get what you want*, sang the chorus. *You can't always get what you want*, and falling into bed, she pulled me down on top of her. *But if you try sometimes, you just might find*, "ahhhhhha!" she screamed in rapture, *you'll get what you need*.

Toward evening, hunger drove us into the kitchen looking for food, the setting sun bathing the room in a reddish, golden glow. I threw dinner together from leftovers. Sitting naked in bed, we held our palates on our laps. "Hey! This is good," she said, and snuggled close.

"I'm glad you like the way I cook. How come you never learned?"

"There was no one to teach me."

"Didn't your mother teach you?"

John-Paul Cernak

"Mom died when I was a little girl. I think she cooked, but I don't remember."

Her frankness surprised me. Whenever I asked about her childhood, she refused to answer and replied only that she had a brother and sister. "How old were you when she died?"

She drew away before answering and sat stiffly. "I was just seven."

"It must have been hard not having a mother."

"It was hard, especially when you have a father like mine."

"What do ya mean?"

"He wasn't there for us. That's what I mean."

"Where was he if he wasn't there for you?"

"He was there alright but not for his kids. After my mother died, I hardly saw him. He sent us to boarding school, and we spent summers with uncles and aunts. The only time I saw him was when we displeased him, and he dispensed punishment. Then he married that witch. She's why I came to the West Coast."

When she said, 'that witch,' I felt like the prince in a fairy tale who came to rescue the princess, but I also felt vaguely concerned. I always suspected the quality of the father-daughter relationship, as well as the mother-son's, was an indicator of what future relationships with the opposite sex would be like. I hugged her in sympathy, not knowing what to say, and our kisses quickly ignited our passions into a raging blaze. Who could think about stuff like that when things were going so well?

———⌘———

October, 1974

IN THE HOPE OF PICKING UP A PASSENGER TO SHARE EXPENSES ON my next trip to Oregon, I pinned a message on the bulletin board at the food co-op down on Sanchez Street and received a call from a woman heading up to a town north of Centerville. On the morning I left, thick fog and heavy commuter traffic slowed travel to a crawl. I could feel the gloom from the people in their cars around me heading to their nine-to-five jobs. On the other hand, I was going into the woods, and my heart was singing a song of joy. I was leaving behind all the pettiness and stupidity of society. I was free, no more traffic jams for me. I was finished with the frustration of dead-end jobs, putting up with self-serving, backbiting people, and with bureaucrats puffed up with their self-importance. I felt sorry for friends who cut their hair and took regular jobs. It was doubtful I could ever fit back into straight society, although when I looked back, it seemed I never had.

The fog lifted when I reached the address my caller gave me on Dolores Street in the Mission near the park. I stopped in front of a large, gray Victorian converted into apartments. A slim, good-looking chick answered the door and looked me over. "Hi, I'm Nancy."

She was a knockout in her early thirties, and I was instantly captivated. With a modest and unassuming approach, she reminded me of Willow. But unlike our Native American Princess, who always seemed ill at ease and displayed characteristics of an animal wanting to flee, Nancy looked relaxed and comfortable in the world.

She parted her dark shoulder-length hair in the middle giving balance to the two halves of her face, which matched perfectly, and along with vivid blue eyes and a gorgeous smile, she didn't need jewelry or fancy clothes to adorn herself wearing only jeans, a white blouse, and casual shoes. What added to her attractiveness and gave her poise was her firm athletic body that radiated strength and glowed with health and vitality. She looked as if she belonged in the country. What surprised me was her firm grip when we shook hands.

Traffic flowed smoothly once across the Bay Bridge and on Interstate-80. I settled back for the long drive taking occasional glances at my attractive passenger. She seemed to be dozing. As I approached the bridge over the Carquinez Strait—the entrance from the Sacramento River Delta into San Francisco Bay—a large, late model sedan swung over from the next lane and cut me off.

I hit the brakes easily avoiding a collision, but became quickly aware he cut me off intentionally. When I caught up, he gave me the finger and swore. Even more perplexing was he wore a suit and drove a large expensive automobile. I lost him in the long line waiting to pay their toll. "What was that all about?" asked Nancy, who awakened from her reverie.

"Your guess is as good as mine. Did you notice that vehicle somewhere earlier?"

"No! I never saw it before, but I wasn't paying attention. He sure looked mad though."

At the tollbooth, I dropped my money into the funnel and drove off. As I shifted into fourth gear, there he was waiting at the side of the road and pulled our behind me. "There he is again!" I shouted, feeling panic, and watched in my rear-view mirror as he quickly approached. "What does the son of a bitch want?" I felt a strong jolt when the big Lincoln bumped my little pickup. "This guy's a maniac." The fear brought to mind a TV movie. In it, a large eighteen-wheeler forced a little car off the road. He quickly approached again. I held on for a second hit, but at the last second, he changed lanes, gave me the finger as he passed, and disappeared into the distance. "Glad to see him go." she said. "I don't even want to speculate what was going on in his head."

"Let's hope we never find out. Has anything like this ever happened to you before?"

"I've run into unstable people, and you never know what'll trigger an outburst. I had a roommate who was a total crazy. She ended up committing suicide. This guy seemed to have an agenda though."

"His wife must have cut him off," I joked.

"Some people just don't like hippies."

"Why are you heading up to Oregon?" I asked, now that the ice between us was broken.

"I'm going up to look at a community near Oakridge. I'm burned out on the city, but I haven't found the right country situation yet. I looked at several communes in the Santa Cruz Mountains around

Ben Lomond. Everything felt closed and didn't feel I could fit in. I'm still not convinced communal living is for me. I'm willing to give it a try. Maybe I'll have better luck in Oregon."

"If you find living collectively is not for you, would you still want to get out of the city?"

"I don't want to live in town anymore, but I don't have enough money to buy a place of my own. Even if I did, I wouldn't want to live alone. So it seems my only choice is to connect with someone or with a group."

The more we talked, the more she enchanted me. When she ran her fingers through her hair, it reminded me of another woman who was once close. "There's a community from San Francisco called the Whole Earth living up in the valley where I purchased land."

"Are they the big one in the Haight?

"That's them."

I wouldn't be interested in connecting with them."

"Why not?"

"I hear they're scammers and into hard drugs. I like smoking a little grass once in awhile, but I'm not into all the heavy stuff. What's your scene?"

For the next few minutes, I described Ash Valley and its isolation. She listened intently without interruption. "If it's that far from civilization," she questioned, "how are you going to earn money?"

"I'm not sure. Something'll work out."

"Your place sounds interesting. I'd like to see it sometime."

"Would you like to come up and see it before I drive you to Oakridge?"

She looked at me as if it was for the first time. "Sure! Why not! It sounds fun."

After I invited her, I felt a pang of guilt and questioned if I was being disloyal to Meg. Throughout our conversation, I never mentioned her. I'm not sure if it was intentional. The guilt quickly eased when I remembered her infidelity with Bruce. Moreover, after Meg told me about her difficult relationship with her father, the intuitive voice warning me that to be with her would lead to disaster returned, and I was going to give this chick a good look.

It was near sunset when we reached the road leading up to the valley. She seemed fascinated by the mountains and dense forest, and we hardly spoke for the past hour. Driving up from the river, a herd of black tail deer darted past heading down to the creek, their eyes shining in the headlights. The valley lay in soft twilight with the sun hitting the top of the mountain and the barn barely visible in the distance. Nancy gave a quiet exclamation of delight by sucking in her breath. "Nice, isn't it," I said.

I lit several kerosene lanterns, and we toasted our safe arrival by drinking wine from coffee mugs. She walked around examining the barn. "Stark, isn't it?" she said.

"It isn't the Ritz, but it's home."

"Where's the bathroom?"

I opened the side door, pointed to the outhouse on the hill, and handed her a flashlight. We talked all evening, and her presence fascinated me. She looked good in daylight but even better in the soft glow of the kerosene lanterns. When our conversation suddenly ran out, I prepared for bed by carrying my sleeping bag up onto the deck and assumed she would choose a spot below. To my delight and at the same time to my fearfulness, she carried her gear up and placed it next to mine. She looked ravishing wearing a floppy nightdress when we ran into each other at the sink to brush our teeth. She wore little makeup, and her skin turned rosy pink from the cold water. After I blew out the lantern, I felt her vibe strongly next to me. I reached out several times to touch her but each time pulled back. From frustration, I began to shiver. After what seemed like hours, I fell asleep.

The morning was cold. I built a fire for the first time in the woodstove made from a fifty-gallon metal drum. We sat silently drinking coffee and absorbing the radiant heat like two lizards lying in the sun. She wore a sweatshirt and jeans and looked disheveled the way most people do in the morning, especially with no bathroom. I always believed the best way to judge a woman's beauty is to see her in the morning when she first arises, and Nancy was beautiful. "Are you in a hurry to get to Oakridge?" I asked.

"Are you trying to get rid of me?"

"No! I like your company."

"I thought I'd play it by ear."

"How about some breakfast?"

"Why don't you let me help?"

Later that morning, we exited the barn for a hike, and I discovered the leaves of the maple tree across the road had turned a bright yellow in my two-week absence. "Where are we hiking," she asked.

"Up there," I said and pointed to the mountain with the clear cut at the back of the valley.

"How far is it?"

"I think Hughie said it's two miles each way. Can you handle it?"

"Four miles? God, that's far. Isn't there a streetcar we can catch on the way back?"

"I can always call you a cab."

A quarter mile up the road, we passed the Whole Earth Communal House. Several vehicles were parked in front, but we didn't see anyone. Down by the pond, a huge white goose ran towards us at full speed, its neck straight up and squawking loudly. "I don't think that gander is welcoming us," she said.

With it long neck straight out, it attacked immediately nipping at our legs and backsides. We ran into the woods and reemerged on the road when safely past. "I don't know if you're safe to be around," she said. "Do you always attract strange creatures that want to harm you?"

"How do you know it's me who is doing the attracting?" I countered.

We walked in silence each focused on the beauty of the forest and the cool morning perfect for hiking. Piles of scat and the feather remains of a kill lay on the road. The road climbed when we crossed over the cattle guard and into the national forest. I wasn't uncomfortable, but my legs knew I was walking uphill. I set a fast pace with Nancy matching me step for step to the top. Meg would have bitched all the way.

All day, Nancy helped around the barn, and that evening we talked again until our conversation ran out. As in the previous night, her presence lying next to me filled me with excitement. Marshaling all my courage, I reached out and put my arm around her. When she didn't respond, I quickly withdrew. She hadn't pushed me away, but I felt rejected, nevertheless.

In the morning, I felt foolish to have believed there could be a connection between us, and felt guilty that I would have cheated on Meg. I made an immediate decision to drive her to Oakridge, yet I felt confused. After breakfast, she disappeared and didn't return for a long time. I peeked out the front door, and she was bathing up by the water tank. She was friendly when she returned, but my attitude towards her changed. I no longer saw her as a beautiful woman but as someone causing me embarrassment. "I think its best I take you to Oakridge this morning," I said with a cutting edge.

"If that's what you feel is best" she retorted but looked perplexed.

On another level, I understood my assessment of her was incorrect. She was bathing to become my lover, but my embarrassment pushed me into a dark tunnel that only let me think of removing her. On the drive to Oakridge, we hardly spoke, and I will always remember her look of longing and of loathing.

—⦿⦿⦿—

November, 1974

THERE WERE SEVERAL UNFAMILIAR VEHICLES PARKED IN FRONT OF the main house when I drove past on my return to the valley. The next day, the woman who lived in the main house with her two young daughters visited. I spoke to her only once briefly. She seemed to have a connection with the Whole Earth, but I wasn't sure how.

"Some men think I'm pretty," she said. "Do you think I'm pretty?"

"Yes!" I said, "very pretty."

"I know that some men don't want a woman with children, but I'm really very nice and would treat you well."

I felt confused. It sounded as if she was offering to be my old lady. The next day, Hughie stopped by to tell me about a new guy moving into the valley. We drank coffee at a small beat-up table I purchased at a second-hand store. "His name's Brad," he said, "and he purchased the main house and a hundred and seventy-five acres."

"No kidding. That must make you feel good."

"Yeah! I can pay off some of my wife's doctor bills."

"When's he moving in?"

"He's already in, and his girlfriend'll join him in a couple of months when they'll be married. Come down, and I'll introduce ya."

"What's going to happen to Cancer Nancy?"

"I'm afraid she'll have to leave." He shook his head sadly, and his face showed regret. "She doesn't want to leave but has no choice. She's such a sweet kid and a good mom, too."

"Won't she move in with the other members of the commune?"

"Don't think so. They won't take her in. I let her live in the main house when they kicked her out before. Her boyfriend was the one in charge of the money when they had their firewood drive."

The following morning on my way out to meet the new guy, a great horned owl sat on a fence post a short way up the hill. I remembered reading about them in nature studies class. He was a large bird standing over two feet high. Although I was only a few feet away, he sat calmly and unafraid and turned his head almost all the way around to watch me pass. I stopped and looked back. He hadn't moved. Was it another omen? But I refused to speculate; sometimes an owl is just that and nothing more.

At the curve in the road, a large herd of cows grazed on grasses that grew abundantly after the recent rains that I missed again. In the distance, I could see a group of people gathered on the road in front of the main house. Standing next to Hughie was a tall man along with David and Lisa the hippie couple and members of the Whole Earth Commune who lived in the one-room log cabin on the road. David was a tall, slim, quiet man in his late twenties and wore a full beard and ponytail. My first impression was that he was secretive, introspective, and somewhat reclusive. Lisa was his opposite, short, pretty, social and aggressive. As I approached, David nodded and disappeared inside. "There he is," said Hughie. "Meet your new neighbor, Brad."

"Welcome to Ash Valley," I said, reaching out and shaking hands.

Brad was in his early thirties and was tall, lean, and athletic. He was the Jack Armstrong all-American boy type and reminded me of a young John Wayne. He was clean-shaven, his hair cut short, and had broad shoulders and square jaw. He was younger, taller, and better looking than I was and exuded confidence. From the way Lisa looked at him and hung on to his every word, I could tell she was already smitten. I felt a moment of envy. "Have you ever lived in the country?" he asked.

"No! I'm a city guy. Maybe, you can give me some pointers."

"Be glad to. I'm heading out tomorrow for a load of fence posts and firewood. Come along if you'd like."

The next morning when I knocked on his door, the sun hadn't yet risen above the mountain. "Help yourself to coffee," he said, "while I get my gear."

I was curious to see the inside of the old log house. The kitchen had a definite backcountry feel with knotty pine walls but with a modern gas range and other labor-saving devices. "Does this house have an indoor bathroom?" I asked.

"Sure does," he yelled from the other room. "Let me know if you ever want to take a shower. I'd have to charge you something for the hot water though."

"How do you heat it?"

"With propane, same as for the range, I haul in from Tiller."

"I just might take you up on that from time to time."

The Odyssey of a Hippie Marijuana Grower   87

Brad drove deep into the mountains that morning on roads used primarily for timber removal. It was my first trip into backcountry. He pointed out different species of trees and how to identify each by their distinctive needles and bark. "Doug Fir and Madrone," he said, "are best for firewood. Western Red Cedar and Yew are best for fence posts."

There was something magical about working in the woods, and although we filled Brad's large pickup with firewood and fence posts, there was no need to cut down any standing trees. Fallen logs of all sizes littered the forest floor. Brad's chainsaw was large and heavy with a thirty-six inch bar and chain. Before he cut, he held it with the bar pointing up towards the sky and gunned the engine. I did the same. It kicked like firing a gun. It was the first time I used one, and I loved the feeling of power it gave me. The highlight of my day was splitting a cedar log cleanly in two using a wood maul. I felt like Abraham Lincoln.

Returning to the barn that afternoon with every muscle and bone aching, I dragged myself into the kitchen for a cup of hot chocolate and fell into a chair. All I could do for the next two days was stare out the window and wonder how long it would take my weak city body to grow strong.

Meg was coming to Ash Valley to spend the long Thanksgiving weekend. It would be her first visit since purchasing the land, but I was feeling apprehensive. It seemed I became territorial about the place. Her coming gave me the feeling she was invading my private domain. I would pick her up at the bus station in Centerville on Wednesday evening, spend three days together in the valley, and after cooking a small turkey on the stove top, we'd return to the city in time for her to be at her job on Monday morning.

Hughie wasn't at his feed store on Wednesday afternoon when I drove in early to try chainsaws. I waited in a restaurant drinking coffee. I picked her out immediately from the people exiting the bus. She rushed into my arms, and it felt good to have her with me. Her hair seemed lighter, and she looked more beautiful than

I remembered. She must have made friends with some guys on the bus who stopped and watched as we hugged and kissed. They knew what we were going to do that night. I wanted to yell out to them: "Eat your heart out!"

———◦∞◦———

December, 1974

IT WAS WARM AND CLEAR WHEN I ARRIVED, AND I AGAIN MISSED the rain. It seemed the weather in the valley wasn't much different from that in San Francisco. I was changing, however, and as the transition to country boy began, I watched the sun during the day and the stars and planets after dark. Seeing a large ring circling the full moon high in the sky on a visit to the outhouse that night, I felt in my bones a weather change was about to happen in a big way.

Early the next morning, high clouds moved in from the southwest, and from the valley, the croaking of frogs intensified. They hatched out in pools after the recent rains and were heralding the coming storm. In early afternoon, a second thicker layer of clouds moved in low and fast, and the rain began in a heavy downpour. There must have been a million frogs, as their croaking became deafening. To add to the crescendo was the pounding of rain on the metal roof. I thought my head would explode.

Night came early that afternoon, and with my head buried under the covers and toilet paper stuffed in my ears, I went to bed without eating dinner or starting a fire. I awakened at first light. Everything was quiet. During the night, the temperature dropped. I could see my breath. I shivered violently dressing and quickly had the sides of the woodstove glowing red, while snowflakes as large as silver dollars floated silently to the ground. The snow fell in whiteout conditions throughout the day, and by nightfall deep drifts accumulated. As a boy living in the city, I eagerly awaited the first snowfall, but alone in the mountains, I felt uneasy.

The next day, the wind howled and the storm intensified. Cold air came in through every little crack in the barn, and I burned large amounts of firewood. At bedtime, I envisioned freezing to death. In the morning, my intuition told me I was safe. As my concerns eased, I reveled in the beautiful white world as I had when a boy and went out into the storm to build a snowman. Towards evening, I walked up the road in the raging blizzard to see how far I could walk in drifts reaching my hips. After a quarter-mile, I returned to the barn exhausted and ate a hardy dinner.

The snow turned to rain the next morning and continued unrelenting for three days until the beautiful white was replaced with drab greens and browns and the valley floor a lake. As the rain diminished, puffs of fog hugged the ground near the creek. With the sun making occasional visits, rainbows appeared sometimes two or three at once. The rain pounding on the roof and the croaking frogs, so vexing earlier, became unnoticeable. For almost a week, I hadn't seen another person; yet I felt peaceful and calm. For the first time in my life, I was self-contained and needed no one else.

AS CHRISTMAS APPROACHED AND WITH MY TIME IN SAN FRANcisco ending, we took sentimental trips around the city and visited a few favorite restaurants to experience them one last time. The first was a pair of miniature Russian bakeries on Clement Street across the street from each other. Besides having wonderful old-world pastries, each had a few tables in the back that served delicious food cooked by little Russian women wearing babushkas. Regrettably, both bakeries closed. A passer-by stopped. "I loved these bakeries," he said, "as I'm sure you did too, but the owners became too old to continue working and retired. I sure miss them."

The next day, we drove across town to North Beach to visit the Gold Spike, my favorite Italian restaurant. Although Meg lived in San Francisco over a year, she hadn't overcome her fear of driving over the steep hills and held tightly to the bar above the door. The traffic light changed halfway up on a particularly steep incline, and the long line of cars came to an abrupt halt. I stopped without rolling back, the little truck clinging precariously to the hillside. I could feel the tension from the people in their cars around us. "Anyone who drives a stick-shift in this town is crazy," she said.

"Trust me," I retorted. "I know how to handle them."

When the light turned green, I smoothly accelerated ahead. "I don't know how you do that, Jack," she said.

As usual, it took twenty minutes driving around North Beach to find a parking spot. We walked up Broadway arm in arm on a cold, foggy, and windy evening through crowds of people, flashing lights, and topless bars. "What's so good about The Gold Spike?" she asked.

"It's a family-style restaurant, and everyone sits together at large tables. The food is home cooking, and it's the best Italian food I ever ate. They serve a six-course meal, and when I first came to town, it was two bucks and twenty-five cents for homemade wine. It's a lot more now but so is everything."

The restaurant was crowded, and a talking mynah bird greeted us as we entered. Paraphernalia from the 49er days covered the walls. There was a photo of the tracks coming together from the west and the east and the gold spike hammered in to connect the transcontinental railroad. The restaurant looked the same, but the minestrone tasted different. While it was still good, something changed. I asked the waitress. "The old folks retired," she said, "and we have a new cook."

We strolled up nearby Grant Street after dinner. The street climbs to Telegraph Hill and Coit Tower. We were going only half-way up to the Coffee Gallery. "What happens there?" she asked.

"It's a little coffee and beer bar with a history. The place was a beatnik hangout in the 50s, and a few were still around when I started going there. It was where I learned how to play chess, but mostly, I went for the music. There's a stage in back. Up-and-coming bands and singers performed for tips. Before they were big,

Janis Joplin, Bob Dylan, and a bunch of other big stars played at the Coffee Gallery."

Everything looked the same when we entered, but pool tables filled the area where the stage was. A few evenings later, when walking through the Noe Valley neighborhood looking at the Christmas displays, it was noticeable there were fewer lights than in previous years due to the oil embargo, and celebrating seemed flat wherever we went. I was disillusioned. "All the little things that made this town great are gone," I said, "and it won't be as difficult leaving San Francisco as I imagined."

In January, I finished the new floor and built a sturdier ladder up to the sleeping deck. I didn't make a trip north in the short month of February. All unfinished jobs would have to wait. I needed time to pack our belongings and finish any city business. On each trip north, I carried as many items as would fit into the small pickup. For the final move, I rented a large U-Haul. With the truck packed and Meg waiting, I gave the empty flat a last inspection and said a short prayer to speed us on our way. It wasn't the most beautiful place I lived in while in San Francisco, but it was the last. The landlord came to say goodbye. He looked disappointed. "You were good tenants, and you're leaving it in better condition than you found it. Drop us a line now and then."

They were nice folks, but I knew I wouldn't.

CHAPTER 6

───⟐⟐⟐───

March 1975

I<small>T WAS PAST MIDNIGHT WHEN WE ARRIVED IN THE VALLEY.</small> I packed our bedding near the rear door of the truck, and we spent the first night comfortable on Meg's queen mattress. Two days later, we dropped the big truck off in Centerville and stopped at Hughie's feed store to try chain saws. I wanted one as large as Brad's but settled for one smaller after learning the price. The next day, we went into the mountains for our first load of firewood. That afternoon, after returning with a load of almost dry fir, exhaustion set in, and it was again two days before I could work. Bringing in that first load taught me to never cut wood below the road.

We rented a post office box at the Tiller Store the following week and had lunch at the Tiller Tavern. We were on our way to Medford to file Meg's unemployment claim and do our food shopping. Stubby and Dorothy owned the tavern. He ran the bar and she the restaurant. The food she served to her mostly logger and Forest Service customers was home cooking and perhaps some of the best in Southern Oregon.

The road out of Tiller was all curves, and when we passed a tiny store about five miles out of town, with nothing visible but mountains and forest, I wondered out loud where their customers came from. Meg quickly intruded into my thoughts. "Good question," she retorted. "Speaking of business, my unemployment isn't going to last forever. Have you figured out how we'll earn money?"

"I've been thinking about it. What do you think of a truck farm? We'll grow vegetables and sell them to locals in town and maybe to restaurants."

She reacted immediately. "Get real, Jack! You're so far from civilization your gas will eat all your profit, and your vegetables will wilt by the time you reach your customers. Besides, there are not that many restaurants."

"Maybe you're right. My other idea is to start a nursery."

She quickly cut me off again. "We don't have anything set up. Wouldn't we need greenhouses and other equipment? In addition, we don't have any plants started. Isn't a nursery something that'll take three or four years before it makes any money? You're going to need to come up with something better than that."

"Well! What do you suggest?"

"I thought you had it all worked out."

"I'll think of something."

All through March, the weather stayed cold and rainy. Storms rolled in off the Pacific one after the other impossible to know when one ended and the next one began. We walked when the rain was light but never encountered anyone. The subject of generating money came up again. We just passed the Whole Earth Community House and the large goose living down by the pond launched an attack. I was prepared and turned it away with a long stick. "Have you had any more ideas about how we'll earn money?" she asked.

"There doesn't seem to be any way, except."

"Except what?"

"Except grow weed."

"Is that all you can think of? Do you want to land us in jail?"

"Lighten up Meg!" I waved my arm around at the tree-laden mountains. "We're so far from civilization nobody gives a crap what we do up here. No self-respecting cop comes within a hundred miles of this place. What people do up here is grow pot. I'll bet everyone from Centerville to here's a grower. If we lived closer to civilization, I'd be hesitant too, but out here, we won't have any problems. Besides, I don't see any other way."

"I don't like it, Jack. I don't like living on pins and needles."

"Are you with me or not?"

Spinning around, she walked fast back towards the barn. I didn't attempt to catch her.

While waiting for the sun to shine, we readied our gardening tool and planted vegetables and marijuana seeds in quart and half-gallon paper milk and juice cartons we saved for months. Each morning and evening, we shuttled our little starts in and out to protect them from frost. I worked outside as much as weather permitted digging fence postholes and constructing a small green-house out of 2x4's I covered with clear plastic. Heavy rain often forced me inside to a warm fire.

I made a decision we would grow our garden without power tools, using only shovels, hoes, and rakes. The truck and chainsaw were the only gasoline driven tools I couldn't do without. All others were luxuries that would keep us dependent on the outside cash economy. My mother grew a large garden using only hand tools, so why couldn't we? I was sure our garden would take up only a half acre.

Around the first of April on a cool, damp, overcast morning, we walked out of the barn each carrying a bucket. With pockets of fog hugging the ground and the valley floor awash in yellow dandelions, we filled our pails with flower heads without moving more than a few feet. Meg was making wine. She stuffed them into several large five-gallon jugs, like those used in water coolers, added sugar, yeast, oranges, and water and placed an air lock on the neck of each to allow the carbon dioxide gas to escape as the mixture fermented. Each day after the third week, she siphoned out some of the not quite finished mixture for tasting, and for the next hour or so, we wouldn't get much work done. After all the sugar turned to alcohol, we bottled it in gallon jugs and hammered in corks. The dandelion wine tasted a little like sake, the Japanese rice wine, and had a kick like a mule.

I noticed a small tear in the corner of the bread wrapper one rainy morning, while Meg cooked breakfast and I made toast. "Oh! Oh!" I said. "It looks like we've been raided by small creatures."

Using both hands, she carried the heavy frying pan filled with scrambled eggs and vegetables over to the table. "Is the toast ready? I've been hearing noises at night. I'll bet this place is crawling with mice."

"We need a cat," I said, helping myself to the food.

"And a dog," she asserted as if she had been thinking about it.

She drove to Centerville the next morning and returned with a dog and a cat. "How easy it was. A little girl in the Centerville Market parking lot had a basket full of kittens, and I found the dog through a flyer on the bulletin board. This was their last one."

The cat was a tiny ball of gray fur and the dog a black lab mix. We named the cat Papocha and the dog Pablo. That evening, sitting near the woodstove on our old leather couch, the cat seemed to like me the best, and the dog spent the evening lying at Meg's feet, when he wasn't exploring and leaving behind small surprises.

Lisa visited on a cold wet afternoon several days later. She and her mate David lived in the one-room log cabin across from the main house and were the only members of the Whole Earth Commune who welcomed us. We gathered around the woodstove on another cold, wet, and wintry day. She came to invite us for a visit to meet the people of the commune. "Stop by tomorrow," she said. "As you probably noticed, Hughie sold the herd, except for Bully and a few females he's keeping for breeding, and he gave me one of the milkers. She gives more than we can use. Come by any morning, and I'll sell you a gallon for fifty cents. But bring your own container. I'm finally getting the hang of milking."

"Sounds great," I said, looking at Meg. "We can make tapioca pudding." I turned and spoke to Lisa. "I do have one request. When we start our garden, I'd appreciate you herding your cow through the valley instead of on the road until I get a fence up. I wouldn't want your cow getting into our garden." Meg quickly changed the subject and the importance of my message was quickly lost. "Who are the women driving an old car I see leaving the valley and returning a few days later?"

"That's Darlene and some of the other women. They're on California welfare. They truck down each month to pick up their checks. She and Donald were the first to move in four years ago and took it hard when the deal to buy the valley fell through. Her old man is more laid back, but she's high octane."

"Who is the guy with the dog?" I asked.

"That's Mountain Man and Chaquese. They're inseparable."

The next day, we walked the quarter mile up to the Whole Earth Communal House. Five or six members sat at tables talking among themselves. Darlene worked in the kitchen assisted by two women. Although invited, we were ignored. Meg stayed close by my side after feeling the cold reception. Mountain Man came around and introduced himself. "And that's Chaquese," he said, pointing to his dog, a handsome Belgium Shepherd with bluish tones. He lay with his head on the floor and looked up at us in acknowledgment.

Mountain Man was tall and athletic and in his early thirties. He wore his long hair in a ponytail and had a bushy moustache. He was the only member of the commune living in the valley without a mate, unless you counted the dog. "Goddamn it, can't you do anything right?"

When I heard the strong language, I looked into the kitchen. Darlene was in a fury, and the two women assisting her looked harassed. We stood around a few more minutes and were about to leave when she rushed past holding a wooden spoon. "Would you people want to be part of our community?"

Everyone stopped talking and looked at us as if we had just arrived. It surprised me when she asked if we wanted to become members. We went only to meet the people, and with the exception of David and Lisa and now Mountain Man, none of the others were friendly. I never spoke with several members, and they didn't even return my wave when driving past. I couldn't imagine being a part of their commune. "No!" I said, without hesitation. "We'll remain solo, but you can continue using the garden. I have no plans to use the land."

As we were leaving, Larry and Carolyn's vehicle drove up, and for some reason just seeing their truck gave me an uneasy feeling.

———◦◦◦———

It warmed in April, but heavy rain continued through the month and into May. Swallows appeared and zoomed around like little fighter planes catching insects on the wing. I didn't know if they came back to Ash Valley each year on the same day as they did in San Juan Capistrano down in Southern California, but I liked them. The sky cleared for several days, but the ground remained too wet for planting. "Where will you plant the marijuana?" Meg asked.

We stood pressed together in our small greenhouse inspecting our seedlings. Marijuana starts grew side by side with vegetables. The answer to her question was one I had considered for a while. Standing behind her, I teasingly kissed the back of her neck. She shrugged her shoulder annoyingly. "Stop it Jack; be serious."

"We haven't even broken ground," I retorted, "and I'm already feeling overwhelmed with all the work that'll need doing once the rain stops, so it looks like in the garden with the veggies."

She turned, facing me, her hands on her hips. "You mean out in plain sight in front of God and everyone?"

I held up a marijuana plant for her to look at closely. "Aren't they beautiful? We'll plant corn in front to hide them."

"That won't work, Jack! They'll be seen."

"You said to be serious. Well, I am serious! Who cares if they're seen? Half the people won't know what they are, and the others will turn a blind eye."

"I don't like it, Jack. We're taking a big chance."

"Maybe, but we don't have any choice. It's either in the garden or not at all. We're living in the middle of a national forest. The rules that applied in civilization don't pertain to us anymore. We make our own laws here. If you're gutsy enough, you can get away with anything."

——◦◦◦——

DRAGONFLIES HATCHED OUT AT THE END OF MAY, AND THERE seemed to be millions in our little valley, deep in the mountains where nature was in balance and free from insecticides and herbicides. Over the months, the birds took their share, but many lasted the summer. Redwing blackbirds built their nests among the swamp grasses along the creek and quickly became my favorite bird. I never tired of hearing their unusual high-pitched calls.

It wasn't until the middle of June that the sun made regular appearances and planting began. I dug up large areas of sod and using shovels and hoes worked the soil. It was backbreaking labor. Meg bitched but buckled down and did her share. We went to Brad's a few times to shower, and a few times Lisa and David, Mountain Man, and Hughie stopped to chat. Otherwise, we did no socializing. Each day, we worked from early morning until the light faded and after a late dinner fell into bed exhausted.

On a cool, cloudy but rainless morning, Meg went to town with the dog. I stayed behind to dig planting holes for fruit trees in the orchard on the north side of the barn. With only the big trees up in the ancient forest looking down at me like sentinels and the cool weather perfect for the heavy labor, I focused on my task. I was jolted out of my mediation when my body registered something threatening. When I looked up, a wolf was sitting on the road just a few feet away. As I readied my shovel to use as a weapon, everything cane into perspective. The animal wasn't a wolf. It was a large coyote. Dressed in a thick fur coat, he was almost as big as his larger cousin and didn't look anything like Wile E. Coyote who chased Road Runner in cartoons. He sat looking at me, unthreatening. Finally I said: "Hello, Mr. Coyote" but felt perplexed. Since when did wild animals make social calls on people? All the while, a voice in my head was urging me to walk up close. I never did. My fear held me back. After a few minutes, he disappeared into the woods above the road. I never told Meg about his visit believing it was for me alone.

———ฅ/ฅ/ฅ———

Now that the valley had new landowners, the Forest Service sent in a surveying crew to help distinguish private land from public. While a crew of three surveyed and buried metal boundary corners in concrete, their supervisor sat in his vehicle reading. We called him the Colonel. He occasionally stopped by, and Meg would invite him in for tea. When the sun shined, we sat outside next to the garden. After he'd drive off in his green Forest Service vehicle, she'd have a few anxious moments. "Do you think he knows what they are? He's an intelligent guy; he must know that's marijuana growing out there."

I shrugged my shoulders. "He didn't let on if he did."

With over a hundred already in the ground and some over two feet high, the corn planted in front to hide them grew only inches.

For most of the spring and summer, when weather permitted, we slept outside under the stars on Meg's waterbed set up on the flat area across the road under the maple tree. I couldn't remember sleeping as soundly all through the night and awakening as refreshed as that first summer. We experienced a few mosquitoes and no-see-ums at nightfall when working in the garden but never while sleeping outside. Neither mosquitoes nor any other creatures bothered us, although we often heard rustling in the underbrush only a few feet away, possibly a bear. Meg claimed it was Big Foot.

Slowly our bodies hardened and the work became easier. All through July, the weather remained cool with frequent showers that sent us scurrying inside, and depending on the time of day, to a glass of dandelion wine. I longed for warmer temperatures after dwellings for years on the cool, foggy, California coast and became heat-deprived.

Living isolated in the mountains had an unanticipated benefit.

When residing in town, I often felt the negative, free-floating vibes from people nearby. What affected me the most were their feelings of dissatisfaction. Most days, I easily blocked them. The volume and intensity on Sunday evenings often broke through my defenses and overwhelmed me. I called the phenomenon, "The Sunday Night Blues." Now I wasn't even sure what day was Sunday, as everyday seemed like the weekend living on the land in a natural lifestyle away from the prescribed routines of society.

About that time, our neighbor Brad paid us a visit to introduce his new wife, Beth. On another rainy day, we sat at the kitchen table drinking tea and wine celebrating their marriage. The sun broke through intermittently heating the barn and stirred the flying insects. I grabbed a yellow jacket that tried to drink my wine, and it stung me. They both laughed. "Don't you know any better than to grab a yellow jacket?" said Beth.

"San Francisco didn't have any, and I didn't know the buggers could sting that hard."

I was surprised and taken aback by the harshness in her voice and her disapproving attitude. When the topic of the Vietnam War came up, I mentioned I participated in several antiwar demonstrations. "Are you one of those radicals," she countered, "who disrupted society with their foolishness?"

"It's was righteous to protest a stupid and illegal war," I said.

"It's people like you and that Jane Fonda woman who gave support to the enemy. I'll bet you're the type of person who believes in astrology and other such nonsense."

Although her disapproving and arrogant attitude irritated me, I tried giving her the shadow of doubt and kept quiet. She was tall, blonde, and with freckles, and dressed cowgirl-style in jeans, a western shirt, and boots, but I didn't find her attractive. She wasn't bad looking. It was who she was inside that projected through and gave her a severe, hardened look. I imagined her the head nun in a strict cloistered convent, and I laughed to myself when I thought of it. The humor quickly faded when she made several more insulting and derogatory comments, and I had enough. "I do believe in astrology," I said. "In fact, we're planting our garden using the Farmer's Almanac for the best astrological planting days." She gave me an ugly look and rose to leave. After they left, I said to Meg that I wouldn't want to spend much time with her.

———⌇⌇⌇———

WITH ALL THE RAIN, EVERYTHING GREW RAPIDLY, AND I NEVER realized it was Hughie's cows that kept the grass short. As the weather warmed, it was suddenly four feet high, and when the wind blew, it undulated like ocean waves. I had only a small hand sickle for cutting around the barn and garden, and it was an endless task. The more I cut, the faster everything grew. Chicory with small blue flowers took over the shoulder of the road, and Shasta Daisies growing in great profusion carpeted the hillside near the outhouse. Wild chamomile with white flowers and yellow centers and borage with brilliant blue flowers peeked up through the grasses wherever I'd sickle. The following week, Hughie paid us a visit. "The grass is getting mighty high," he said. "If you let me cut it for hay, I'll give you three dollars a bale."

For the next few days, I watched Hughie, assisted by Brad, cut and rake the grass into long rows and bale it. All through the process, they seemed aloof and unfriendly. I hadn't approached Hughie; he offered to cut it. After Brad and his wife's visit, an air of animosity and mistrust seemed to permeate the valley, and the last time we showered at their house, an incident occurred.

The sun was setting when we walked the quarter mile down to Brad's house. David and Lisa were visiting from their one-room log house across the road, and they barely acknowledged us and moved back into the shadows letting the spotlight fall on Brad, his wife Beth, and on Meg and me. They must have been talking about us, and we startled them. Feeling suddenly trapped, I wanted to run out the door. I must have had an out of body experience, because in the next instant, I was viewing the scene from outside my body like a spectator. "We'll shower together," I announced after feeling their hostility.

"How risqué," Brad broadcast loudly, his tone reeking of sarcasm and his face ugly and filled with antagonism. "Are you sure you can afford it?"

"We'll pay for two showers."

Beth added something under her breath I couldn't hear, but from her malevolent expression and tone of voice, I knew her comment was pejorative.

Without staying to socialize, we immediately walked back to the barn. Stars twinkled in a coal black sky on a warm evening. I was feeling anger at what I experienced and remembered the owl sitting on the fence post the morning I went to meet Brad. At the time, I refused to consider it an omen but changed my mind after dealing with him since. I remembered reading about Indian tribes in the Pacific Northwest who believed the birds were sinister and called out the names of people about to die. It was believed evil shamans changed themselves into the large night birds, and I no longer had any doubts that the owl sitting on the fence post was an omen, an evil one. "What are you feeling about Brad's comments?" I asked, breaking the silence.

"He was putting us down and so was his new wife. I didn't feel comfortable, and I don't think we should bathe there anymore. It must be that he's not pleased with the arrangement and doesn't know how to tell us."

"It's something more. This is not the first time I felt crappy after visiting Brad, and it gets worse each time I see him. The few times I showered there before you moved up always left a bad taste in my mouth. I'd feel apprehensive and nervous for hours afterwards. It's like his vibe is toxic and poisons me. The last time we talked, he came across as if he was king of the valley."

"King shit is more like it," she added.

"I think he was actually expecting me to kiss his ass."

"Remember the head games kids played in high school. It was

a putdown to make themselves feel more important."

"They were power trips," I added. "What a bummer to have neighbors with such a perverted mentality. They're the kind of people I fought against all my life."

As we approached the barn, I stopped and pointed towards the eastern sky. "Look!" I said. The full moon was rising over the mountain and looked ominous. We watched until it was fully visible. Half was covered in a dark shadow, and the other half glowed blood red. It was in eclipse, and the troubled feeling it gave me added another daunting layer to the owl omen and increased the feeling of looming catastrophe I felt since their visit.

Because we no longer showered at Brad's, each afternoon at the warmest time of day, we bathed in the creek. Meg had no trouble jumping into the icy water, but with little fat for insulation, I found it excruciatingly difficult. Nonetheless, the cold water left me feeling refreshed and relaxed. We soaped and rinsed off out on the bank to prevent polluting the creek.

On a sunny morning after weeks of working without a break, Meg suggested taking the day off. Piling the breakfast dishes into the sink, we drove off without a destination in mind. After driving some miles upriver into the mountains through thick forest, I crossed a bridge and found a parallel gravel road on the opposite side of the river. After driving a short distance, I parked along the bank under towering trees. After toking on the pipe, our kisses quickly became passionate. "You look especially luscious this morning," I said, caressing her inner thighs and unbuckling her bib overalls. She suddenly stopped me. "What's wrong?"

"You're the most gorgeous man in the world," she proclaimed, kissing me passionately. "The truck's too confining. I want to stretch out and really feel you in me!"

Out in the sunshine, I looked across the river for the main road but saw only a mass of green. Walking hand in hand along the bank and stopping to kiss and fondle each other keeping us on edge, we came upon a huge flat rock that jutted out into the river and narrowed it to half its usual width. To our delight, it was covered with a thick layer of moss like a huge, green rug. Sitting near the edge, we had a perspective of being in the middle of the river, and thick foliage growing all around gave us the feeling of protected privacy. I again scanned the forest across the river looking for the main road but hadn't seen or heard another vehicle all morning. "What a wonderful soft rug the Gods gave us," I said, feeling her excitement rising. "I wonder what they had in mind?"

With our next kiss, her mouth imploring me to give her fulfillment, I unhooked her bib overalls, and this time, they slid off unobstructed. She looked ravishing lying naked on the plush, green rug, my hand caressing the soft, blonde hair between her legs. Soothed by the sound of rushing water, a soft, warm, summer breeze caressing our naked bodies, and a floating, euphoric feeling from the marijuana, we united in the middle of the South Umpqua River.

Within moments of entering ecstasy, a loud roar infiltrated my consciousness. At first, I tried to ignore it, but it grew progressively louder demanding attention. Reluctantly, I glanced up, and what I saw revolted me. A log truck was charging rapidly towards us. Hidden by thick shrubbery, the main road ran directly next to the river instead of far back as I assumed. Anyone driving past could easily see us locked in our lascivious embrace fifty feet from any cover.

The driver gave us a prolonged blast from his air horn as he passed, and seconds later, I heard squealing tires. To see two people balling out in the open must have stunned him, and he almost lost control on the curves ahead. Amid laughter and feeling only mildly embarrassed in the knowledge our identities were anonymous, we retreated to our little truck and finished our lovemaking. I'm sure the hippie couple who were fucking out in the open were the talk of every sawmill and logging operation throughout the South Umpqua Valley that day—and perhaps for weeks to come.

It was late evening on a day in the middle of July when we finished planting our garden and still hadn't eaten dinner. "I know there's a lot more work to do," I said, "but we've reached a plateau."

"Thank God, I'm wiped out."

"Let's celebrate and take a few days off."

The next morning after breakfast, I went out to inspect the garden but especially the area that was planted the day before. Long rows of vegetable seedling grew around me and gave me a feeling of pride and satisfaction at seeing how vital and healthy everything looked. It was a major accomplishment, after all, using only hand tools to plant a large garden in virgin soil, and we were well on our way to becoming self-sufficient. When I reached the area planted the day before, my feelings of pride and achievement quickly turned into disgust and anger. Deep animal tracks trampled and destroyed it. Meg! Meg!" I shouted, "Come look at this."

"My God! What happened here?"

"This was done by Lisa and her fucking cow. All that work down the drain. Didn't I ask her nicely to herd her cow through the valley?"

"I remember you telling her, but she wasn't listening."

"I knew this would happen, and I'm going to make sure it doesn't happen again."

Later that morning, as we worked to repair the damage, Lisa came by on the road herding her cow. She carried a small stick for smacking it on the rear when it stopped to graze. She was moving fast, as if she didn't want us to see her. "Lisa," I yelled. "Did you see the damage your cow did to our garden? Didn't I ask you nicely to use the valley when moving your cow between houses?"

She stopped and looked at me. "Don't yell at me, Jack Cernak," she shouted back. This valley is open range, and I can run my cow on the road if I please. Even if the road goes through your property, it's a right of way."

Turning, she ran up the road after her cow. "If I catch it in our garden again," I shouted after her, "I'll shoot the fucking thing."

"Weren't you a little hard on her? And you shouldn't have said that you'd shoot it."

"It was her attitude that pissed me off. I wasn't expecting her to throw herself on a suicide fire. A simple, 'I'm sorry' would have sufficed. All I got from her was some claptrap about this being open range, and that it was our fault her cow trampled the garden."

"What's she talking about anyway? What's open range?"

"It's an archaic law devise by cattlemen when they controlled the west. Cows have a right to go wherever they want. I don't know why it's still on the books. It's as outdated as the horse and buggy.

"Do you mean the owners of cattle don't need to enclose them, but everyone else must fence them out?"

"That's how it works."

"That doesn't seem right."

"Hell no, it isn't right, and I don't give a crap about their stupid law. This is my land, and they better keep their cows off."

Within a few minutes, Brad's wife Beth appeared all fluffed up. She stood on the road and waved her hands in angry gestures. "What right do you have to harangue Lisa that way, Jack Cernak," she bellowed. "This valley is open range, and this road is a right of away. She has every right to run her cow through here, and you have no right to badger her. It's up to you to get your fence up."

She turned and stormed off up the road. All through her tirade, I stood impassively. But what I wanted to do was throw rocks at her. Within a half-hour, Hughie's red pick-up slowly rolled down and stopped near where I worked."That's my cow you're threatening to shoot," he snarled, his hands on his hips and his short body frame hunched over in a combat stance, "and there'd be dire consequences if you did."

"I don't give a crap about your fucking cow or your threats," I yelled, totally losing it. "It trampled my garden, and if I catch it here again, I'll fill it with so much lead, you'll need your cat to move it. And I'll kick your ass to boot."

I stood daring him to make a move, although feeling a little surprised and shocked at what I said. I hadn't meant to go quite that far in threatening to boot him in the butt. I casually leaned on my shovel pretending I was feeling confident. He glared at me menacingly but made no move. After a few minutes, he drove off mumbling to himself.

I took a chance challenging Hughie and believed he wouldn't come onto my property to fight me. Although he was uneducated, he was no dummy, and I wasn't physically or psychologically ready to fight him. Hughie was master of the valley and for good reason. He was strong and powerful. I heard stories he backed down everyone even the biggest and strongest of the hippies. No one ever got away with what I said, and the incident broke open the smoldering hostility I felt from Brad, his wife Beth, Hughie and to a lesser degree from Lisa and thrust it into open conflict. All I wanted was to live in the mountains and be left alone. My act of rebellion wasn't meant to create the firestorm it had, but Hughie and Brad were acting as if they were the bosses of the valley. When I threatened to shoot his cow, I unintentionally challenged their assumption and warned them I wasn't about to take any of their crap.

They retaliated immediately by giving us the silent treatment. Now whenever they drove past, they looked straight ahead pretending we weren't there. We had become persona non grata and the lepers of Ash Valley. When Larry and Carolyn drove past, they purposely increased their speed to kick up dust. I vowed that someday I'd make them eat it. "What's with these people?" Meg asked. "Why do they resent us?"

"Because we don't fit in with their program and do their bidding. We're independent and do as we choose."

"Does our autonomy threaten them?"

"It must. They can't imagine anyone going it alone, and it frightens them."

Although I talked confidently, the next few weeks were difficult for us both, and I wondered if I went too far in proclaiming independence. At first, I perceived the incident as a defeat. In staying true to myself, I later saw it as a win. The conflict cleared the air, and everyone knew where they stood. And without the pretense of friendship, I didn't have to watch my back. Their silent treatment was an attempt to punish us for being free and independent, and they believed we'd soon beg them to take us back, our tails between our legs. I've seen that tactic work before. The facts were, I couldn't give a rat's ass if they never spoke to me again. They were intimidated by my challenge, and their silent treatment was a childish attempt to make it seem they were in control. On top of that, Lisa never ran her cow on the road past our garden again.

Still feeling distraught a few days after the cow incident, I was faced with another difficult decision. The dog killed the cat. We cried when burying its little body up in the woods. "What are you planning to do? " she asked, as we walked down off the hill.

"I know the dog can't stay, but I don't want to shoot him. A bullet seems so final. If we lived closer to town, I'd try to find him another home."

During the night, I made a decision and in the morning fed him a large meal. That afternoon, I drove almost to Centerville. Stopping on a back road, I opened the tailgate, and the dog jumped out. I took off down the road. I will never forget his look of panic when he realized I was abandoning him. Maybe someone will find him, or he'll find his way into town.

While waiting in line at the Centerville Grocery checkout on our next trip into town, a woman with dark, deep-set eyes waited in the next line and smiled when we looked at each other. She was in her mid-thirties, had premature strands of gray in her long dark hair, and her exotic beauty was reminiscent of A Thousand and One Nights. We finished at the checkout lane at the same time and walked out together. "My name's Ginger," she said, "and I live with my old man a few miles upriver. Stop by for some coffee and conversation."

Ginger wasn't a hippie. She was counter-culture more like we were. We followed her back to her homestead. She lived with her mate, Bob, in a small, unincorporated community of six or seven houses each on a few acres a half-mile up from the river. Driving in, I saw chickens, rabbits, and several goats and like most country folks a large garden with flowers. I also noticed power lines going to their house. Bob welcomed us by rolling a doobie, and we sat on their patio becoming acquainted. I felt from the beginning that I knew Ginger all my life.

<hr />

Mountain Man was the only person living in the valley who still talked with us. He was a loner and lived with his dog in a small, leaky, illegal house covered with shakes up in the national forest. I never saw him wear anything but shorts and worn out sneakers. The few times I walked with him, he moved easily up hills and through the woods with his dog at his side. On one occasion, he unhesitatingly walked over a narrow, thirty-foot log spanning the creek. When it was my turn, my body refused to cooperate. I edged across holding on to branches of a tree growing in the creek bed. On his visits, we'd sit outside in the sunshine next to the garden. "You're really devoted to that dog," I said.

"Since I got him five years ago, we've never been apart. We're buddies. Four years ago my first winter here, the temperature plunged below zero for two weeks straight. Separately, we were freezing, but when Chaquese got into my sleeping bag, we stayed warm."

"I remember that winter," I said. "It was cold all along the West Coast. For all the years I lived in San Francisco, I hardly remembered a frost. That year, the temperature dropped below freezing for a long stretch. I lost a bunch of plants. I didn't know you spent winters here."

"I didn't last winter. My father sent me a train ticket home to upstate New York. When I learned Chaquese would have to travel in the cold baggage car, I bought a pair of dark glasses and passed him off as a seeing-eye dog, so he could stay inside with me. You should have seen all the strange looks people gave us when we sat up in the observation car. "How's your pup doing?"

He was pissed when I told him what I did as I knew he would be.

When Meg drove to town to find us another cat, she came back with two, a gray tabby we named Geraldine and a calico we called Gretchen. For the first few days, the tabby wouldn't come to us and hid anywhere in the barn she could. On the third day, she decided we were okay and allowed us to hold her. Within a few hours, she caught her first mouse. We cheered her triumph. She looked proud as she devoured her catch.

A large feral black cat with long hair named Midnight impregnated both females. He lived in the wood before we came and belonged to a hippie who long since left the valley. Whenever possible, he'd sneak into the barn and eat our cat's food. I shot at him several times but always with the intentions of missing. I admired his ability to survive in such a harsh environment. I heard later Brad shot and killed him. It was like him to shoot something free he couldn't control.

We kept the runt of Gretchen's litter. Sammy was small but ferocious like his wild father and impossible to be around until he was fixed. He then became a great cat. He was a climber. A blue jay sat on the branch of the maple tree across the road taunting him loudly. "You can't catch me; you can't catch me!"

The small, sleek, black cat playing it cool moseyed over towards the trunk pretending he didn't care about the jay. In two long leaps, he was up the tree and missed catching the stunned bird by a whisker.

In late July, we experienced the warmest weather of the summer. The temperature reached the upper eighties a few days, and with all the rain, everything in the garden seemed to get larger by the minute.

WHILE MEG AND I WORKED TOGETHER IN THE GARDEN ONE morning, we looked up simultaneously at hearing the sound of machinery coming from down the valley. It was Brad riding Hughie's tractor and working the land. "What's he planting?" she asked.

"He's not planting anything. He's spreading fertilizer."

"Why don't you plant something? We have all these acres with nothing growing on them."

"Probably wouldn't make any money even if I planted the whole twenty acres. Besides, I don't have any farm equipment, and since the cow incident, the short, stout fellow won't let me use his."

"If you hadn't threatened to kick his ass, maybe he'd let you use his equipment too."

"Unlikely. When Brad moved in, he became Hughie's sidekick, and besides, I'm not a farmer. If I wanted to farm, I'd have found a place more suitable closer to civilization. I do not intend to plant crops, nor do I intend to spread phosphate fertilizer as Brad's doing and have the runoff pollute the creek. In the Midwest where all the corn and soybeans grow, there isn't a river or creek unpolluted because of the runoff. Since I have no plans to develop the land, I have no need for his equipment. I'm a little worried though." She looked at me questioningly. "We don't have title to the land yet, and now that he's made me the bad guy, I don't trust him. I think we should see a lawyer. I'll ask Ginger if she knows a good one."

Jim's office was in the back of his Victorian house in Ashland, Oregon, and I felt an immediate connection with him. He and his wife Mary were from the East Coast and came to Oregon to experience the Great Northwest. He tied his long hair into a ponytail and was without facial hair. He wore Levi's, an expensive looking dark green shirt, and sandals. Mary was straighter-looking. They had one child, a two-year-old boy. I could tell he was a devoted father in the way he held and talked to him. He spoke in

John-Paul Cernak

a professional tone after Mary whisked the little one away and sat in deep contemplation after hearing our concern. "I'll make you folks a deal," he said, walking to the window and touching the sill. "I love this room but dislike the paint covering the beautiful wood. I checked, and there's only one coat. If you strip the paint off the windows and the woodwork, I'll make sure you get your title, and I'll pay for all the materials. Mary and I are leaving town for a week. You can move in while we're gone and do the work." I looked at Meg, and she quickly nodded her approval.

He gave us a key, and we returned the following week. I marveled at our total focus in accomplishing the task. I attributed our super concentration to the yoga we practiced daily. The job took four hours a day for three days, and for the remainder of the week, we enjoyed living in the beautiful Victorian house with electricity and hot water and with ample time to explore the town of Ashland. On Thursday, we attended a performance of Othello at Ashland's Shakespearean Theatre and drank beer most afternoons at a tavern on the Plaza.

———— ❦ ————

IT WAS TIME TO MAKE A PURCHASE, TWO PURCHASES REALLY. THE first was an old-fashioned Kenmore wringer washing machine, and the other, a Honda generator. Going to the laundromat consumed most of our time on our trips into town. Now we could do our wash at home, and the generator gave us electricity to hear music. In most instances, the valley was too far into the mountains to pick up any stations. An exception was a western AM station out of Portland and a few others that came in clear but only after dark and if atmospheric conditions were right.

Through the middle of August, the weather remained cool with overcast skies and persistent showers. With all the rain, the first of the marijuana planted grew to over six feet high and almost as wide. The corn planted in front to hide them was doing a poor job. Everyone knew it was there.

On an evening a few nights after the full moon, I lingered outside after dark inspecting the garden. The waning moon rising over the mountain barely gave enough light to see. I was experiencing a strange sensation in my gut. Brushing it off as something I ate for dinner that disagreed with me, I awoke the next morning feeling the same sensation. While in bed, I tried to analyze and uncover the source of my discomfort. Meg was up and dressing. "Are you feeling anything different this morning?" I asked. "I'm feeling weird."

"What do you mean, weird?"

"I'm not sure how to explain it. It's like a hollow feeling in my stomach."

"Are you ill?"

"I don't think so."

I started my day watering. When I looked out over the garden, something looked different. Puzzled, I scanned from top to bottom without detecting what caused the distortion. I checked a second time. When I finally saw what the problem was, my psyche refused to believe what I was seeing. I convinced myself it was an illusion. After I was unable to deceive myself any longer, waves of nausea swept over me. Feeling angry and violated, I finally accepted half the marijuana was gone. "Meg! Meg!" I shouted. "We've been ripped off."

We stared in disbelief at the empty spaces. I never considered anyone would steal them, because they grew next to the barn. Sixty were gone. "Who did this?" I asked.

"I don't know," she said. It's not that we have a lot of friends in the valley, and everyone knows we're growing. They were in plain sight. It could be anyone."

"How could they have gotten them out? Sixty is a lot of plants, and they were large. I didn't hear any vehicles last night, did you?"

"No! They must have parked off somewhere at a distance and carried them to their vehicle, and whoever did this must be hard-up for money. The plants were immature and not very good smoking. They won't get much for the leaves."

After she went inside, my frustration mounted. I stood silently looking around. Everything felt normal when I looked down the valley towards Brad's place. When I shifted my focus to the mountain with the clear-cut behind us and to the small cabin across the creek, where a Whole Earth Communal Family lived until the beginning of June, I received a psychic hit. I looked into the cabin after they left and saw clothing and a shotgun. I didn't touch anything believing they would return to claim them. The thieves must have hid in the cabin until after sundown. It seemed unlikely they carried sixty plants up the mountainside to the road above in the dark. It was over three hundred feet straight up. Then I remembered standing in the garden the night before and feeling the strange sensation in my gut. The thieves must have been lying in the grass watching me. "Ahhhhhha!" I screamed at the sky overwhelmed by frustration. The cry echoed between the hills of the narrow valley three or four times before evaporating into space. The Gods looked down to see who was making all the noise.

Word of the rip-off spread quickly throughout the South Umpqua Valley all the way to I-5, as growers everywhere looked for ways to protect their crop. Even Hughie brought his son's dog up from town to guard the plants he grew. "Shucks," he was overheard saying, "A few plants pays me taxes, and I'm not about to let anyone steal 'em."

Mountain Man stopped by with an insight he wanted to share. We sat outside in the sun looking at the empty spaces, his dog lying at his feet. "As I see it," he said, "this is an inside job."

"I don't know what you mean by inside job?"

"Look where this valley is located. No visitor could possibly pull off a heist here. If you came here only a few times, would you know this place? I don't think so. It's so remote and wild, there's no possibility anyone not living here could do it. The thieves knew this place. This was an inside job."

"But a lot of people knew we were growing."

"There's a big difference in seeing it growing and getting it out in the middle of the night. Only someone who's familiar with the location could do that."

"How about some of the people who lived here in the past like Harry the Carpenter? He knows his way around here."

"No! I know Harry well, and he's not into ripping off people's dope."

Everyone I mentioned, Mountain Man proclaimed they were not the thieves. This left only those living in the valley, and he said no to everyone until coming to Larry and Carolyn. "Where do they go when I see them leaving the valley?" I asked.

"They have a commercial thinning contract with the Forest Service somewhere in the woods. I don't know where. I believe they're working in the Glide District, and you have to remember this, Jack, only someone living here would know you no longer have a dog."

Early the next morning, we were on the road looking for Larry and Carolyn. I was carrying the twenty-two rifle, the weapon with which I was most accurate. "Why are you bringing a gun?" she asked.

"Just in case."

"Just in case of what? I don't want any trouble, Jack, do you understand me?"

"Well, if they're the thieves, and we confront them, who knows how Larry will react. I hear he's a hothead. You want me not to have a weapon to protect us?"

"Just be careful."

The Glide Ranger District was on the north side of the forest fifty miles over backcountry roads. Under heavy overcast skies, we headed up river into the mountains. The gravel road took us up to five thousand feet at French junction and back down to two thousand at the main highway on the north side of the forest. Although it was well maintained for timber removal, there were steep drop-offs with no guardrails. A few times, I came precariously close to the edge and scared myself. Meg sat gripping the bar above the door. We arrived late morning.

John-Paul Cernak

The ranger station was a large complex of log office and storage buildings painted deep reds, yellows, and browns on the bank of the North Umpqua River and was the headquarters of the Umpqua National Forest. My guess was that the Civilian Conservation Corps, the CCC, built the compound in the depression years of the 1930s. I was hoping to find where they worked without having to ask. If there was a shootout and either of them was hurt or worse, I didn't want anyone to identify me. There was no other way. The area was vast and stumbling upon them in the woods was unlikely. A Forest Service employee told us where they worked and the quickest way there.

We drove under towering trees that made the dark day even bleaker. Suddenly, there was Larry's truck parked off the road. To avoid attention, I drove past, but because of a steep drop off on each shoulder, I had to park on the road surface. Silently, we entered the thicket of the unit above where they worked. To our amazement, they were directly below us, and we could hear some of their conversation. They didn't seem to be doing anything in particular. Larry kept looking into a large plastic bag. They must have cleaned the leaves and stashed them in the sack. I watched feeling anger and not knowing what to do. I was holding the twenty-two rifle, but I wasn't into shooting anyone. Without warning, they began walking out of the unit. When they reached the road, they'd see our truck. Impulsively, I dashed out to confront them. "Larry, you son of a bitch," I shouted from a distance, "you ripped-off our marijuana." They raced to their truck and roared off up the road. We sprinted to our truck. It wasn't until I climbed in behind the wheel that I realized I was holding the rifle. They must have thought I intended to shoot them.

Retracing the route taken that morning sliding and skidding around curves and sending up a huge cloud of dust, I missed colliding with a log truck by inches rounding a curve. At the summit, I broke out into brilliant sunlight blinding me and almost lost control. Clouds spread out around us like a huge blanket with only the higher peaks of the Cascade Mountains visible in the distance. But regardless how fast I drove, they maintained their lead. Moreover, I wouldn't have known what to do had I caught them. "Jack! Jack!" Meg shouted, shaking my arm. "Slow down or let me out."

Caught up in the frenzy of the pursuit, I was hardly aware of her. "I don't want to get killed chasing them. At least we know for sure who did it. Let's handle this more calmly and get home safely."

All during supper, I felt their desperation and knew another confrontation would end in a shootout. At dusk, their truck sped past the barn leaving the valley. After waiting to make sure they wouldn't return, I drove to the back and holding the twenty-two rifle entered their small makeshift house. Two chainsaws lay on the floor. I confiscated both. It would make up in part for what they stole. Holding the larger of the two with the bar pointing up towards the sky, I felt its power. Now I had one as large as Brad's.

The news that Larry and Carolyn were the thieves spread rapidly throughout the South Umpqua Valley. It was a death sentence for them socially, and they left immediately. Growing marijuana was a major industry, and it would have been unhealthy for them to remain. After I put a notice on the bulletin board at the Centerville Market, I sold the smaller of the saws within an hour. Over the next week, the mood in the valley returned to normal. Mountain Man and Lisa stopped by to find out what happened. Brad and Hughie remained distant. After our lawyer put the screws to Hughie and forced him to refinance, I received word he wouldn't pay us for the three hundred bales of hay he harvested off the land, and the war between us escalated.

The next week, the Forest Service called a meeting of all the landowners in the valley to discuss their logging plans. At the meeting, Brad tried to act as spokesperson for everyone. I let them know he wasn't speaking for me. In his attempt to assume leadership, he stammered and stuttered inanities and looked foolish.

The meeting was called under the pretense of talking about their five-year plan. In reality there was no discussion. They weren't

John-Paul Cernak

interested in dialog, only in acquiescence. It was a charade to make it seem the people had a voice and to head-off another possible lawsuit if they logged again. "Our plan is to log all the trees in the valley," said Jeff Blackwood. He was a chief forester sent in from the regional office. "I can't give you a precise timeline, but it's in our five-year plan. There are also plans to spray after we log."

"What kind of chemicals will be sprayed?" I asked.

"There will be a variety of herbicides but primarily 2-4D."

"Are you people looking for another court battle?" I said. "You won the last one, but I guarantee you won't win this one if you spray 2-4D in my watershed.

He glared at me with an expression that said: "Who are you to challenge the Forest Service." Huddling, the brass spoke in whispers too quiet for me to hear. "As you all know," I added, "2-4D's major ingredient is Dioxin and is one of the most virulent poisons known and the major component in Agent Orange, the herbicide the military is using in Viet Nam. It's a known carcinogen and causes birth defects."

The meeting ended abruptly once they saw the people of Ash Valley weren't buying their declarations. They had all the power and didn't hide the fact that they were going to do as they pleased regardless of the damage they caused. "What a sham the Forest Service is," I said to Meg. "They pretend to protect the forest when in reality destroy it."

When leaving, a biologist gave us a friendly greeting. We stopped to talk. He was not in agreement with the official policy of logging everything. "Who is this Jeff Blackwood guy?" I asked.

Smiling, he moved a little closer. "He's the son of high-ranking Forest Service official in Washington. Probably won't be around here long. It wouldn't look good if he moved up too fast and not spend any time in the woods. I'm sure he'll be moving to Washington soon."

"How interesting! Nepotism in the Forest Service. Thanks for the information."

On a rainy morning a few days later, Meg looked out the window as she did the breakfast dishes. "Sure was a nothing summer," she said. "Now that half the marijuana's gone, I don't know how we'll make any money."

"We still have half," I stated, trying to put a positive spin on the situation, "and I hope the rain keeps everything mellow. I don't know how much more excitement I can handle."

In the next instant, she let out a loud shriek: "JJJaaacccckkk! We're busted!"

Rushing next to her, I looked out the window. An Oregon State Police Car stopped on the road opposite the garden. A trouper jumped out and focused his binoculars on the plants. Turning, he spoke with two occupants in the cruiser. The cop with the binoculars was Trouper Brady. He was the local game warden. I didn't know the driver, and Jeff Blackwood of the Forest Service was in the back seat. "Son of a bitch," I said, under my breath.

What happened next surprised me. Officer Brady jumped back into the cruiser, and they drove off. "They don't have a warrant," I said, "and we're too far into the mountains for them to use their radio. The nearest phone's at Crooked Creek, and it'll take them over an hour to get back."

In haste and under a light drizzle, we pulled the remaining plants, stuffed them into plastic bags, and dragged them far up the mountainside.

"Maybe it wasn't such a good idea after all to grow in the garden," I said, as we walked down. "Larry and Carolyn did us a favor by ripping off half the plants. It would have been a bitch pulling them all if the largest sixty were still in the ground."

"Shouldn't we warn the other people in the valley?" she said.

I looked at her as if she was crazy but quickly reconsidered. "Yeah! Maybe we should."

Brad was out in his field sowing seeds, and as we approached the fence separating the properties, he moved slowly towards us, his manner unfriendly and his expression deadpan. He stopped twenty feet short of the fence. "The cops were in the valley," I said, "and they saw our marijuana. They didn't have a warrant and went to get one."

"What did you do with your plants?"

"We pulled them." Without another word, he moved off. "And Lisa's not home," I said to his back. "You better pull hers."

He turned and gave me a blank stare. "Do you think he'll do it?" she asked.

"He and Lisa are close, but I know he won't."

"You pull them then."

"Not a chance, especially after the rip-off. What if the cops don't come back? How could I explain why I did it? It would seem like sour grapes. She wouldn't believe me in a thousand years."

"You're in a no-win situation, Jack, dammed if you do and condemned if you don't. If you don't pull them and the cops come back, she'll blame you for getting busted."

"There's one small chance. She's at Crooked Creek with her hippie friends. Let's go get her and bring her back. It's a long shot, but there's no other way."

The tires squealed going around the first curve on the river road. After five miles, a police cruiser sped past heading up river. I watched in the rear-view mirror as they turned and came after us. Meg jettisoned a joint we were smoking. I slowed to let them easily catch us. We did our best. Lisa was on her own.

"Sir," said Trouper Brady. "We saw marijuana growing on your property. Please follow us back to the valley."

I gave him no argument. As we pulled up to the barn, he quickly jumped out of the cruiser and was standing next to the truck almost before it stopped rolling. "You have the right to remain silent," he said, reading me my rights. "You have a right to, " and he cut himself off in midsentence when he realized the plants were gone. "You people work fast."

I played innocent. "Pardon me officer."

He stood scratching his head. "Are we under arrest?"

"No!" he said, after a long pause, "but you're not free to leave just yet; we'll need to make a complete search."

"Search all you want."

"Our warrant will be here shortly."

But their warrant didn't arrive for another two hours. Since it seemed inhospitable to leave them waiting outside, Meg invited them in for tea. On this trip, Jeff Blackwood was not with them. Sitting at the kitchen table, we discussed the pros and cons of legalizing marijuana. Both cops favored decriminalization, and I was surprised at Officer Brady's progressive attitude, because of a prior run-in I had with him.

Unaware it was the day before the opening of spring fishing season, we hiked up to a ten-acre pond deep in the woods to take a few photos. The forest was dripping wet with moss clinging to everything. The green was so vivid, it seemed almost to glow like phosphoresce. As we approached the pond, a cop suddenly jumped out from behind a tree and scared the crap out of me. It was Officer Brady. He reminded me of Dudley Do Right from the Bullwinkle TV Show and pounced on us like a cat on a couple of mice. "Are you people fishing?"

I pointed to my camera, the only item I carried. "Does it look like we're fishing?"

"Just answer the question," he shot back in an unpleasant and surly manner.

"No! I am not fishing."

"What an arrogant son of a bitch that cop is," I commented on our hike back. But that day in our kitchen, he didn't seem self-important. He seemed an enlightened officer of the law. After an hour, they asked if we would allow them to check the garden. I turned to Meg. "When their warrant arrives, they won't have to ask."

After counting the planting holes, Trooper Brady dug into the soil and found several marijuana leaves. "Here!" he said, handing them to Meg. "You forgot these."

Along with a group of deputies, the Sheriff of Douglas County delivered the warrant in person. He was a big, rugged guy with a deep, gruff voice. "Don't rub my nose in it, kid," he said, getting into my face. "If I see it growing, I'll bust ya, but I'm not going to look for it. So, if you must grow, plant where I can't see it."

Those were the words verbatim of the elected sheriff of Douglas County. They all piled into their vehicles and headed up the road toward Lisa's plants.

The next day, we received a visit from a low-level Forest Service Manager. Meg invited him in for tea. I wondered why he came. "We received word," he said, "that the police saw marijuana growing in your garden."

I was stoned after we just finished smoking a bowl, and I felt daring. I looked him straight in the eye when I spoke. "The cops came, but they were mistaken."

I searched his face for any sign that he didn't believe me, but he never revealed his feelings. He left shortly afterwards. "What was that all about," she asked.

"They're probing. I'll bet he was sent by Blackwood to find out if we saw him in the back of the cruiser. The son of a bitch turned us in."

"Blackwood was never here before yesterday. Who was here was the Colonel of the surveying crew. When you challenged them at their meeting, he informed Blackwood who went to the cops. How did they know Lisa was growing? Because they surveyed the whole valley and knew precisely where they were."

"Hmm! You're probably right."

A week later, while working in the generator room near the road, the hair on the back of my neck stood up when an angry voice startled me. I turned to face Lisa. "Jack Cernak! Why didn't you pull my plants?"

"I couldn't pull them," I replied meekly.

"Why couldn't you pull them?" she asked again crying hysterically. "Because of you, I got busted. They're charging me with a felony, and you could have prevented it. Was it asking too much to pull them?"

"I told Brad to pull them."

"Was it asking that much?" she continued not hearing anything I said and walked off sobbing.

"I'm sorry you got busted," I said to her back.

That same week, the surveying crew found Mountain Man's illegal house in the woods and demolished it. Without a place to live, he immediately left the valley. With only four members remaining, the Whole Earth Commune was disintegrating. In the months ahead, the court lowered Lisa's felony charge to a misdemeanor and fined her two hundred dollars.

———✦———

THE SUMMER OF 1975 WAS THE SEASON THAT WASN'T. WE HARvested many vegetables but only green tomatoes. While brushing my teeth one morning, I walked out the side door and around to the front and almost bumped into Larry standing in the road holding a double-barrel shotgun. He held the gun loosely in front of him but didn't point it at me. "I want the saws," he said.

As adrenaline shot into my system, I walked towards him without breaking stride holding his gaze. "You son of a bitch," I said, spitting each word into his face. He backed perplexed by my aggressiveness. After all, he was the one holding the shotgun. After twenty feet, he stopped pointed the gun at my head and snarled. With contempt on my face, I looked deeply into his eyes for a long minute. Casually turning, I walked around the corner of the barn and never looked behind me. If he was going to shoot me, it would have to be in the back. It was the longest short walk I ever took. The instant I entered the barn, I began shaking involuntarily. My whole body trembled. "Larry's outside with a shotgun," I shouted.

Meg dropped to the floor behind a cabinet. I pulled down the 30-30 rifle off the rack and pushed the door open with my foot. If he was there, I would shoot and ask questions later. The road was empty. Trying to determine which way he went in the woods, I quickly abandoned the idea of pursuing him. He might be laying in ambush, and if I found him, for sure there would be the gun battle I so far avoided.

That afternoon when everything calmed, Meg brought out the pipe. "I walked towards him," I said, "not knowing if the gun was loaded. I heard you should never show fear, and it worked."

"You took a chance doing that, Jack. You're lucky to be alive. The gun was probably loaded."

"I should have taken it from the cabin when I had the chance. Now that we know for sure they came down the mountain from the road up in the clear cut, it must have been a horrendous task carrying the heavy plants up the steep mountainside in the dark. Maybe the truth was it took two nights."

"What do you mean two nights?" .

"On the morning of the rip-off after you went inside, I received a psychic hit from the cabin but never went to investigate. In retrospect, I can't imagine not searching it, unless I was feeling danger."

"Danger?"

"Larry waiting for me with the shotgun and half the plants they probably carried up the second night."

The following week, we went to the courthouse in Centerville to file papers. I was taking Hughie to small claims court for non-payment of the hay. "Are you sure you want to do this?" Meg asked.

I held the pen ready to sign. The clerk looked at me questioningly. "Yes! I want to keep the pressure on him. I can play hardball, too."

She frowned. "If you back off, maybe things'll get better."

"Hey! Whose side are you on?"

"I just think this can be handled differently," and she signaled the conversation was over.

I signed the papers.

EVERYTHING WAS LATE IN RIPENING BECAUSE OF THE UNUSUALLY cool summer. Through September, we canned vegetables and picked fruit at u-pick orchards located throughout the Medford area. At a roadside fruit stand, I choose two luscious peaches from a large display. The sign said forty cents a pound. A dour old man with several front teeth missing worked the cash register. The fruit weighed under a pound. "Eighty cents," he said.

I didn't catch the overcharge but Meg did. "You hateful old man," she said, pulling me away.

"Dirty hippies," he snarled.

In early October, we visited a dentist in Ashland our lawyer introduced to us. We spent several days helping him with projects in exchange for dental work. After checking in with the receptionist, I took a seat in a large waiting room filled with patients. After a few minutes, I rose to select a magazine from a large circular table in the center of the room. As I scanned through the pile, my eyes landed on a six-month old, April 1975, issue of Time Magazine. The headline read: "Vietnam Falls." The cover photo pictured helicopters evacuating people from the roof of the American Embassy in Saigon. Stunned, I felt empty inside. "Look, Meg!" I said, excitedly, "Vietnam fell. All those people killed for nothing."

Several patients in the waiting room chuckled. I felt sad for everyone hurt or killed in the war and was glad I was no longer a part of society. I remembered graffiti written on a wall in San Francisco during an anti-war demonstration that read: "If voting could change the system, it would be outlawed." I vowed never to vote again.

The sun shined each day that it failed to do all season and gave us a long, warm, Indian summer. The blustery wind that usually blew up the valley hardly stirred, and the leaves of the surrounding maple, ash, and alder trees turned bright yellows and reds. We made daily forays into the forest for firewood using the new, larger chainsaw and put the garden to bed for the winter by covering carrots and other root crops with leaves to protect them from freezing. For days, the only clouds we saw were contrails from aircraft streaking across the sky at altitudes high enough to barely hear their jet engines and the only reminder there was another world beyond the mountains.

When it was just too nice to be inside, we prepared dinner outside on the flat area across the road where I constructed a fireplace. We sat around the fire until well after dark. It was like camping out, except we did it every night. One evening as the first stars twinkled in the eastern sky and the forest already in deep shade, I heard a vehicle enter the valley and was feeling something I didn't like. "We're getting company," I said.

"What are you feeling?"

"Someone's coming to see us."

"I don't hear anything."

I held up my hand listening intently. In the distance, the sound of tires popping on loose gravel became barely audible. "Do you know who it is?"

"No, but I don't like whoever it is."

With its parking lights on, a dark pickup appeared at the top of the low hill and glided to a stop next to our kitchen. Tension built, and Meg moved the wooden crate she sat on behind me. Two men climbed out and aggressively walked toward us. I stood and faced them. One was Harry the Carpenter. The other was a long hair dude I saw at the Tiller Tavern but didn't know. They appeared drunk. "I hear you've been telling people I ripped-off your marijuana," said Harry.

He was a big burly guy with a ruddy complexion. His partner was slim but not in good shape. As far as I could tell, neither carried a weapon. "You have it wrong, my friend," I said, standing my ground and speaking calmly. They remained on the periphery

"The word is going around I was your prime suspect." He paced nervously, "and I want you to know I don't like it."

"I don't know where you heard that, because it isn't true. I'm sure your name was mentioned but so was everyone who lives in the South Umpqua Valley. I wouldn't take it personally."

"I do take it personally."

"Well let me tell you my friend, if I thought you were the thief, you'd have been the first to know."

In the way they approached aggressively walking fast toward me, I thought I would have to fight them. Quickly, the wind left their sails. I wasn't backing down, and they had to make a decision to either fight me or leave. Harry said something under his breath I couldn't hear and stopped pacing. His partner remained in the background and never said a word. Harry grunted, and they walked back to their truck and drove off. "They must have been drinking at the Tiller Tavern," she said, "and the alcohol gave them courage to come harangue us."

"Yet another fallout from growing the marijuana in the garden," I mused. "I won't make that mistake again."

—◦◦◦—

WHEN IT FELT SAFE, WE BROUGHT THE PLANTS DOWN OFF THE mountain. With the generator running, two naked bulbs burning overhead for light, and rock music playing on the stereo, we sat cross-legged on the floor and cleaned plants. "They paved paradise and put up a parking lot," sang, Joni Mitchell from her Blue album. The music came from speakers on the shelf against the wall.

"I'm feeling a little left out of the process," said Meg.

"What do you mean?" Her words of dissatisfaction surprised me. "You're involved in everything that happens around here."

"It's your place. If it's ever sold, you'll get all the profits, and I'll get nothing. I put in as much energy as you do, but there's nothing in it for me."

"This marijuana's half yours."

"That's not what I mean, Jack. I don't feel like a full partner. I feel like a hired helper."

"What if we get married?"

Her expression softened. "That would be nice."

I felt shocked at what I said, although I must have been thinking about it. "Let's drive to Ashland. We can do it before we go to San Francisco."

"Oregon has a three-day waiting period. It'll mean driving to Ashland, applying for a license, and driving back in three days to get married. Nevada has a no waiting period. Let's get married there."

"Where, in Reno?"

"No! Everybody gets married there. Somewhere else."

I scanned over the Nevada Roadmap I spread out on the floor and pointed to Winnemucca, a town in the center of the state on Interstate 80 near the Oregon border. "It's an interesting name," I said. "I've never been there, and the drive would be an adventure."

My only dress clothes were several wild print shirts with large collars and bell-bottom trousers left over from the sixties. Meg packed her best dress, and we began the long drive through the Cascade Mountains and sagebrush country of Eastern Oregon. Because it was still early in the season, snow hadn't accumulated at the passes, and traveling through the mountains was easy. It snowed heavily entering Winnemucca, and the town was mostly deserted. The desk clerk at the large, hotel casino where we stayed rented us the honeymoon suite with two rooms and a hot tub for the price of a regular room. The next morning, we applied for a marriage license at the courthouse. A Justice of the Peace married us in the afternoon. We ate our wedding dinner at a Basque hotel and family restaurant. Everyone sat together at large tables like at the Gold Spike and served themselves from platters of delicious home-cooked food.

Later that evening, we went down to the casino. The room was large and in semidarkness with hundreds of slot machines and gaming tables and all covered with green tarps. A small crowd gathered around several craps and blackjack tables in a lighted corner and attracted us like moths to a porch light. With the tourists of summer gone, the professionals came out to play, and the action was hot and heavy. Although we had no money for gambling, it was exciting to watch the high rollers bet thousands on each toss of the dice and turn of the card.

On the return trip, I received a citation from a Nevada cop for making a dangerous turn. The ticket was not for making an unsafe turn. It was for having long hair. While driving back through the Cascade Mountains, a snowstorm hit unexpectedly. Using all my concentration, I drove steadily in almost whiteout conditions until reaching lower elevations. The ticket and the snowstorm made me aware getting married was easy, and the trouble came afterward.

Several days later, as we drove on the River Road toward Centerville to do our grocery shopping, a sheriff's vehicle followed closely behind. "He's had plenty of opportunities to pass," I said.

Meg turned and looked over her shoulder out the back widow. "He's looking for a reason to pull you over."

His flashing lights finally came on after another mile. With the river flowing past twenty feet below, I parked on the shoulder of the narrow road, and watched the trooper approach in my side view mirror. He was tall, wore knee-high boots, and mirrored sunglasses and reminded me of the prison guard in the movie, Cool Hand Luke. He stood close to the door in an attempt to be intimidating, but I wasn't feeling threatened. It was the second time in less than a week I was pulled over because of my long hair, and I was pissed. May I see your driver's license and registration?"

"Why was I pulled over?"

He seemed taken aback by my question, as if it was illegal to ask. "I can't read your rear license plate, and I'm writing you a citation."

Meg and I quickly exited the truck and walked around to the rear. The license plate holder slightly covered one of the numbers but was still easily readable. He moved back to his vehicle to write the ticket but was close enough to hear when I said loudly: "The son of a bitch is harassing us." He immediately removed a camera from his trunk and photographed the license plate. "What court has jurisdiction in this case?" I asked, when he handed me the citation.

"The Justice of the Peace in Centerville."

We drove directly there. The justice was a portly woman who worked out of her home and turned her living room into a small courtroom. I told her I received the ticket because of my long hair. "He's the kind of cop that gives all police a bad name. It's the same holder that came with the truck." We went outside to examine it.

"You're right," she said, "This does not warrant him giving you a citation. I'll dismiss it and talk to him but to be on the safe side remove the holder."

She provided a screwdriver and wrench to do the job immediately.

After doing our food shopping, we visited Ginger and Bob. Ginger greeted us at the door. "Hi, you two. What's new?"

"I'll bet you can't guess what we did," said Meg.

"OK! I'll bite. What did you guys do?"

"We just got back from Nevada where we got married."

"Bob! Bob!" she yelled up the stairs, "Come down quick. We have some celebrating to do."

Out came the food, Ginger's homemade wine, and Bob's best dope, and we partied for the rest of the day. When things settled down later that evening, I told them about the ticket and about our talk with the Justice of the Peace. "I'm proud of you, Jack," said Ginger. "The only way to handle a bully cop is to stand up to him the way you did. The same holds true whether the bully is a thug on the playground, the cop on the beat, or an official in business or government. Most people are afraid to stand up and fight for their rights. They'd rather pay the fine, and that gives the bullies more power. We have the kind of people running our government that we deserve."

On November 12, we appeared in small claims court against Hughie. When the judge saw my long hair and beard, he didn't attempt to hide his disgust. We sat in the back row of the small courtroom. Hughie and Brad sat across the aisle and glanced in our direction. "Did you see the look the judge gave me?" I whispered. She looked at me with reproach.

"I knew it was a mistake. What did you expect? Hughie's a 'good old boy' and has a business in town. Did you think the judge would find in your favor? You're a hippie."

"I guess I'm an idealist," I said, speaking loudly. "All I'm expecting is a fair shake."

"You'll learn," she said.

The bailiff standing next to the bench walked over. "No talking in the courtroom," he said, and pointed at me.

I fought off an urge to flip him off. The judge found in Hughie's favor, and I never even had a chance to tell my story.

CHAPTER 7

EVERYTHING WAS READY FOR OUR TRIP TO THE CITY. IT WOULD be our first since moving to the valley, but we worried about our cats. They sensed something unusual was happening in the way they tangled around our legs mewing and seeking affection. They relaxed after we explained to them we'd be gone only a short time. We'd leave them a large amount of food, but they would have to supplement their diet with hunting. I packaged the marijuana in boxes and taped them shut. We planned to leave in the morning. Meg was having last minute jitters. She sat on the couch looking nervous. Her brow was creased, and the tenseness in her body reflected the anxiety she expressed. "With your long hair and beard," she said, "you belong to a group of people cops love to stop. What if we're stopped like we were on our return from Winnemucca?"

"I'm not as concerned about getting stopped as I am with the agricultural inspection stations at all the border crossings. There's no way to avoid them regardless of which road we take. "

"Yeah! Wouldn't it be safer to sell locally?"

"It would be safer, but we'd receive a fraction of what we'd get in the city. We'd be like most farmers who do all the work and let a middleman make all the profit. I'm not going to let that happen. I'm willing to take the chance."

"Do you think the difference is worth the risk?"

Holding her hand, I sat down next to her. "It is and not to worry. I'm looking forward to visiting the city. I know enough people with money who'll pay a good price for our weed. As for the agricultural inspection stations, they're looking for live plants where insects can hide and not marijuana. With the boxes taped shut, we're cool."

"I hope you know what you're talking about, Jack!"

It snowed the morning we left giving the forest and mountains a coating of white and added an element of excitement but not deep enough to hinder our progress. Although I felt calm, there was a background of nervous tension. At Interstate-5, I headed the truck south. Once past Ashland, the last town in Oregon, the freeway climbed to the Siskiyou Summit. At over forty-three hundred feet, it was the highest point on I-5. Luckily, the mountain received only a sprinkling of snow, and chains were not required. On the long downgrade, a large sign welcomed us to California, and the tension built. Another sign announced the agricultural inspection station was ahead, and all vehicles must stop. "Look relaxed," I said, "and smile."

"Do you have any plants or fruit?" asked the woman dressed in a forest green uniform and standing close to the truck. "None."

She stepped back, looked suspiciously at the boxes in the bed of the truck, and waved me on. I let out the clutch and smoothly accelerated back onto the freeway. "That wasn't so bad," I said, confidently, although my underarms were a bit moist.

As we neared the bay, the smell of salty air filled me with excitement, and what a feast for the senses it was hearing the tugboat whistles, the call of the seagulls, and seeing Alcatraz Island and the Golden Gate Bridge in the distance. Once on the Bay Bridge, the city was on the horizon and the fog was in. I was reminded of my first crossing.

It was the summer of 1961. After driving across the country, I spent the night at a gas station and slept in the car. I came out of the central valley where the temperature was a hundred and ten degrees. Driving across on the Bay Bridge, I could see the fog hanging low over the city. I wondered what it was. It looked like a shroud and gave everything a depressing look. As the temperature dropped, I rolled up the windows and turned on the heater and for weeks not feeling warm enough. I drove around that first day looking at the city and passed the large hotels on Nob Hill. After seeing tourists huddled together dressed in skimpy summer clothing and shivering in the cold fifty-degree temperature and forty-mile-an-hour wind, I understood Mark Twain's famous, enigmatic statement: "The coldest winter I ever spent was a summer in San Francisco."

Now twenty years later, I still experienced the same exhilaration I did that first day. After seeing all the familiar places, I had a moment of regret wondering what I missed. The city felt different reminding me I was a visitor now. I remembered a conversation with Steve who came to say goodbye in February before we moved up to the valley.

With boxes of household goods stacked against the wall ready to move, we sat in the living room in the flat on Castro Street on a sunny day reminiscing old times. There was a long pause in our conversation as Steve stared out the window. "So!" he said, glancing at the boxes, "you're really going to do it. I was hoping you'd come to your senses before it's too late. It's beyond me how you can leave this beautiful city and live isolated in the mountains without electricity or a bathroom. You'll miss all the great happenings."

"For one thing, Steve, everything's become somehow repetitive. For a long time, the river. flowed past my door, and everything came too easily. I stopped growing." After hearing what I said, I became aware I voiced the real reason I was leaving. "Besides," I added, "what could happen more exciting than the 1960s?"

He looked at me for a long moment deep in thought smiled and slowly stood up. "You're probably right." At the door he gave me a hug. "Happy trails, man," he said, and walked out.

While in town, we stayed with Meg's friend, Marge. They met while going to school in Germany. When we lived in the city, we occasionally had dinner with Marge and her steady boyfriend, Tim at a German Restaurant on Church Street. It reminded the women of their stay in Europe, Tim wanted to take their relationship to the next level and live together, but Marge wasn't ready to make the commitment. They were the perfect straight couple relaxed and fun to be around, and they smoked marijuana when they were with us.

Marge lived with three feminist, bisexual women in a large house with five bedrooms in the Inner Avenues district near the University of California Hospital. It was the beginning of the time when sleeping with someone of the same sex was in. Different men and women always hung around, and I could never figure out who was sleeping with whom. On the day we arrived, a tall, beautiful, head honcho woman gathered all the men together. With her arms folded across her chest, she proclaimed: "This is a women's house. Any man leaving the toilet seat up will be shot at dawn."

The next day, I visited Jeffery, a gay, printer friend whose shop was on Geary Boulevard in the Richmond District. I lived in the neighborhood briefly when I first arrived in the city. It was near the Golden Gate Bridge and experiences heavy fog. Most nights, the deep baritone voice of the foghorn on the bridge lulled me to sleep.

Geary was a wide, heavily, traveled boulevard lined with shops, and although I was enjoying the bustle of the city, the noise distracted me. When I entered the shop and closed the door, it quieted, and I relaxed. Jeffrey was running an antique, hand-fed letterpress with a big, iron wheel. The shop smelled of chemicals. Anyone who has ever printed soon becomes addicted, and I felt at home. Looking up from his work, he did a double take. I wore my hair parted in the middle with a braid on each side. It was probably how I looked when I lived on the plains in my past life. "Jack!" he said, smiling. "How delightful to see you."

I always enjoyed Jeffry's bubbly personality and his humorous perspective on life. He stood about five feet six and was showing his age by spreading in the middle. He had black ink smeared on his cheek and in his graying hair. Stacks of paper and printed material lay everywhere, and the shop was a mess. Yet he looked as if he was enjoying himself. "What's happening?" I asked.

"Just working!" he answered with emphasis and a bit of sarcasm letting me know he wasn't getting any. "What brings you to San Francisco?"

"I'm in town to sell my crop."

"What are you selling—trees?"

"I'm a marijuana grower."

Shocked, he failed to feed a sheet into the press. "Good God Jack! What made you get into that business? I didn't think growing giggle weed was your style." I shrugged my shoulders. "Hold on. I'm almost finished with this job. Let's run across the street to the coffee shop and talk."

We sat at a counter against the front windows where I could watch traffic and absorb the excitement of the city. When I gave him the details of the summer, he displayed pain and sympathy. "It's okay, really!" I said. "It was still great. Will you print some cards for me?"

"Sure! What do you want to say on them?"

He removed a pad of paper and pen from his apron pocket. "For Oregon's finest, call Jack and a line beneath where I can write in a phone number. I don't want to use the word marijuana. Whoever reads it will understand what it means."

When I reached for my wallet, he placed his hand over mine. "Put your money away, Jack. This one's on me. You and Isabel did enough for me when you had your shop. It's my turn. I'm just sorry you're no longer in the printing business."

High wind and thick fog buffeted the Golden Gate bridge but quickly cleared as Highway 101 funneled traffic through the tunnel with the rainbow around the entrance and down the long Waldo Grade to Mill Valley and Throckmorton Avenue. It was the exit to Reggie's frame shop and gallery. Cars moved slowly along the tree-lined avenue filled with small apartment buildings and shops. I always liked the Marin County town where, unlike the city, the sun shines regularly. Three large pricey-looking abstract oils with splashes of color sat on easels in the gallery window. The inside was empty. I looked at the art on my way to the back. Reggie appeared from behind a screen. "Hey, Matey! Long time no see! Come on back. Some of the lads are here."

Although I talked with him on the phone, I hadn't seen him in over three years, and he changed. His hair was longer, and he lost his boyish youthfulness. I flashed back to when he first arrived.

It was 1967, the year of the "Summer of Love." There was a different feeling about the times. In part, it was the music but was more how people talked with each other that gave a feeling of brotherhood and optimism. It was the year Isabel and I bought the Victorian in the Haight. A little old lady living alone in the large house was freaking out when thousands of hippies flocked into San Francisco and took over the Haight-Ashbury and Golden Gate Park. She took a liking to Isabel and sold us the house at a price far below its market value. After a long drought, my favorite DJs on KSAN, FM Radio began playing a new Beatles Album. "Sergeant Pepper's Lonely Hearts Club Band" blew my mind, and I knew it was going to be a far-out year.

When Reggie arrived, Isabel and I still lived in a rented house on 20th and Pennsylvania. Perched at the edge of Potrero Hill, it had a panoramic view of the bay. Evenings, I watched the lights of the city of Oakland coming on across the water and never tired of seeing ships sailing up and down and those anchored in the middle. With a house full of people, Isabel's friend, Deirdre brought Reggie to a Sunday afternoon get-together. He was tall, ruggedly good looking, with blond hair, vivid blue eyes, and a brash self-confidence. Wearing jeans, a black leather jacket, and a red scarf tied around his neck, he carried a six-pack of beer under his arm. "Hope ya don't mind me crashin' your party, mate."

When he spoke in his thick, British accent, every woman in the room turned and looked at him. "Interesting brogue. Where're you from?"

"London, mate!"

"You a Beatles fan?"

"The Beatles are fine, but the Kinks are my crew. They're from

Muswell Hill in North London where I grew up."

"What brings you to California?"

"I'm on a round-the-world trip, mate, and I've always wanted to see Frisco." He pointed towards the bay through the large picture window. "See that tramp steamer tuggin' at anchor out in the middle? That's the one that brought me and a few of the lads across. We boarded her in Gibraltar and traded work for our fare. She's Greek with Liberian registry called the *Eastern Star.* Came up.through the Panama Canal. She'll be sailin' for Singapore with the tide in the mornin'. But Deirdre here thinks I should stay and get to know your city. So many lovely birds, and you Yanks are such hospitable folk."

The beautiful Deirdre and the excitement of San Francisco in the 1960s derailed him from his trip around the world. They took an apartment together in Mill Valley. From the beginning, he didn't strike me as someone ready to settle down. Several months later, I paid them a visit in the midst of trouble. After breaking the hearts of countless men, the lovely Deirdre was about to learn how it felt to be on the receiving end. He paced smoking a doobie. "Fuckin' birds are all alike," he complained, angrily. "They wanna know what you're doin' every minute, and if you look at another bird, they go into hysterics. This relationship is over. I'm moving out."

Thereafter, each time I saw him he was involved with someone new. "I'm not the marryin' type," he'd say.

Reggie quickly adapted and found his niche opening an upscale frame shop and art gallery in Mill Valley and connected with the affluent people of the county. He and his friends had the money to pay top dollar for their marijuana, and I intended to be one of their suppliers.

As Reggie worked framing pictures, three guys stood around his workbench drinking beer and smoking a doobie. I met all three. I couldn't remember being at Reggie's shop when some of his friends weren't visiting. "Looks like I arrived at the right time," I said.

A short, slight man in his late twenties with a squeaky voice handed me a partially smoked joint. Buttons was a regular and lived in an apartment above the shop. Evenings, when Reggie would hang out at any one of several bars in town, he and the others in the Englishmen's entourage were usually there. "What is it?" I asked.

"Oaxacan."

I took a hit and passed it back. He clamped the edge of the paper with a roach clip and handed it to the next guy. Andre was another regular and the owner of a local soup restaurant. He often dropped by after the lunch crowd was gone and before he had to go back to work for dinner. The third guy was a short, stocky Hispanic who lived up the street. He was telling a story of how he shot twenty crows for no other reason than to kill them. Bad karma, I thought. "Where're you living, Jack?" asked Andre. "You look different these days."

"I moved up to Oregon and growing weed."

"You're growing marijuana? He looked around at the others. "Have any of you guys ever smoked homegrown? No one responded. "Can you make a living?

"I'm hoping I can. I've only grown one crop and made a few mistakes, which I hope to correct next season."

"What's the weather like up there?" asked Buttons.

"It was snowing when I left."

He put his hand in his pockets and held his arms close as if he was cold. "I'll stay right here in sunny Mill Valley."

"Any wildlife up there?" asked Reggie.

"Any cars on the freeway?" I responded.

I handed Reggie a small package when he walked me to the door. "It wasn't much of a crop this year," I said. "It's only shake but try it out. I'm sure there'll be better stuff next year. I'm hoping you'll move some for me."

"Thanks mate. I'm heading out tonight for a few bevies at an English Pub. Why don't you and Meg join me? They have good food, and we sings a bit. Remember, I've never met her. If you can make it, drop by about seven. Cheers, mate."

My next stop was back in the city to see Isabel. After moving out of Cole Street, I saw her only once when she invited me to an outing with her large Italian family, and against my better judgment, I attended. I wanted to say goodbye to people who were warm and supportive. At the outing, they turned hostile. Isabel was their darling, and there was never a divorce in the family. I couldn't blame them for being protective, but I thought they had more class.

Where Haight Street ends at Market near the Zen Center was where she moved. Her eyes grew wide in surprise when I entered on the second floor of a small office building. She was dressed in a white blouse and slacks. Peppered with strands of premature gray, her long black hair and her white skin reflected.both her Irish and Italian lineage. She was slim and petite with an hourglass figure, and with green eyes and everything in proportion, she didn't need makeup to look beautiful. "Jack! Is that you behind that big beard?" She was smiling. "How's life in the country?"

"Everything's great!"

Hugging, I was reminded it was Isabel who taught me how to hug. It was something the family I grew up in never did. "I'm sorry you missed Frank's memorial service," she said. "I tried getting in touch with you. But when you moved from the shop, I didn't know where you were." Tears formed in the corner of her eyes.

"It was the strangest thing, Isabel." I said. "When you phoned, I somehow knew you were calling to tell me Frank was dead. Who attended?"

"Margo and I organized it. Fifteen to twenty people came. I was surprised many of his old friends didn't show. We scattered his ashes up in the Marin Headlands where he shot himself. He didn't leave a note." She dabbed at the corner of her eye with a handkerchief. "Why did he kill himself? He was such a good person."

"The 60's were over, and the world was changing back."

She looked at me quizzically. "What do you mean? He was talented and had so much to offer. Couldn't he see another way?"

"How I saw it, he found his niche in the 1960s. Society was in chaos. It was more like an insurgency, really, and Frank was a pioneer of the sexual revolution. It put him on the cutting edge and gave him the notoriety and prestige he wanted."

"But why did he kill himself?"

"When the 70s rolled around, the sexual revolution was old hat. Everyone was doing it, and he was an ordinary guy again. For all the years he was president, the league supported him, and he was free. The ride was over when he turned the chapter over to Steve and took a nine-to-five job. You were already gone and didn't see him becoming more depressed each day. What a comedown it must have been for him. Then there was the backlash of the straight community. That probably affected me more than it did him. I talked with one guy who wanted to put hippies or anyone else who was different into concentration camps and gas them like in Nazi Germany."

"Certainly not everyone in the straight community feels that way."

"No! But more than you can imagine. The good thing is most people still believe in diversity and tolerance, and the haters don't have much power. If someday they get power, all of us had better watch out. I felt sad to hear Frank was gone. Pulling the plug was his choice. I didn't like the direction things were heading either, and I left. I'm just glad he blew his brains out in the Marin Hills instead of upstairs in his studio."

"You're so understanding, Jack."

"How's Gene?" I asked, ignoring her sarcasm.

"He's not doing well right now, and I'm no longer on speaking terms with Debra."

"Reeeaaally! What happened?"

"The truth is, I came down with a dose of the clap. He was still having sex with her, and you know what she's like. She was going

John-Paul Cernak

to a different fuck party every night. I told him he had to make a choice. When he told her he wasn't going to sleep with her any more, she kicked him out and filed for divorce. It was nasty. He lost everything even his pension, and can you believe, she blamed me when it was all her crap."

"God! What a mess. I'm sure glad I got out when I did. I knew this would happen."

"Oh, yeah! You're the one who created the problem when you split the scene. She was never the same afterwards. You're the one who screwed it up."

"I was saving my life. We were all exploring new territory. But hey! I didn't come to squabble. I'd like to take you out to lunch tomorrow and have you fill me in on what's happening with our old friends."

"Jack, I'll take your money anytime you want to spend it."

"I'll come by around one."

As I walked out, I stopped and turned holding the door open. "Oh! By the way, Meg and I got married last month."

We met Reggie that evening at an English Pub in San Rafael. The bar was a meeting place for people from all over the British Commonwealth. We met people from Australia, Canada, New Zealand, and the islands of the Caribbean and spent the evening playing darts and drinking Bass Ale. Reggie was on speed and talking so fast that along with his accent, I could hardly understand him, or for that matter, anyone else. Accompanied by a piano, a master of ceremonies led everyone in singing songs that were popular during the war. It seemed strange, because the war ended over thirty years ago. The songs from that era must have given the Brits a feeling of unity living amongst the colonials. We had a jolly good time, but more importantly, Meg and Reggie met and established rapport for future cooperation.

Because of a major shortage of marijuana, we sold our crop quickly. People were eager to buy even though it was only shake and the quality mediocre. The price went up big-time. In the past,

Colombian sold for as little as ten dollars an ounce. We asked thirty-five, and no one blinked an eye. Meg was in a disaster mood on our trip back to the valley. "What are we going to do, Jack. I knew we wouldn't earn enough money and my unemployment's run out. Do you realize how little money we have left? We'll be totally broke in a few months."

"It's okay! We'll be fine."

"How can you say that when we have real-estate taxes to pay?"

CHAPTER 8

——❦——

1976

OUR CATS WERE WELL AND GLAD TO SEE US. WE GAVE THEM extra attention and additional food that came from an unexpected source. While we were gone, a large tree fell during a storm on the Valley Road near the bottom, and it was first come first serve. Brad or Hughie would cut it up for firewood unless I got to it first. As I worked in a light rain, I soon needed to pee. It seemed it was something I needed to do more often when it rained. Instead of moving off into the woods, as I would usually have done, I stayed on the road. In summer, the traffic on the Valley Road was light, but the chance of anyone driving up in the dead of winter was remote.

To my dismay, the second I began, I heard a vehicle charging up the road towards me. Trying to stop, I wet my trouser leg. Seconds later, a dark, older Chevrolet stopped next to me. The driver was a stranger, his face with chiseled features. His hat looked a little like the one worn by the gangster, Al Capone, only his was black with a western flair pulled down low over one eye. "Howdy! My name's Slim." I laughed to myself; what else would it be? "Do you live in the valley?"

"Yeah, why do you ask?" I felt put out for urinating on myself and that a stranger was asking where I lived. "Do you folks like beaver meat?"

"I don't know. I've never eaten any."

I stood sideways to hide my wet pants. "I might be having some I wouldn't mind giving you folks if you could use it. I'm a trapper.

I was hired to stop them from building dams and flooding out the back of the valley."

I felt certain that as an Indian living on the plains, I trapped animals for their meat and fur. I took what I needed for survival. There was something that rubbed me the wrong way when done for profit. Nevertheless, I invited him to stop by on his way out.

After splitting and stacking the firewood, I sat by the fire getting warm and drying my pants. In a few minutes, I heard his car coming back down the road. "Howdy, Ma'am," he said to Meg with exaggerated politeness.

He was taller than I thought, and like his hat, his medium-length green coat with large buttons didn't fit any category. I felt uncomfortable that he carried a large revolver in a holster on his hip. His manner was abrupt and aggressive, and he possessed a primal quality that probably mimicked the animals he trapped. Standing with his coat open and his thumbs hooked onto the waist of his Levi's, he could have been an old, wild, west gunslinger, and I didn't like the way he looked at Meg. "That sure is a big gun you have there," I said.

He tapped it lovingly. "Not really big enough. Trapped animals are vicious. This six shooter has saved my bacon many times. Even animals that aren't usually aggressive will tear you to pieces. I set several traps. I'll return in a few days to check 'em. I'm sure I'll get a few back there. I keep the skins and the tails. They're the best eatin'. If you folks like, I'll give you the rest. Beavers weigh up to fifty pounds."

He explained that he was one of the last two remaining trappers in Oregon who made a living selling skins.

On our return from town the following week, we found a package on the porch next to the side door that contained two animals gutted and skinned. We had steaks for dinner, but the flavor was too strong and gamey for us. Our cats became the beneficiaries of all the meat. We had turkey for Christmas, and they had beaver. The taste wasn't too strong for them.

ON OUR FIRST MAIL RUN TO TOWN, WE STOPPED TO LOOK AT THE bulletin board at the Tiller Ranger Station. Posted were advertisements for summer jobs in recreation at Diamond Lake in the High Cascades. "Do you think jobs in recreation are teaching little old ladies how to play shuffleboard and things like that?" I asked. She shrugged her shoulders. "But I really don't want to leave the valley."

"If you don't get a job, we'll be out of money soon. What about working for the hoedads? They have an office nearby."

"Their office is close, but they don't necessarily work locally. They plant trees throughout the forest and in most instances too far to come home evenings. Trudging around on steep mountain slopes in rain, sleet, and snow carrying a heavy load of seedlings is not my idea of fun. Besides, they work only in the rainy season, and it's almost spring. As much as I hate 'working for the man,' it seems the only way

During our first week back, Donald drove by each day, and I knew something unusual was happening in the valley. He was the mate of Darlene, the head honcho lady of the Whole Earth Commune, and it seemed unusual, because I rarely saw him. Although I lived in the valley almost two years, we never spoke. Lisa informed us that Darlene ended their relationship and left the valley. In a few weeks, Donald was also gone. The Whole Earth Commune was officially dead in Ash Valley. Only Lisa and David remained, and they moved from their one-room log cabin across from Brad's house into the now vacant Whole Earth Community House and made payments to Hughie.

The large angry goose that lived by the pond disappeared. It was assumed he became too old to defend himself against predators. For most of the winter, a female coyote hunted in the valley down by the creek stalking and pouncing on small prey. She must have had pups to feed hidden in a den somewhere up in the forest. No snow fell since the day we left for California, and although the dawn often revealed white at the top of the surrounding mountains, by noon, that too melted off. It was a wet but mild winter. We drove into the forest to replenish our firewood whenever the rain let up, and it was still possible to find dry firewood if the downed log somehow remained off the ground.

I had cabin fever, and after weeks of rain, the walls were closing in on me. I hadn't seen the sun since returning from California. In March, the showers let up, although the sky remained overcast. Holding a map of the Umpqua on my lap one morning after breakfast, I pointed to a shelter marked on the chart high on White Bird Mountain. "I'd like to check it out before the rain returns," I said.

"How far is it?"

"It's deep in back country, but if I don't get out, I'll go mad."

The engine of the small truck whined as we climbed through the heavy overcast and reached a small sign along the road marking the trailhead up to the shelter. "They could have at least built it along the road," Meg complained.

With the trail often covered in mud or deep snow, the hiking was difficult at around five thousand feet. I stopped and waited when she lagged behind. "It can't be much farther," I said. "I'll push ahead and rendezvous with you at the shelter."

After another short hike, the refuge lay ahead on a flat area surrounded by a thick undergrowth of mazanita, shrub pine, and stunted firs. It was a small, wooden structure open on two sides. I paused when something among the underbrush didn't fit. The puzzle quickly came together when the head of a huge bull elk wearing a gigantic rack lifted from grazing. I froze, but it was too late. He saw me. Squatting to make myself as small as possible, I made hand signals to Meg coming up the trail urging her to hurry, while all around me the heads of many animals lifted from grazing. Concealed by thick shrubbery, I walked undetected into the middle of a large elk herd.

With the warning sounded, they began to move slowly at first and then with greater urgency perhaps aware of Meg's approach.

I held my arms up to protect my head as they galloped past—the ground shaking like in an earthquake and everything in a blur. She arrived just as the last elk disappeared over the crest of the mountain. "How many were there?"

"Fifty, maybe sixty."

"Couldn't you hold them until I got here?"

—◦◦◦—

I KNEW I WAS SMOKING POWERFUL WEED WHEN IMMEDIATELY MY lungs expanded, and I was forced to expel the hot smoke in a coughing jag. A large woodstove radiated delicious warmth on a cold, dark, stormy, winter afternoon. Aluminum-backed foil insulation showed on the walls and ceiling of the unfinished house. Ginger stood at her cook stove preparing a dinner of soup, vegetables, and yearling goat they slaughtered in the fall. "He weighed about fifty pounds," she said. "We'll keep his sister, and she'll replace the one we're milking when we have her bred. I want you to taste young goat before it's all gone."

As the marijuana took effect, my perception changed, and I understood the subtle nuances from what Ginger said and watched the expressions change on Meg's and Bob's face. I heard my heart beating inside my chest, felt the blood surging throughout my veins, and was keenly aware of my emotions. I felt the usual chill and the change in breathing that signaled I was stoned. When the joint came around again, I took a second hit even though I was already high.

Before we smoked, Bob showed me his stash. It looked different from the imported Colombian or Mexican I usually smoked. It was reddish brown in a series of tightly packed buds instead of the mixture of green leaves, stems, and seeds I was accustomed to. When I looked closely, I saw tiny, sparkling crystals.

"That's THC," he said. "When you see the glitter, you know your dope is stony. I grew ten plants in the garden surrounded by large bamboo."

"Did you do anything special to get the sparkle?"

"Not really. I dug the holes down two feet and gave them all the fertilizer and water they could use. This is the fourth year I've grown far-out weed."

"Is that the secret of growing stony marijuana?"

He paused before answering. "I think the secret is *Los ojos del campesinos.*"

"What does that mean?"

"The eyes of the grower," he replied.

⸺ ⌇⌇⌇ ⸺

"It's already spring," said Meg one morning as we relaxed after breakfast, "and you still don't know where you'll grow the crop. I hope not in the garden again."

"No! I've learned my lesson. I'm taking the sheriff's advice and growing it where it can't be seen. At the moment, I'm a grower without a place to plant."

"How about down by the creek? There's plenty of water down there."

"The problem is the same as growing in the garden. It's further from the road but not secluded enough."

"Well Jack!" she said, "If there's no place to grow on our land, why not plant on their land? I'm sure the government wouldn't mind you borrowing a few of their million acres."

"I've considered it. I've just haven't figured out where on their land."

"It's almost April. If you're going to grow, you better find a spot fast."

The rain finally stopped, and the wind blew sweeping the sky free of clouds. During the storms, debris washed down from the forest above and clogged our water intake reducing the flow into our storage tank. On a warm, sunny, spring-like morning, I headed uphill to clean it out. High water swirled just beneath my feet on the narrow bridge that crossed over the small creek separating national forest from private land. As I climbed steeply through a jungle of tall grass, young conifers, and huge bracken ferns, everything glowed in brilliant shades of green nourished by deep volcanic soils and a great abundance of water. I lovingly touched each plant as I passed knowing it was where I belonged.

I paused scanning the terrain above looking for the water pickup buried somewhere among the greenery. Dressed in late winter catkins, alder trees grew in a thick tangle along the creek, and through their naked branches, I spotted a clearing. Above where the stream narrowed, I jumped across. Instantly, a voice whispered in my ear that I entered a sacred place. In a trance, I walked around the gently sloping terrain feeling a deep reverence that a higher power just led me to an almost perfect growing area.

⸺◈◈◈⸻

As you entered the barn through the front door, immediately to the left was a small workroom separated from the main room by a half-wall made from rustic old barn wood. It was where I stored my tools and did my dirty work. One afternoon as I sharpened the chainsaw, Meg returned from a mail run with a letter from the Department of Agriculture addressed to me. "Leave it on the table," I said. "My hands are oily."

She reappeared after several minutes holding the letter. "Open it. I'm curious."

"The Forest Service is part of the Department of Agriculture," I mused. It took several moments after reading it before the information sank in. "Hey! I have a job at Diamond Lake, and I'm to report for work at the end of the month."

"Thank God for small favors," she replied, "We're almost out of money. Does it say anything about what you'll be doing?"

"All it says is that it's in recreation. In a way, I was hoping I wouldn't get it. I'm really not that keen on leaving the valley and you being alone most of the summer."

"Will it give you enough time to get the plants in?"

"If the weather holds."

In the greenhouse between the tomatoes and peppers grew ninety marijuana seedlings ready for transplanting. While Meg planted vegetables in the garden below, I labored up on the mountainside digging planting holes down two feet and using my shovel in a piston like motion worked the virgin soil into a fine loam. A major benefit of growing on the slopes was that the water drained off more rapidly, and the soil dried faster allowing me to plant sooner. But my greatest benefit was that I was now a hardened veteran. My body continued to develop, and with each passing day, I was stronger. All of the easy-living city fat melted off and became muscle. I never felt more energetic and looked forward to the hard work. Running effortlessly uphill, I determined this was what my body was like when I lived as an Indian in my last life. With three-quarters of the plants in the ground, the rain returned in the third week of May and brought everything to a halt. The rest would have to wait. I was now a weekend farmer.

AT DAWN ON A CLEAR, SOFT, SPRING MORNING, WITH PUFFS OF FOG hugging the valley floor near the creek, I kissed Meg goodbye and headed the little truck upriver into the mountains using the same route taken when looking for Larry and Caroline. Turning east at the Glide Ranger Station on the opposite side of the forest, I drove up the main highway that follows the North Umpqua, the larger of the two rivers. Wearing waders and standing waist deep in water, fishermen cast their lines into the fast, flowing stream. This was the same good fishing waterway Zane Gray wrote about in his novels. In the distance, two snow-capped peaks protruded above the trees and glistened in the morning sun. At almost ten thousand feet, Mt Thielsen to the east had a volcanic plug sticking out of its center and looked like a hand giving the world the finger. Shorter and with a soft round top, Mt Bailey was to the west. At the fifty-two hundred feet road marker sandwiched between the two peaks, the beautiful.

blue waters of Diamond Lake opened before me. At the front gate, a young woman wearing a green Forest Service jacket stepped out from a small booth. "How long will you be staying?" she asked.

"Hi! I'm Jack. I'll be working here."

"Oh! Hi, I'm Becky."

"Who's the guy in charge?"

"That would be Jim."

"What's he like?"

"He's a grouch and does everything by the book."

At a mile high, the air felt chilly walking from the parking lot to the office. Coming off the lake, fishermen held long lines of trout. The bodies of countless black flies lay everywhere and crunched under foot. I entered an empty office in a row of prefab buildings. Wearing a Forest Service shirt and jacket, an unsmiling fellow entered a few minutes later. He gave me a long, slow, suspicious look. "What do you want?" he asked.

"I'm Jack Cernak."

Without saying a word, he handed me a folder and pointed to a table. Although he spoke little, his attitude and his vibe spoke volumes. The people of San Francisco accepted that I looked hippie, but this was backwoods Oregon and the Forest Service. I was joining their organization, and as much as I resented it, I would need to conform to their standards and cut my hair. "You'll be working with Charles in recreation," he said, without looking at me, "and the two of you will be running the campgrounds."

"I don't know anything about the place. What do you mean running the campgrounds?"

"Charles'll fill you in." He looked at me with quick side-glances. "This is his second year, and he knows the ropes. He turned towards me and gave me a distasteful look. "I hope you're not like the guy we had two years ago. He pestered me constantly and couldn't make any decisions on his own. I'm a busy man and don't have time to do my job and yours, too. I don't want to be bothered unless it's absolutely necessary. Do I make myself perfectly clear?"

The Odyssey of a Hippie Marijuana Grower   153

"Whatever you say," Mr. Grouch, I said to myself.

After a quick conversation on the phone, he turned towards me. "You and Charles are in charge and responsible for everything that happens."

"And what is it I'm responsible for?" He ignored my question.

"I'm assuming you have the credentials they were seeking when they hired you. Charles is studying law and in his last year at the U of O in Eugene. He'll be here shortly." Without another word, he walked out.

After a few minutes, a man entered wearing jeans and a plain, beige jacket. He was in his mid-twenties, around five-nine, with short, sandy hair, and brilliant blue eyes but with nothing physically outstanding about him. Yet his presence immediately grabbed my attention. If this guy is going to be a lawyer, he's going into the right business. "You must be Jack," he said reaching out his hand. "I'm Charles. Welcome to Diamond Lake. I've been waiting for you and wasn't sure when you'd be here."

"You've been waiting for me?"

"I'll need to get out of here in a few weeks, and I want to show you as much as possible before I leave. A class opened that I need for graduation, and this summer is the only chance I'll have to take it. My plan was to be here all season, but it looks like you'll be running the show by yourself."

"What show are you talking about?"

"Nobody filled you in?" He shook his head. "You've been hired to maintain the campgrounds."

"I'm not going to be showing little old ladies how to play shuffle board?"

"No!" he said, stifling a giggle. "We don't have shuffle board here. This is a Federal campground, a large one, not a luxury cruise liner. Your job is to clean up after the campers and clean the toilets and the fish cleaning stations. There'll be some police work like catching speeders, but your main job is cleaning the crappers each day."

"How exciting. Recreation means cleaning toilets! I need cre-

154   *John-Paul Cernak*

dentials for that?"

"That's what you've been hired for. It's not that bad. You'll have a large crew, the summers up here are delightful, and nobody's breathing down your neck."

"It's not what I thought it'd be."

"Sorry for the bad news. When you work for the Forest Service, nothing is as it seems. This is a large lake. There are three campgrounds, and each has a bunch of toilets and fish cleaning stations. Let me show you around."

The sun rising over the mountain reflected brilliantly off the blue waters of the lake, and it became comfortably warm. We drove up a short hill to three military style buildings. The first was the men's bunkhouse, the second the kitchen, and the third the women's barracks. Charles stopped to chat whenever we passed people working, and everyone greeted him with handshakes and backslaps. When he introduced me, a few gave me strange looks. "Most of the people are friendly," I said. "What's with this guy Jim? Why's he so uptight?"

"He's having problems with the brass, and I think they're trying to find a way to oust him. Last year he got himself into trouble that nobody'll talk about, and his wife's threatening to leave. He's poison. Stay away from him as much as possible, and since we're on the subject of people to avoid, watch out for some of the wives. A few hate the Forest Service for keeping them isolated up in the mountains away from the bright lights and shopping malls and look for a little diversion. I didn't get involved when one of the wives put the moves on me last season. The place is small, and it's easy to get caught. You can do what you want, of course. I'm telling you because my predecessor warned me, and I'm passing it on."

That evening, I drove back to the valley to pick up items I'd need for the following week. Meg questioned me the minute I walked in the door.

"So, what's the job all about? Are you working with people in a recreation center?" I hesitated. "You're not going to tell me?"

"The job's cleaning toilets."

We rolled on the floor laughing. "Hey! Mr. Forest Service Ranger," she mocked, "teach me to play shuffle board."

At the lake the next day, twelve people arrived, and eight were assigned to Charles and me. In the barracks that night, I became aware I would have to make other arrangements. All the guys were in their late teens and early twenties, and it wasn't until the wee hours of the morning before it became quiet enough to fall asleep.

The weather turned warm and dry when I returned to the valley for my two days off. It felt magical up on the mountainside working with my plants in the new growing area. The surrounding vegetation provided shelter from the incessant winds that blew in the valley, and the beauty of the surrounding tree-covered mountains and the singing of birds up in the canopy of the big trees soothed and calmed me. I planted an additional twenty-five for a total of seventy-eight. I had room for more but feared I wouldn't have the energy to carry all the water they'd need.

The only irritant that broke my exquisite concentration were the biting deer flies. They buzzed and circled around my head annoyingly. They were fast, and I learned quickly trying to swat them didn't work after several administered painful bites. Turning the tide in my favor, I devised a system of retribution. Holding a bare arm out as lure, I held the other up to strike. After taking the bait, it would sit nervously watching me. If I acted prematurely or even moved, it would take to flight, and I would have to start over. It used its front legs to part the hair on my arm, and when it lowered its head to bit, my raised hand would follow it down with a slap and send it to fly heaven. The system worked so well, I was never bitten again.

I wondered why there were more flies than the previous year. Hughie was rebuilding his herd. I saw many cows when driving past. The insects laid their eggs in deer dung but also in cow patties, and the more cows the more pests.

On the second evening home, we worked out in the garden until dark. Meg was in a strange mood all day, and before going inside, we stood next to the side door hugging and kissing. "You seem pensive." I said, stroking her arm.

"I guess I'm not feeling good about being the only one here with all that marijuana growing up there." We entered the barn to have dinner without comment.

Our evening meals were intimate affairs sitting on pillows on a plush rug under a small table. The yellow flames of three kerosene lanterns illuminated the area around us but with most of the large barn in darkness. "There's nothing to worry about," I said, continuing the conversation from outside. "It's not like last year when everyone saw it growing in the garden. No one knows it's up there."

"Don't be naïve, Jack. Even if they can't see it, everyone knows were growing. They just don't know where yet."

"Out of sight, out of mind," I said.

She dipped her spoon into her stew and nervously stirred it around. "That's easy for you to say, but if the cops come, I'm the one who gets busted."

"Better you than me."

I stretched across attempting to kiss her on her cheek, but she drew away. "Ha! Ha! Very funny."

"Don't worry, the police won't come. Remember the sheriff said they won't look for it, and if this new job works into something more permanent, we'll stop growing" We both knew I was lying. "For now, there isn't any other way."

Her mood softened. "Are we safe, Jack?"

"Yes! Of course we are, baby," I took her hand. "Absolutely."

Although I talked confidently, I remembered the pain from last season. I always considered farming risky and doubly so for growing weed. I heard many stories from growers that sounded like fishermen's tales of the big one that got away. All were close to bringing in a crop but losing it at the last minute. The prospect of another rip-off, the cops finding it, or losing it from another way yet unforeseen loomed over my head like the "Sword of Damocles" hanging by a single hair. "But no matter what happens," I said, "we'll be fine. We'll just become more self-sufficient, and isn't that the reason we moved here? We have our garden, a forest full of game, and a nearby river full of fish; what else do we need? We don't need much money to survive. Where can we spend it? Maybe we could find another crop to grow, and I was thinking of doing some hunting this fall. When I was alone the first winter, I shot a few birds. The forest is full of grouse and other game. Even if we have no money, we'll never go hungry."

"You went hunting!" her voice rising. "How could you shoot those poor little birds?"

I returned to the lake the next day with a one-man tent and erected it behind the barracks. As I crawled into my sleeping bag on the first night back, the rain returned. I prepared by adding a second tarp tent over the one I slept in. On the second day, the storm intensified, and the campgrounds emptied. It was fine with me. The rain would keep the Umpqua National Forest lush and green and that included my marijuana.

Several weeks later on my days off, I decided it was time to do the deed. On the drive to Centerville, we stopped to pick up the mail at our Tiller post office box. The sun shined brightly for the first time in two weeks. Meg ran in to get the mail and came out holding a letter. "It's from Brandy. She wants to visit. I'll write her directions when we get home."

I drove around Centerville until I found a beauty salon. Several older women sitting under hair dryers stared at me as we waited. My hand trembled slightly holding a magazine. The next day at the lake, everyone did a double take when I entered the workroom.

Although I looked less hippie with shorter hair and a trimmed beard, it wasn't enough to change the opinion of Roger Morgan, a low-level manager out of Glide. He stood five foot two, had the personality of a pit bull, and carried a chip on his shoulder as large as a boulder. Each time he spoke, he offended someone, and the more people he insulted the better he liked it. His job as drill instructor was to indoctrinate employees into Forest Service culture.

John-Paul Cernak

I rebuffed all his attempts. His attacks came from frustration that I cared little about becoming a permanent member, and he found it intolerable that a hippie with long hair and a full beard worked for his beloved organization.

—————✺✺✺—————

UNLIKE THE PREVIOUS YEAR, THE WEATHER TURNED HOT BETWEEN storms. Meg went out first one morning to begin her day, and when I followed a few minutes later, she removed all her clothes and worked nude in the garden. She occasionally removed her top on the few warm days we had last.season but never fully naked. "What'll you do if someone drives by? She pointed to a dress lying near the garden.

I thought about her naked body all the way up the hill, but once in the growing area, the plants quickly absorbed my attention. Most stood over three feet high and almost as wide, and I was delighted with their growth. With all the rain, I anticipated an easy weekend, but it was dry when I dug my hand into the soil at the base of several plants. That morning, I made thirty trips to the creek holding a bucket in each hand and sweating in the hot sun. For the first time, I also removed all my clothes. I enjoyed feeling the sun and air on my skin but worried that certain parts never exposed before were in danger of becoming sunburned. Although nobody could see me, each time I filled my buckets, I looked around making sure I was alone. On the other hand, Meg was completely comfortable without clothes even if it was certain someone driving past would see her bare bottom.

Around noon, I looked up to see her jump over the creek and enter the growing area, her blonde hair shining in the midday sun. She was barefoot and wore a short, flimsy dress that clung against her moist skin and revealed the curves that firmed and became more desirable over the months. She carried a basket with lunch and two pillows, and I knew we wouldn't get much work done that afternoon. "You sure look delicious all nude and everything," she said, hugging and kissing me passionately.

WHEN I DROVE IN FROM THE LAKE THE FOLLOWING WEEK, I FELT irritated at finding an unfamiliar car with California plates parked in my spot under the maple tree. My annoyance quickly changed to fascination when Meg and our guest greeted me with hugs and kisses, and both were in the nude. Brandy was an old friend from San Francisco. Last winter while in the city selling our marijuana, I reconnected with her. "It was my idea to greet you naked," she said. "I thought you'd like that. We made a great dinner with homemade bread, and Meg made squash pie for desert."

"Whatever you wanna do is fine with me."

During the evening, Brandy did most of the talking, and that too seemed unusual, because Meg's strong personality usually dominated. It wasn't the first time I saw Brandy nude. During the Sexual Freedom League days, Isabel and I attended a few parties, and she was usually there. Everyone partied in the nude, and I remembered admiring her from afar. For a woman in her forties, she had the body of a much younger woman. A peculiarity was that the two halves of her face didn't match, as if at birth she received a half that belonged to someone else. It somehow worked for her. I couldn't call her beautiful but interesting. She had the combination of sensuous body, unusual looks, and provocative personality men couldn't resist. Brandy was a good cook, kept a clean house, and was artistically talented. She worked as a nurse and was a no-nonsense person but with a proclivity for sex I believed came from a deep need to be of service to her fellow man.

Any pretense of work was abandoned the next day with the exception of watering the plants. Brandy was the first outsider to see the new growing area. After touring the valley, we drove to the top of the mountain with the clear-cut behind the barn. Although the area was just behind the valley, the road getting there was a complicated nine-mile drive through the mountains. We didn't see another vehicle all morning and the huge forest seemed like out private playground.

Under a cloudless blue sky on a warm, summer afternoon, Brandy immediately removed her clothes. What again seemed unusual was that Meg remained clothed. She was usually first to disrobe. While Brandy and I frolicked among the young trees growing in the clear-cut, laughing and playfully teasing each other, Meg remained off to the side shooting photos. In what seemed innocent at first, Brandy kissed me. From there, the situation quickly escalated. With her second kiss, her tongue probed deeply, and she pressed her pelvis hard against me. "You've changed, Jack," she said, her voice a breathy whisper. "Your body is so hard. You turn me on."

I knew Brandy for years, and nothing sexual ever happened between us. I was flying high from the massage they gave me the night before, and holding her nakedness in my arms, I knew I lost control. With my excitement now apparent, I led her to the pickup and spread a large towel over the lowered tailgate. She climbed aboard and lay back keeping her knees up. With a blank expression, Meg stood close watching. I drew her near and kissed her passionately in an attempt to include her. She neither rejected nor returned my kiss. Feeling it straining to be liberated, I unzipped my pants. Every creature living in those beautiful mountains held their breath enthralled at hearing Brandy's prolonged song of ecstasy. As my climax approached, I shuttered and experienced wave after wave of release along with a feeling of satisfaction in collecting an old debt—left uncollected—since Meg's infidelity with Bruce two years earlier.

———⌇⌇⌇———

WAITING OUT ANOTHER DRENCHING STORM IN THE UMPQUA, WE spent my two days off the next week up on the sleeping deck sipping wine and getting high smoking weed. Meg lounged in her bed with a copy of *Ms. Magazine* in her lap. I read the *Mother Earth News*, a magazine for people like us who moved back to the land.

Feeling confident and a little assertive, I introduced a subject I was hesitant to bring up until after the clear-cut incident. "Have you been reading the personals in the magazine?" I asked.

"I've glanced at them. Why do you ask?"

She took a hit on the pipe and returned to reading. "There are inquiries," I said, "from people seeking a place in the country. Some are seeking communes and others want to live with families." She turned and looked at me with her glasses down on her nose. "So!"

"Why don't we run an ad and advertise for a woman to live with us?"

She looked at me for a long moment her face expressionless, except for one eyebrow that rose almost imperceptibly. "Why?" she asked finally.

"Well, you complained there's too much work for one. She'd be someone to help around the place and now that I'm gone most of the week, a companion. We can advertise for someone just out of school or maybe a little older."

"Write the ad," she replied, almost too nonchalantly.

"Will you help?"

"Sure," she said, tersely.

The ad appeared in the next three issues of Mother Earth News and simply stated that we were seeking a woman to join us. Responses trickled into our post office box. We must have written a good ad, because in later issues, other ads appeared worded identically to ours.

When it rained, I worked inside and replaced an old window above the kitchen sink with two new ones. A stained glass crafted by an artisan from the Applegate Valley hung in the new opening. We met him at the Ashland Food Coop where we volunteered a half-day each month giving us a discount on our food purchases.

———✺———

IT FELT LIKE WINTER. THE RAIN POUNDED ON THE WINDOW OF the lunchroom at the lake, and a blazing fire burned in the potbelly stove. The conversation was loud and lively between the eight guys sitting at the table. They came to Diamond Lake to spend the summer outside. I felt their gloom as another storm dumped heavy rain on the forest. When I withdrew a small box from my shirt pocket, everyone stopped talking and watched. Slowly opening it, I removed a doobie. "Does anyone have a match?" I asked.

After taking a hit, I handed it to Jake sitting next to me; he was my second in command. He looked at me and the joint and smiled. "I wondered if this would ever happen. With Charles, I knew it wouldn't, but when I first saw you, I told myself this might be a fun summer."

Jake was a smooth big-city kid from LA. He was short like Roger Morgan but more easy going unlike the uptight manager out of Glide. He graduated from college two years earlier but hadn't yet decided on a life's path, except he wanted to stay in the Northwest and expand on his interest in ecology. He was playing around with several ladies but most particularly, Brenda, a short, sexy chick about his age assigned to Broken Arrow, the campground on the south end of the lake. I saw her riding in Jake's yellow Camaro. Whenever I'd run into her, she'd greet me with: "Hi, Jack" in her low, sultry voice.

Linnel sat next to Jake. He was a lanky, black, big city kid from the east the Youth Conservation Coprs placed in the job. He played amplified guitar, and his dream was to become another Jimi Hendrix. He took his hit and was ready to take a second when Mitchell yelled from across the table: "Stop bogarting the joint, Linnel."

"Fuck, ya," he said but quickly passed it on.

Mitchell was a college kid from Medford who also played amplified guitar, and he and Linnel competed in everything they did. It started early in the spring during firefighting practice when each began digging at a furious pace to see who could dig the deepest hole in a given time, while the others cheered them on. Mitchell claimed victory when it was apparent Linnel's hole was deeper. The lanky kid from the east turned to me and asked. "He didn't win that, did he, Jack?"

"Looks to me like Linnel won that one."

Thereafter, they asked me to officiate and call the winner on several occasions when each claimed victory. Both went along with my decision without complaint. Throughout the summer, the victories were about even, and I often used their need to compete as a way to get the work done faster. After the joint went around, the noise level elevated, and I felt the need to be alone.

"Stay out of the barracks," I advised, getting up to leave, "in case Jim or Roger Morgan come around. They know there's nothing to do, but if they catch you guys hanging out, they'll be obliged to find work. I don't care where you go as long as you're back by 7:30 tomorrow morning when maybe the sun'll shine."

I headed to the main hall of the lodge with the intentions of reading and kicking back. The large firewood racks outside the main entrance bulged with lodge pole pine logs, the major species in high country. The big hall was empty, except for the desk clerk and a few employees hanging out and talking. I sat on a couch in front of the large, stone fireplace and close to a side door where I could quickly exit. The flames flared when the desk clerk added a huge log.

Several young girls entered who I recognized as employees, and my thoughts drifted back to a few days earlier. While walking through the hotel, I passed a tall maid cleaning rooms. I usually didn't bother with the uptight local chicks, but this one was especially attractive. "How are you?" I asked.

Not expecting a response, I walked past. "Could be better and you?" she said to my back.

Surprised, I faced her. "What's the matter? Don't you like liquid sunshine?"

"Doesn't the sun ever shine around here?"

"I don't know. I've only lived here two years." I quickly became aware she was somehow different. "You're not an Oregon chick, are you?"

She paused before answering as if she wasn't sure she should reveal anything about herself. "I'm from Michigan," she said.

"Really! You are far from home. I spent some time in Michigan. What town are you from?"

When I stopped and took a good look at her, I realized how pretty she was. At close to six feet tall and wearing a short skirt, she had gorgeous long legs and a beautiful face. With a small delicate nose, gleaming white teeth, and her blond hair falling in soft folds around her shoulders, it gave her a wholesome girl-next-door look. Yet she was classy enough to have just stepped out from the cover of Vogue or Cosmopolitan magazine and was the kind of chick headed for stardom. "You probably don't know this town," she answered. "I'm from Ironwood. It's way up north in the Upper Peninsula on the Wisconsin border."

"You're not going to believe this," I said, feeling I had an opening. "I know it. I've been there."

"How did you get to know such a small community in a far-off corner of the country?"

"While exploring Northern Wisconsin around Ashland and Eagle River with a group of friends, we spent the night in Ironwood. Do you know those towns?"

"Of course I know them. I have friends in both. We play them in football and hockey."

"You must be Swedish being from up there."

"I'm Norwegian. I've seen you around; do you work for the Forest Service?"

"Yeah! I'm Jack. How'd you get a job way out here all the way across the country?"

"I answered an ad for summer jobs in a hunting and fishing magazine. Living in a small town was driving me crazy. I had to get away from all the young guys. They wouldn't leave me alone. They're so juvenile."

"Where are you staying?"

"I'm in the dorm with the others."

She looked at me long and hard without saying another word.

Picking up some towels from her cart, she walked into the room. Hmm! I didn't get her name.

In late afternoon, I left my warm seat in front of the fireplace and headed to the kitchen to cook dinner. The kitchen and barracks were empty. The guys must have taken my advice and drove to Medford. As I crawled into my sleeping bag, stars twinkled for the first time in a week. Tomorrow, the campers and fishermen would return.

————◦∂◦∂◦————

ALTHOUGH CHARLES LEFT AFTER THREE WEEKS, HE HAD A PRO-found influence on everyone. Even Jim the grouch and Roger Pit Bull Morgan fell under his spell. We threw him a party before he left, and folks asked about him all summer. For lunch, we often went to the café at the lodge where he seemed to know everyone. He walked around greeting people making small talk and telling jokes that kept everyone laughing. I followed him around like a lost stepson but with a motive. Charles was a cool dude, but I reasoned what he did couldn't be that difficult. His departure would create a huge vacuum, and everyone knows how nature abhors the emptiness. I was just as cool as he was, only no one yet recognized it. After he left, I intended to take his place, become the second Charles, and have as much influence as he had. So, I watched and listened learning how he operated. We sometimes sat with Pete and Claudia, a middle-aged couple from LA who seemed to have loads of money and who often bought lunch.

It took several weeks after Charles left before I built up enough courage to make my grand entrance. Feeling a little nervous on the chosen day of my inauguration, I entered the café confident I would soon take my rightful place as king of Diamond Lake. I intended to walk around greeting people, tell a few jokes, and charm everyone as Charles had. Approaching several Forest Service ladies having lunch, I turned on the magnetism and tried striking up a conversation. They ignored me and looked annoyed. When I tried engaging a pretty girl Charles always made laugh, she turned away and ignored me, also.

166   *John-Paul Cernak*

Waitress! Waitress! I called out. But she also zoomed past and didn't even slow down. Wait a minute, something's wrong. I wasn't getting the same response Charles had. With an uncomfortable feeling, I looked around at the room filled with people, and I was dead in the water. Blood rushed to my face in embarrassment when I realized I was making a fool of myself. I felt like the Titanic after hitting the iceberg, and sitting at the next table was Pete and Claudia.

As usual, Pete was reading the financial pages. Charles moved easily into his world talking about stocks and bonds as if he were a broker. "Hi folks," I said, as warmly as possible, although I was crumbling inside. They both smiled but didn't ask me to sit as they always had when I was with Charles. "May I join you?"

Pete pointed to an empty chair and went back to reading. Claudia had a faraway look and said nothing. I sat silently stewing in the juices of my failure. This was not the outcome I had in mind. After sitting for some minutes in complete silence, pressure built inside. I felt compelled to say something. "What's happening in the market?" I asked.

Pete glanced up looking annoyed. "It's weak," he said, and went back to reading. Claudia just stared into space.

I contemplated making a dash for the door. After another long silence, the pressure built again. I struggled to hold everything inside. Words I could no longer contain came bursting out. "What's General Motors doing?"

Looking exasperated, Pete stood and reaching across dropped the paper in a heap on the table in front of me. "Check it out for yourself," he said, curtly.

Holding the daily in front of my face and pretending to read the jumble of figures on the page, I felt the icy waters of the North Atlantic slowly wash over me.

———

"COME ON GUYS," I YELLED, "LET'S HUSTLE. JAKE, TAKE MITCHELL and Linnel and do the three bathrooms and fish-cleaning station down on the south end. We'll finish here. I'd like to get done fast today."

I was pushing the crew to finish early, because I had a date. They knew I was married, and I didn't want anyone finding out. Yesterday, I found a note pinned to the tent: "Jack, meet me tomorrow at 7:30 in front of the hotel." The note was signed, Olga. A vision of the tall Norwegian chick flashed in my mind and gave me a warm feeling.

After a quick dinner, I went up to the barrack. No one was around. Wondering where the guys were, I was glad for the solitude and wouldn't need to explain why I was showering a second time that day. Before going up to the hotel, I stopped for a six-pack of beer, and parked inconspicuously off to the side. People and cars came and went on a warm, pleasant evening. Olga appeared around eight. She looked around until she spotted the truck and walked over. "The hotel's jammed with a square dancing convention," she said, "and I haven't had time to shower. I'll be back in a while."

I waited over an hour and almost left thinking she wouldn't show. As the sun dropped below the mountain, she reappeared dressed in tight jeans, high heels, and the tails of her red plaid shirt tied together in front revealing a bare midriff. She looked stunning walking towards me in a fast gait suggestively swinging her hips and reminded me of a model on the runway strutting her stuff. I received a good look at her long legs and slim body as she entered, rather gracefully for a tall chick, and sat pressed against the door letting me know she wouldn't be a cakewalk. I smelled soap. "Where would you like to go?" I asked.

"Wherever you'd like," she murmured.

"Drink beer?"

"Yeah, sometimes."

"Are you old enough?"

"I'm nineteen and old enough to drink beer in Wisconsin," she said with emphasis.

The darkness closed in around us when I pulled out onto the

John-Paul Cernak

deserted highway. With only the double yellow line visible in the headlights and the glare from the hotel fading fast in my rearview mirror, I drove towards a side road I remembered seeing up in the mountains. "Did you have a hard day?" I asked, making conversation.

"It was okay."

I found the road after driving several miles. It was unused, and when the little truck began to lurch and heave from ruts and potholes, I stopped and turned off the engine. Everything went black. We sat silently until I determined it was safe to be there. She moved without resistance when I pulled her close. "You're married, aren't you?" she said.

Bummer! "Yeah! How'd 'ya know?"

"I saw you with a blonde woman."

She must have seen me last week when Meg needed the truck for a doctor's appointment and drove me to the lake. "Why did you leave the note when you knew I was married?"

"You were nice to me and not many people around here have been kind. Everyone's cold and angry. I thought maybe we could be friends, and older men are more understanding."

"I think that you're nice too, and I'll be your friend."

"You're the first person I met since I came who's not from here. I don't think they understand me. I haven't made any friends. They treat me like poison just because I'm from out of state. They won't even talk to me."

"Sounds familiar. Outsiders aren't accepted, and I don't know how long you have to be here before they do." I put my arm loosely around her shoulders in a friendly, understanding way. "I know how you feel, and you can talk to me as much as you like. Would you like another beer?"

"That'd be nice."

We drank silently, and after a few minutes, I turned her face and kissed her gently. Her lips were soft. I liked the sensation and how they tasted and wanted to linger but broke it off. "I know how difficult it is when folks won't associate with you." Taking the beer can out of her hand, I placed it next to mine against the door and kissed her again. When her lips parted slightly, my tongue brushed her upper lip, She didn't react. "It must be lonely not having friends." The next time, I kissed her passionately, and my tongue darted in. Her reticence quickly collapsed, and she hugged and kissed with total abandon, as perhaps months of loneliness and frustration poured out. When I slipped my hand into her shirt and cupped her small breast, she quickly unbuttoned her shirt and allowed me to unhook her bra. But when I reached to unbuckle her jeans, she stopped me.

"Wait! Wait!" she stammered breathlessly and put a hand on my shoulder holding me at arm's length. "I want you to know I'm a virgin, and I intend staying virgin until I marry." She leaned forwards and put her arms loosely around me. "But you're such a nice man, I hate disappointing you. It doesn't mean we can't do other things. We can do whatever you'd like as long as you promise not to fuck me."

When I reached down the next time, she quickly unbuttoned her jeans and let me remove them followed by her panties. For a few minutes, everything was a tangled mix of heads, arms, and legs going every which way in the small, cramped front seat of the truck, but somehow we achieved the perfect position. "Mature men are more understanding," she sighed after a long silence.

On my drive back to the valley the next day, I took a slower road through the woods that gave me time to think about Olga. I wondered if Meg would sense a difference. We didn't actually have intercourse, but I felt apprehensive, nevertheless. She hadn't expressed any remorse when she ran off with Bruce. So, why should I hesitate to have fun with a lonely girl when it doesn't take anything away from her? In fact, I felt playing around restored balance in our relationship, and when I suggested we run an ad for a woman to join us, I felt the pendulum swinging back in my direction.

CHAPTER 9

I PULLED INTO THE PARKING SPACE UNDER THE MAPLE TREE across from the barn and looked around. Weeds stuck out from between stacks of firewood left over from last season, and tall chicory took over the shoulder of the road. High grass almost hid the new fence posts and gave the place an abandoned look. I cut small areas around the barn and garden with the sickle, but with all the summer rain, it grew back twice as thick. Hughie cut the grass for hay last season. After the cow incident, that solution was out of the question. I talked with Meg about the problem at dinner. "The grass is heading out," I said, "and the seeds are blowing into the garden. Worst of all, it looks ugly."

"Why don't we buy a lawn mower?"

The next day in Medford on our monthly supply run, I purchased a cutter on closeout. Although it had a five-horsepower engine, I was skeptical it was the right tool for the job and uncomfortable purchasing an additional piece of gas-burning equipment hooking us deeper into the outside cash economy. As I began mowing the next day, even the large engine wouldn't cut the tall grass. The only way was to push down on the handle and stand the cutter up on its rear wheels. Then, slowly lower it with the engine at full throttle. If I dropped it too fast, the tall grass smothered the blade and killed the engine. I spent most of the time pulling on the starting cord and cleared only a small section around the garden after working all day.

On my two days off the following week, Meg asked when I'd finish the fence. "I don't know. Why do you ask?"

"The deer are raiding our strawberries."

"I'm not Superman, I shot back, feeling irritated at yet another demand on my time. "I can't do everything in the short time I'm home."

"We won't have strawberries then."

"The fence is a long way from completion, and I didn't know how hard it'd be finding straight posts. With working at the lake, watering the crop, and now mowing, I don't have much time to devote to the fence."

"Don't you think protecting the orchard and garden are more important?"

"I won't have Hughie and Brad gloating that we can't even get our grass cut."

While in the workroom the following week, Meg looked in at me over the short wall. "Why are you sharpening the chainsaw?"

"Well, after you complained the second time that deer are raiding the garden, I'm going looking for fence posts."

"Great! I'm coming with you."

Driving through large, old-growth forest deep in the mountains, I spotted several yews and parked off the road behind large bushes. Although close together, they were crooked and unusable. While deciding what to do next, I sat on a large, downed log and set the big chainsaw on the ground next to me. Meg stood waiting patiently. Several large carpenter ants milled around on the log and quickly disappeared down a small hole when I nudged them with a stick.

"There should be more yews around here," I said, looking around at the thick mass of greenery surrounding us. "You walk one direction, and I'll walk in the other in a large circle and rendezvous down at that fir." I pointed to a large tree about a quarter mile down a gradual slope. "You remember how to spot them, don't you?"

Resting the long bar of the saw on my shoulder, I walked uphill scouring the undergrowth for the telltale red that was the signature of the yew. Shafts of light penetrated the thick canopy, and a light breeze kept me cool on a hot summer day. After walking halfway around, I paused thinking I heard her whistle. Listening intently, I heard only the wind rustling through the trees. As I continued, there it was again. This time I was sure, and I moved rapidly in her direction skidding and sliding on loose gravel but managed to stay upright, the long bar of the saw bouncing against my shoulder. When I heard panic from her next call, I urged every ounce of speed from my body jumping over logs and around obstacles, now holding the big woodcutter in my hands. In the distance, I could see her holding a long branch in front of her fending off a bear, and I knew why I held on to the big heavy thing. As I ran, I pulled the starting cord, but it only coughed. Out of nowhere, a loud voice said in my ear: "Pull out the choke!" On the next yank, it roared into life screaming like a banshee, and the bear retreated into the woods.

With my heart pounding and my coveralls drenched in sweat, the quiet seemed strange after the deafening noise. She looked pale and frightened. "That was a close call, Jack. Thanks for coming so quickly. I'm lucky to be alive. When I saw the cub, I started back peddling. It was too late. I was already between the mother and her child. Luckily she was small, and I held her off with this large tree limb and whistled with everything I had."

When back in the truck, I hugged and kissed her reassuringly. After she settled down, we toked on the pipe, and our kisses quickly became passionate. In an unusual fervor, she quickly removed her coveralls, and I can't remember her being more ardent in her love-making. Her intensity in getting laid must have been an affirmation she was still alive.

Later that afternoon as we worked in the garden, a single-engine airplane suddenly flew in from the south. I followed it as it circled overhead and above the marijuana growing on the hill. It came in so low, I could almost make out the face of the pilot and was confused by the strange markings on its wing. After it retreated to the north, I tried hiding the panic I felt. Meg's face registered horror. "Do you think it's the cops?" she asked.

"Naw!" I said, brushing the incident off as unimportant. "It's probably a fire suppression crew.out on a jaunt and checking us out. They're probably all stoned."

∽

With summer ending, attendance at the campgrounds decreased with one last full capacity on the long Labor Day weekend. After finding different colored stains in a storeroom, I painted ten picnic tables different colors to give them some pizzazz. Jim called me into his office. He was furious. "Are you trying to get me in trouble?" He paced back and forth ranting. "Painting tables red and orange is against the rules."

"A few of them are yellow," I added.

"What? You painted some yellow?" I could see a vein throbbing in his forehead. "What's wrong with you? Where are they so I can have them painted back to the color they're supposed to be? The official color is brown and no other. If Roger or someone from Glide sees them, I'll get my ass canned. I thought you had more smarts. You must have been hiding your stupidity all summer."

I walked out before I lost control and did something unfortunate.

On the last day, Eddie Bower the head ranger from Glide came in and talked to the people in recreation. "We've been asked by Washington to bring down costs, and we're making changes. Beginning next season, we'll award the maintenance of the campgrounds to a private contractor on a bid basis. I'm pleased with how this season went. Jim and Jack, you both did a great job as did the rest of you. It's been good working with you all."

"This is the opportunity we've been waiting for," I said to Meg that evening at dinner. "We'll submit a bid, and if we get the contract, we won't be as dependent on the marijuana. We could make enough money for the year working the summer months, and Eddie Bower said that he thought Jim and I did a great job.

I'm hoping his complement was a hint that I have the inside track. The Forest Service would be stupid to give the contract to someone who doesn't know the ropes, and I have a whole season's experience. I did have a problem with Jim, I mean Mr. Grouch. I don't think he'll give me a good evaluation. I painted picnic tables different colors he objected to."

"You idiot, Jack. Can't you get along with anyone?"

———✧✧✧———

By the middle of August, the marijuana grew over eight feet high, and I pulled fifteen flowering male plants. The following week, I pulled an additional fifteen. I wasn't quite sure of the process but felt all was going well. I was after sensimilla, which are unfertilized female flowers, and I didn't want any males around to ruin the crop. Once they were safely inside, like magic, the females bloomed, and although the sun dropped noticeably south, its rays still bathed the growing area for most of the day.

A week later, Meg and I walked around inspecting the plants. "I've had my eye on this strong female," she said and stopped before a beautiful plant in full bloom. "I'll pollinate her for next year's seeds. From now on we'll use only those that came from plants we've grown. She'll make us good babies next year. I'll collect pollen from a strong male hanging in the barn and pollinate her this afternoon after the wind dies down."

Each morning and evening, I scanned the western horizon for signs of rain. I didn't want a storm sneaking up. But there wouldn't be much I could do if one had. The buds were small and not ready to harvest. As Meg did laundry the following Saturday morning with the generator running, I played with the dial of the receiver attempting to pick up a station with music or news from the outside world. As usual, only static came through. Turning the arrow on the dial to the upper end, I suddenly heard the voice of a weatherman coming through loud and clear. "What luck!" I said loudly over the noise of the washer. "I'm catching a weatherman from a Medford station."

"What's he saying?"

"The jet stream is far to the north, and the Pacific Northwest is protected by high pressure blocking any storms heading our direction."

The weather forecast ended, and the next voice was one I heard before. "Can you guess who that is?" I asked.

She came close and listened intently. "Is that Ronald Reagan?"

"It sure is, and it sounds like he's running for president."

"Do you think he has a chance?"

"I don't know, but it would be a catastrophe for the country if he's ever elected."

"Tune out that tight ass and play some music."

A late summer heat wave settled in, and the blustery wind that usually blew up from the river hardly stirred. For days, the valley seemed deserted without any vehicles passing. Most mornings, I drove into the woods alone to cut firewood and enjoyed the cool under the canopy of big trees. I was feeling joy at being on my own away from the schedule of the Forest Service, and how better to express that happiness than to wander around the forest doing as I pleased.

On a stiflingly hot day, as I stacked firewood on the flat area across the road from the barn, a Forest Service vehicle appeared at the top of the short hill. Feeling suddenly alarmed, I watched as it.glided down and stopped across from me. The window slowly rolled down. The lone occupant was the Colonel from the Forest Service surveying crew. My mind went spinning back to last year when the cops came, and he was the one who turned us in. "Hey, Jack!" he inquired, "Where are you growing your marijuana this year?"

His words cut across me like a knife. "A little here and a little there," I said, unsmiling.

Perhaps feeling my unfriendliness, he drove off immediately. I stood motionless in the hot sun feeling tightness in my chest. With sweat dripping off my brow, I watched his vehicle disappear up the road leaving behind a trail of dust that slowly drifted into the valley.

Several days later, while putting away tools and garden supplies for the season, I heard a vehicle enter the valley. Meg was nude in the garden picking the last of the beans. She was suntan over her entire body. "We're having guests," I said.

Quickly picking up her dress, she headed for the door and looked at me questioningly. "What are you feeling?"

"A vehicle just entered the valley, and I received a hit we're getting company."

In a few minutes, a yellow Camaro appeared at the top of the short hill, and the familiar car glided down to a stop in front of the barn. Who owns a yellow Camaro? Then I remembered. "Hey, Man!" said Jake. "What a great valley!"

Sitting low in his car, he looked like a low rider. "I was wondering if you'd be able to find us."

"Yeah! But it wasn't easy. You sure live in the boonies. I didn't see anything for miles and was beginning to think I was lost."

"You're at the end of the line, man! There's no other private land beyond here, and except for the people living in the valley, our nearest neighbor is over ten miles downriver. Regardless how far it is, it isn't far enough from civilization to suit me."

"Guess what?" He was standing next to his car. "I'm working at a sawmill in Medford, but it's only temporary while I wait for the Service to process my papers, which'll be soon."

"You've applied for a permanent job with the Forest Service?"

"I have, and I've been approved. But I have to wait until there's an opening. They're expecting some retirements in the district, and it shouldn't be more than a few months."

"You know what the Forest Service is like and what they stand for; why do you want to work for them?"

"I know what you're saying, Jack, but when I looked at my other options, working for the Service didn't seem that bad. Where else could I work outside and have input into the environment?"

"I guess you're right," I said and let the subject drop. "You're just in time for dinner. You remember Meg?"

She came out and was standing next to me dressed in a blouse and overalls. "We met," he said, smiling and flirting a little, "the time you drove Jack to the lake."

"I remember. Good to have you."

"We're having dinner outside in our summer kitchen," I said. "Meg's cooking, and I'm building the fire. Help me gather the firewood."

From the forest behind our wood-burning stove, we gathered a large pile of fallen branches. "I want to show you something," I said. He looked around curiously as we walked up the path. I was taking a chance by showing him. After working with him all summer, I felt he could be trusted. Moreover, I was feeling such pride, I had to show someone. When we jumped over the creek and entered the growing area, he stood staring at the tall flowering giants, and all he managed to say was: "Wow!" I had to admit they looked impressive.

Meg brought out the pipe and we celebrated Jake's visit by smoking a bowl. With dinner, we drank wine and toked again on the pipe. As we settled in for the evening in front of a blazing fire, we smoked again and drank more wine. With a crescent moon hanging low in the western sky and night slowly descending upon the forest, it felt good to be home on a velvety evening and have Jake visiting. Our conversation was lively and spirited. We rehashed our time at the lake and remembered all the people who spent their summer high in the Cascade Mountains of Southern Oregon. The evening seemed to fly by, and all seemed right with the world.

As the fire burned low, the conversation slowed. When a coyote howled in the distance, for some reason, I remembered the deer that were raiding the strawberries. In a strange turnaround, my pleasant mood quickly dropped away, and I felt angry and irritable. "I'll bet those deer that are raiding the strawberries are out there right now waiting for us to go to bed so they can plunder them again." Standing, I shined my light into the valley. Three pairs of eyes lighted up. "See what I mean. I'm getting my rifle."

When Jake joined me on the road above the orchard on the north side of the barn, I was holding the 30-30 fully loaded. "You know it's against the law to shoot deer without a license," he said and put his hand on my shoulder. "I don't think you should do this, Jack. I don't want to be a witness to it."

"Hey, Man! You're not working for the Forest Service yet. Besides, it's almost deer season, and I don't intend on getting a license." Rubbing my eyes, I tried shaking out the lingering effects of the wine and marijuana. "Those deer out there have been eating our strawberries."

"You sure you want to do this? You might regret it."

Annoyed at his faintheartedness, I was going to proceed with or without his help. Holding the flashlight against the barrel of the gun, I shined the light into the valley, and the three pairs of eyes lighted up. Aiming at the nearest, I squeezed the trigger. The rifle kicked, and the report echoed like the crack of a whip between the hills of the narrow valley. All three pairs of eyes continued reflecting back. "The one thing I hate about guns," I said, "is the whole fucking world knows you just fired it."

"There's no one around to hear it," he reasoned.

"My neighbors can hear it, and it's just the idea. The less they know the better."

Undeterred, I aimed and fired a second time, but again the three pairs of eyes looked back at me. It was the same after I fired a third time. Now feeling frustration, I cocked the rifle and shot in quick succession until the gun was empty. As before, all eyes continued reflecting back. "Bummer! This gun couldn't hit the side of a barn. Come on, Jake! Let's get that deer."

He followed close behind when I dropped down into the orchard, past where the new fence was coming in and into the valley proper wading through waist-high grass and stumbling on berry bushes and anthills while holding the light on the spot where I last saw a pair of eyes shining. Unexpectedly, I came upon a young spike deer laying in a shallow depression. When I stopped suddenly, Jake ran into me. We looked at it, but it didn't move. "Far-out! I must have hit it." I handed him the flashlight and knelt close.

"Is it dead?" he asked.

"It's alive."

"How can you tell?"

"I can see it breathing."

"Then you must get it out of its misery," he said, his voice quivering with emotion.

I rose, stepped back a few feet, cocked the rifle, and pointed it at its head, but when I squeezed the trigger, the firing pin only clicked when it hit the empty chamber. I repeated the process with the same result. "Bummer! This stupid gun is empty."

"Cut its throat then or something!" Jake said, shaking excitedly. "You must get it out of its misery!"

Unsheathing my knife, I knelt next to the deer. As I reached across with the blade, the buck opened his eyes. Startled, I recoiled. He jumped to its feet and ran off. "Don't let it get away," Jake shrieked hysterically! "Do something!"

"Keep the light on him," I yelled racing after.

I caught him after a short run and hit him over the head with the stock end of the empty gun. He shook off the blow and ran off. "Stay with me Jake," I yelled. After another short chase, I caught him again. This time, I swung with all my strength. In the beam of the light Jake held, I saw clearly the stock of the rifle break-off when it connected with the deer's head and with everything moving in slow motion. He shook off the blow again and ran off, only to suddenly disappear. When I quickly reached the spot where he vanished, I saw he fell into the creek. Jake shined his light into the black abyss. The deer lay on the rocks fifteen feet below, and from the awkward position of his body, I knew he was dead. "I'll be back as quickly as I can," I said. "Keep the light on so I can find my way back."

I returned with a rope and a long 2x4. With the board on our shoulders and the carcass hanging in between, we carried it out of the creek and up to the road. Jake looked pale when I shined the light in his face. "I need to go home," he said. "I'll see you in a couple of weeks."

I didn't remember him driving off. I dumped the deer into the small creek across from the barn to cool the meat. Meg appeared moments later holding a book and lantern. After a quick prayer to the spirit of the deer, I began cutting. "It says to cut around the anus and upwards through the belly." She read from the book, "but don't cut too deeply or you'll cut into the intestines and ruin the meat."

Although I never gutted an animal before, I proceeded as if I did it a hundred times. After removing the intestines, I cut away the liver and kidneys from the bloody mess. Penetrating the membrane that protects the chest cavity, I searched around in the muck until finding the heart. I was determined not to waste any part. We hung it from a high branch of a maple tree and skinned it.

As I climbed into bed, I remembered something odd. "I didn't see any bullet holes," I said. Meg was already in bed. "He was lying on the ground, and I thought a bullet found its mark. With all the noise, he couldn't be sleeping. He had plenty of time to escape. I've never heard of deer playing dead like possum."

"Are you sure there were no bullet holes? It was dark out there."

"I looked the whole time I was skinning it. It was as if he was lying there waiting for me and sacrificed himself."

For breakfast, I ate liver and onions with eggs. Meg refused to eat meat. With large piles of raw meat stacked throughout the kitchen and blood everywhere, it took most of the day to cut up and process the animal. We canned twenty-one quarts and in a crock pot marinated the steaks and better cuts with onion, garlic, vinegar, red wine, and spices. For dinner, I ate the heart sliced thin and sautéed with onions and tomatoes and spiced with rosemary. She ate vegetables with tofu. "You're missing something good," I said, stuffing a piece into my mouth, "and it has a subtle flavor of strawberries."

———◦◦◦———

I awoke before dawn on a morning in late October and lay quietly listening to Meg's rhythmic breathing in her bed next to me. Starlight reflected off tinfoil-backed insulation on the ceiling that came through the large picture window I recently installed on the north side of the barn. The new opening was five feet by five feet and gave us a great view up the valley. It added more light and brought the outside in. With the hole in the wall cut and ready to receive the glass the next day, we slept on the floor in front of the large uncovered space. It was like sleeping outside, but we were inside comfortable on Meg's queen mattress. Lying in the dark that night almost asleep, I saw a bat fly in and out several times. I wondered how it was possible to see it in total darkness, but I quickly fell asleep thankful for the natural insect control.

Snuggling into my sleeping bag on the cold morning, I remembered the woman who almost came to live with us after we advertised in the Mother Earth News. We received over twenty responses. The final choice was a woman who lived in Pennsylvania. Meg called her in September and arranged for her to come out. At the last minute, she changed her mind. I took her not coming as an omen and didn't pursue a second choice. When I remembered the cold wind blowing in from the north yesterday afternoon, I worried about the plants growing up on the hill. Quietly sliding from beneath the covers, I dressed quickly shivering in the cold. As I swung my leg over the top of the ladder starting down, Meg's voice rang out from the darkness. "You're up early."

"Something woke me, and I couldn't get back to sleep. It feels colder. What day is today?"

"I think it's the twenty-third."

"According to the Farmer's Almanac, that's when we should be experiencing our first frost. You might as well stay warm until I build a fire."

After hearing crackles of burning kindling, I hurried out into the crisp morning air. The first light of dawn smeared the eastern horizon. Above and to the west, stars hung like jewels in the raven sky. In my beam, I saw my breath in a white cloud and sparkles of frost along the edge of the road. When it became light enough to see, I hurried up the path. My worries quickly eased. The cold air never settled on the plants and continued down into the valley, another benefit of growing on the hillside. When the weather turned warm and sunny, I almost left them in the ground. Listening to an inner voice, I harvested that afternoon.

For several weeks, I felt foreboding vibes that put me on edge. Standing in the growing area that morning with my eyes closed and in a meditative state, I understood their origins. I was feeling the paranoia of all the marijuana growers in the South Umpqua Valley ready to harvest their crop, and after remembering what happened last year, I wasn't immune. I didn't want anything going wrong after six months of hard work. That evening, with forty-eight female plants hanging in the front of the barn, I couldn't keep my eyes off them and was getting high from their smell.

Meg checked them daily, and after a week reported they were dry and ready to clean. That morning, we would smoke the bud for the first time. The pipe was filled with a small one. She took the first hit. After I toked, I was high instantly. "I've never smoked weed that worked this fast," I said and reached out the pipe. With a little wave, she declined. After drinking my tea, I noticed small cracks in the bottom of my cup. Holding it close, I was suddenly looking into a deep ravine. It was a fascinating world down there. I'm not sure how long I looked into the canyon. It could have been hours or just seconds. My perception of time was altered, and it somehow seemed unimportant.

She didn't speak when I walked past her on my way out. I sat on the steps leading up to the side entrance on a clear autumn day, and seeing the low October sun reminded me winter was coming. It was quiet. I did hear the chirping and chatter of birds up in the canopy of big trees, but those were natural sounds that soothed and calmed me. I heard no sound made by humans. The roar of traffic, the constant hum of electric motors, and the slamming of car doors and garbage cans jangled my nerves when living in civilization. I remembered how the lack of human sounds felt threatening when I first arrived. The silence frightened me. It's impossible to avoid hearing noise living in society. It's so pervasive, I hardly noticed it until my first night in the valley. It took several visits before silence felt normal. I tried blocking out the ruckus when in the city last winter. The clamor was a constant irritant until back in the valley. Silence reduced stress and easily offset the inconveniences of living without electricity.

I immediately became aware that the high from the bud was different from the tips we smoked all summer. My hearing and thinking were extraordinarily sharp. From the moment I toked, my perception shot up into the stratosphere, and it was pure and clear. I don't remember smoking weed that took me as high with such clarity. When Meg and I discussed what we experienced that evening, the name we gave it was, Cascade Clear. I was uncertain of what gave marijuana its qualities. I'm almost certain where the seed came from and the soil and weather are important. I noticed weed grown at high elevations was usually of better quality. Our marijuana had spiritual qualities, and I wondered if it absorbed emotions from the grower? After a few minutes, I felt the urge to climb the hill, as I did a hundred times that season, and sat at the top of section four most of the afternoon feeling complete, tripping, and listening to the birds singing.

———

SEVERAL DAYS LATER, MEG JOINED ME ON THE PORCH WATCHING dark clouds move in low and fast. According to our Medford weatherman—who we now listened to each Saturday morning along with Ronald Reagan's political commentary—the high pressure protecting the Pacific Northwest broke down, and the winter rains were about to start. "What a great year," I said. "It would be nice if they waited until late October each year."

"Count your blessings, Jack. You were lucky this year."

With a blazing fire burning in the woodstove, two naked bulbs hanging overhead for light, and music playing non-stop to keep us in the mood, we sat cross-legged on pillows on the floor and cleaned plants. We worked continuously for three days, stopping only for food, a little sleep, and sex, and all the while stoned from chewing off the resins that built-up on our fingers. As we finished weighing and bagging the bud, she asked about the large leaves. "We've never smoked them," I said, "and I don't know how potent they are."

"Are we taking them with us to the city?"

"I don't think there's a market for shake, at least not in Marin County. I'll stuff them into a plastic bag for future sale."

Jake visited several days later. I could barely see his bright, yellow Camaro through the downpour. "You came at the right time," I said.

"What do you mean by that? Are you planning another hunt or something?"

"Not to worry." We moved toward the warmth of the woodstove. "It's something you'll like. "We want you to be a judge of the crop."

He held a baggie filled with bud and looked at it under the light. "It looks beautiful, but I can't tell much by looking at it."

Meg handed him a joint already rolled. He gave me the same look as when I handed him the joint at the lake. He took a hit and held in the smoke for as long as he could. "Dynamite, it comes on like an express train."

For fifteen minutes, he spaced out. "This stuff takes me away, man! It blows my mind. I can hardly speak after one hit. I've smoked ganja from all over the world. I've experienced the finest from Maui, Humboldt County, and Thailand, and this compares with the best, maybe better."

I wasn't a good critic. What I smoked was average quality Mexican or Colombian with the occasional good stuff thrown in. On the other hand, Jake was a connoisseur, and I trusted his critique that our little valley deep in the mountains of Southern Oregon grew some of the most potent marijuana on earth.

That evening, we served barbecued venison to celebrate bringing in the crop and for Jake helping with the deer. I hadn't eaten any meat since the heart and liver. The moment I laid the platter on the table, he speared a fillet, quickly devoured it, and harpooned a second. He objected to killing the animal but had no qualms about eating it. I couldn't blame him. It was delicious. The meat acquired a slightly sour flavor from the vinegar and wine marinade leaving a nice aftertaste. For the first time in memory, Meg ate meat. "It's okay," she said. "It's organic. The deer was wild and not shot full of antibiotics or hormones like store-bought."

In a downpour on the first anniversary of our marriage, we drove toward San Francisco, the truck loaded with boxes filled with high-quality marijuana tucked snuggly under black plastic. Even with the rain, my insides tingled with excitement. Instead of driving all the way on I-5, I exited the freeway in Grants Pass where the skies cleared. "Driving Highway 101 is a much longer trip," she said.

"I love Mt. Shasta and the mountains of Northern California, but driving through the Central Valley is long and boring. Besides, I'm longing to see the redwoods again."

The trip down to the Oregon Coast on Highway 199 was seventy miles on a narrow mountain road with many curves and cutbacks, and it was as dangerous as it was beautiful. Sitting wide-eyed and holding on to the bar above the door, she gave a sigh of relief when high on the mountainside, the blue waters of the Pacific opened before us. We stayed overnight in a motel in Crescent City, the first town in California. For the first time in over ten months, we ate breakfast in a restaurant, and they served good coffee. "Wow!" I said afterwards. "That was fun."

In the morning, the California Coast was cold, windy, and foggy. As Highway 101 moved inland, the sky cleared and the temperature rose into the mid-seventies. I turned on my headlights in the twilight under the giant redwoods at Humboldt State Park. Our plan was to spend a few days camping and hiking under the big trees. Unfortunately, the campground was closed for the season, and with few motels in the area, our best option was to immediately drive the three hundred miles south. It wasn't until I crossed the Golden Gate Bridge that I realized how much I missed San Francisco. After a short time driving up and down the hills, it seemed I never left.

⎯⎯⎯⎯⎯⎯⎯⎯⎯⎯⎯

WE STAYED AGAIN WITH MEG'S FRIEND, MARGE. SHE GAVE IN TO Tim, and they rented a house together high on Mt. Davidson just below the large, lighted cross overlooking the city. In a town known for its spectacular views, the spreading panorama of the city below was one of the best. I found a safe spot to stash the boxes in a dry basement. We surprised Marge and Tim on the first evening with a delicious vegetarian meal prepared with vegetables from our garden in the valley. It felt good to be spending time with city folks again. They were a cosmopolitan couple, liberal and broad-minded, and different from the narrow and provincial Oregonians. I visited Isabel the next day.

Although our break-up had had a few stormy moments, it ended without excessive rancor. During one intense exchange, she accused me of not doing my share of the housework, and that I was responsible for her dog's demise. She was probably correct about the housework but not about the dog. She had him put to sleep. I was surprised and even shocked. Although I casually mentioned the sick K9 would be a problem when looking for an apartment, I never considered having it killed. It was her decision alone. Beyond the two grievances, I was grateful to her for not seeking alimony. As we prepared to go before the judge, I overheard a conversation with her feminist lawyer: "Make the bastard pay," she said. "If you don't need the money now, ask for one dollar and keep the door open. You can raise the amount later."

To Isabel's credit, she refused to yield to the pressure, and without entanglements, it allowed the healing process to begin.

When I climbed the stairs up to the second floor of a small

office building where Isabel had her business, she was still there, and the name, Cernak & Associates appeared on the door. As I stood outside ready to enter, I received a psychic hit that one day I'd find her office vacant and never see her again. With her back turned, the way I saw her a thousand times before her move, she stood at her orange-colored light table looking slim and beautiful. When she turned, her expression said she was glad to see me, but something was wrong. "Gene's dead," she said.

I felt shock. "What happened?"

Tears ran down her cheeks. "Several months ago, I told him I wanted to see other guys. He took it hard and became depressed. His divorce was final last week. Although I was seeing other guys, we continued to date. We went to dinner a week ago Sunday and made plans to go skin diving up to the Mendocino Coast this coming weekend. His secretary, Julia, called on Wednesday. She was worried. He hadn't come to work for two days and didn't answer his phone. She wondered if I knew where he was. I still had a key to his apartment, and we went in together. He was dead in his bed. It was horrible, Jack."

"What did he die from?"

"The autopsy was inconclusive and baffled the doctors. He was a runner and skin diver and in excellent shape."

He died of a broken heart, I said to myself. "How did Debra take it?"

"What a bitch she turned out to be. She blamed me for it when it was all her doing. The funeral was yesterday. You just missed it. At the wake, I received people downstairs, and she greeted them upstairs acting as if she was still his wife. I was much closer to him than she was."

Feeling despondent after hearing about Gene's death, I walked out into a dark, cold, and foggy San Francisco day and drove along Haight Street and through the old neighborhood in the hope of finding an inspirational vibe to lift my spirits. Instead, my gloom deepened. All the old places were gone, and only a few pseudo-looking hippies walked the street. A drugstore was now where the shop was on Cole Street, and I didn't recognize any of the businesses who were my neighbors. When searching for a familiar face at a coffee shop that opened on the corner, I saw only strangers sitting stiffly and looking into their coffee cups afraid to make eye contact, so different from the easy, friendly laughter of the hippie days. Remembering all the beautiful people and the joy I experienced living there, I quickly left the neighborhood sad and disillusioned. The hippies were gone, and the zombies had taken over the Haight-Ashbury.

The fog lifted along with my spirits after crossing the bridge into sunny Marin. Reggie and Andre sat in the sun on a bench in front of the gallery along with two guys I didn't know. "Hey Matey! It's good to see you."

"Still growing domestic weed?" asked Andre.

"I'm still a growing." I removed a doobie from my pocket for all to see. "It's a sample of the new crop for everyone to try."

Rising in unison, the four guys quickly reassembled inside in the backroom. "I believe you've got it lad," Reggie said, holding a bud up to the light. "Look at all the sparkles. You Yankee boys are getting the old know-how. I was hopin' you'd be in soon. There's a major fucken shortage of smoke."

"What's good weed selling for?" I asked.

"Sixty to seventy-five a lid," Andre interjected, "and around eight to nine hundred a pound."

"The market's gone fucken wild," Reggie added.

"Wow!" I said. "That's up considerably from last year."

After he told me the new higher price, I understood why the name of my marijuana changed. Last year he called it homegrown, this year domestic. Understandably, it would be more difficult charging nine hundred dollars a pound for something grown at home. After everyone toked, it became quiet. Finally, Reggie spoke: "How much can you leave me?"

"Can you move two pounds?"

"This stuff? I can move all you can leave me."

━━━∞∞∞━━━

PACIFICA IS A SMALL TOWN TEN MILES DOWN THE COAST FROM San Francisco on Highway 1. The town's most noticeable features were the fog and its pastel-colored houses. It was where I met Rick. He was a Paul Bunyan-type guy standing 6'4" or 6'5," narrow at the waist and broad at the shoulders. Yet in comparison to Reggie's boisterous and flamboyant personality, he was soft-spoken and possessed an uncommon gentleness and humbleness. He played steel guitar in a band, and with his tall, rugged, good looks had his pick of the ladies who came to hear his music. The difference was he took women and love seriously. Whereas to Reggie, it was all a game, but like the Englishmen, I trusted him immediately. It seemed a paradox how in the marijuana business, which was illegal, I trusted everyone I did business with. In other legal businesses I was in, I hardly trusted anyone. "I've heard of good ganja coming out of Panama, Hawaii, and Humboldt County," he said, "but I haven't heard of any coming out of Oregon. I'd like to try it."

On a sunny, Sunday afternoon, we toked sitting on a comfortable sofa in his elegantly furnished living room in a house he shared with two roommates high on a bluff overlooking the blue Pacific. Afterwards came the customary silence. Sitting back, I watched through a large picture window a sloop glide into her moorings down on the bay. "How long do you intend on staying in town?" he asked, breaking the silence.

"Only as long as it takes to sell the crop, although we'll stay longer if we're having fun."

"If you leave some with me, I'll have the money for you in a couple of weeks."

We visited Brandy. We hadn't heard from her since her summer visit. No one mentioned the clear-cut incident, and the women acted friendly toward each other. She invited us to Thanksgiving dinner at a wealthy, industrialist friend's house who moved to

California from Pittsburg. He lived in a large, palatial mansion in Corte Madra. After smoking our marijuana, he bought six ounces. Almost everyone who tried our product purchased it. Next year, we would have a long customer list, and in dealing, everyone welcomed us. With my shorter hair and trimmed beard, I blended in more easily and didn't look as much like the hippie dope dealer I did the first season. I must admit, I missed the special attention I received from the ladies when looking like a hippie freak.

For the first time since moving to the land, money was available to purchase needed items plus a few fun things. Meg purchased a simulated fur jacket giving her a classy look, and I bought a down vest. Once the money started rolling in, we splurged going to movies, taking Marge and Tim out to dinner, and having a few drinks at the bars. It felt good to have spending money again, although money lost significance. Since moving to the mountains, I simplified. In the past, I clogged my life with material things I thought I needed. Instead, I filled my life with sun, wind, and rain.

Marge and Tim left to visit their families for the holidays, and on Christmas day after Meg went to bed, I sat alone in the dark living room late into the night looking at the lights of the city below and reminiscing the fun times living in that beautiful city by the bay and the wondrously, wild and outrageous 1960s. After stopping for a drink at a bar to bring in the New Year, we spent a quiet New Years Day reading and meditating and returned to the valley at the end of January. We were gone almost three months. It snowed heavily our first night back.

CHAPTER 10

─◁◁oⲟⲟⲟ▷─

1977

THE APPLICATION FOR SUBMITTING A BID ON THE MAINTENANCE of the campgrounds arrived on our first mail run. Sitting close to the woodstove and soaking up its warmth on a cold, rainy morning, I held the application feeling confident and maybe a little smug after a successful trip to the city. Meg sat next to me. "Have you figured out what you'll bid?" she asked.

"With the cost of salaries, vehicles, etcetera, etcetera, it must run them fifty grand for the summer. What do you think if I submit a bid of twenty-five thousand? At twenty-five, we'll make money and save the Forest Service a bundle. Remember it's only a three-month season. This could be our ticket to ride."

"I'll leave it up to you."

I made a second trip to town the next day to make sure the application went out. It snowed again heavily the following week. The sun shined afterward for two weeks before the next storm arrived. By mid-March, it seemed the rains ended for the winter, and I began to hear the word drought in people's conversations. California experienced drought for several years. It seemed almost inconceivable that it could happen in Oregon, after two wet and soggy winters. With drier weather, cold, continental air moved in to fill the void usually occupied by wet but moderate Pacific Air. For two weeks or more, temperatures dropped into the teens.

After I made repeated trips into the forest for yew posts, the fence was racing ahead. In early April, I started a hundred and fifty marijuana plants and spent days digging new planting holes up in the growing area in soil already dry enough to work. The little greenhouse was busting at the seams with starts, and when Meg saw how many, she expressed doubt. "Do you intend on planting them all?"

"As many as I can get into the ground."

"Are you sure you'll be able to carry water to all of them?"

"Of course," I answered with irritated self-assurance. She looked at me skeptically. "Last year was a snap," I said. "This season we'll clean up!"

A month later, it was already time to begin planting. It was a month earlier than the year before. The plants in the greenhouse glowed a healthy green. As I gathered several cartons to carry up to the growing area, a plant fell over. Its leaves looked green and healthy. When I inspected closer, the stem at the soil line looked weak and eaten. After scraping the earth away from several other plants, they were all the same. Something was attacking them at the soil line, and several more fell over. I stuck my head out the door and yelled: "Meg! Meg! Come look at this."

"What's going on?" she asked, squeezing in next to me into our small greenhouse

"Look what's happening to the plants. Have you been over-watering them?" I was feeling panic, and my tone of voice was accusatory.

She examined several and looked perplexed. "I don't know what's going on! They look healthy."

I scraped the soil away from several more. "They're all that way, and it looks like something caused by overwatering. We're going to lose the whole fucking crop. We should be planting now, for Christ sakes. You were in charge of the greenhouse!"

She flashed an angry look. "Blame me for it, why don't you."

"If you weren't up to it, you should've told me."

Turning, she stormed out of the greenhouse and into the barn slamming the door behind her. I ran in and cornered her in the kitchen. "It was your job to see everything was going okay. Why couldn't you have stayed on top of it?"

"I did my best, Jack. It's not my fault."

At the post office a few days later, I sifted through a stack of mail until I found the one I was looking for. I didn't open it until back in the valley. "Is that the mail we've been waiting for?" she asked, looking anxious.

"I think so."

"I hope we got the bid now that the crop looks questionable."

I quickly ripped open the envelope. When I scanned down the list of bidders, my heart sank when I found our name way down the list. "Bummer! We didn't get it. They awarded the job to someone for eight thousand dollars."

"We weren't even close. Can they make any money at eight thousand?"

"If they work for slave wages. The Forest Service'll get their crappers cleaned for cheap. We don't have any choice. We'll have to replant the crop."

After starting new seeds in fresh soil, we stood together a week later in the greenhouse looking at the young seedlings beginning to germinate. "How we'll handle it," I said, "is that each of us will be responsible for half the plants."

"Whatever you want."

Several weeks later, as we again stood in our tiny greenhouse surveying the young seedlings, I was feeling gloom at seeing they grew only a couple of inches. "Are you giving your plants enough fertilizer?" I asked.

"I'm giving them what you told me."

"If you are, why are yours plants smaller?"

"It's your imagination."

"Are you calling me a liar? I can see your plants are smaller."

"Why are you being such an asshole, Jack?"

Feeling all the frustration of the last few weeks, I spitefully block her from exiting the greenhouse when she attempted to

194   *John-Paul Cernak*

leave. I didn't strike her, but there was physical contact pushing and shoving. "Get out of my way you son of a bitch," she screamed and angrily pressed past me.

Although aware I overreacted, I refused to apologize and blamed her for the problem. Over the next few days, we settled into an uneasy truce barely speaking to one another. Several days later, I made the decision to plant the marijuana up in the growing area even if they were only a few inches high. They were growing much too slowly in the greenhouse and maybe planted in a more natural setting would help speed their growth. I planted ten seedlings on the first day. With each, I poured in extra portions of fertilizer but feared burning the tender young plants. They were so small that I could hardly see them.

The next day, already sweating in the unseasonable hot weather, I inspected the seedlings planted the previously day, and it seemed several were missing. They were so small and hard to see, I wasn't sure anything was planted in the spaces but quickly identified deer tracks that put me into a total state of panic. What else could go wrong? In my gloom, all I could think of was why didn't she take better care of the greenhouse. "How are you going to keep out the deer?" she asked at dinner.

"All the entry areas are blocked, except at the top. I guess build a fence."

"What kind of fence?"

"Wire would be fastest, but if anyone from the Forest Service walks past, they'll wonder about a chain fence on government property and discover the plants. The only solution is something more natural looking. There're branches and other debris up on the mountainside under the big trees that would make good fencing material."

We slept up in the growing area that night as a buffer against the deer. I awoke at first light. The sky turned a pale blue, and a pinkish glow smeared the eastern horizon. It was that exquisite time of the morning that happens only in summer when the light is diffused and even the birds haven't fully awakened. For a few moments, I lay looking up at the sky feeling peaceful. Suddenly, I was no longer Jack Cernak in the mountains of Oregon. I was somewhere out on the plains wrapped in a buffalo robe lying next to a river and with snow-capped mountain peaks in the distance. I could feel my palomino nearby but couldn't see him.

As my awareness quickly reintegrated into my present consciousness, I remembered the reason we slept up in the growing area and was feeling something I shouldn't be. Quietly unzipping my sleeping bag, I reached over for the 30-30 rifle lying next to me and slowly stood up. Once past the bush blocking my view, I came face to face with a handsome buck deer across the gully. We both must have been stunned, because we looked at each other without moving for a long time. As I raised the rifle, Meg awoke. "What's happening?"

"Don't get up," I said and squeezed the trigger.

The shot missed, and the deer bounded off. "How could you have missed?" she commented later. "You were only a few yards apart. You must have still been asleep."

In reality, I must have been hesitant to kill such a beautiful animal

For the next few days, I dragged debris down off the mountainside and piled it into a barrier along the top of the growing area. With everything in a straight line, it didn't look quite natural, but it would keep out deer. The final tally after I finished planting was a hundred and thirty-five seedlings, more than double the previous year, and I used all the available space.

Each day dawned bright and clear with hardly a cloud in the sky, and each day I tended my plants from early morning until evening, carrying water, applying fertilizer, and urging them to grow faster. But regardless of how much water or fertilizer I applied or how much urging, they just sat and marked time. By the end of June, they were still less than a foot high, and each day I came down off the hill mentally and physically exhausted. If only she had taken better care of the greenhouse.

During the day, we avoided each other, and nights, I would lay in bed longing to be close. It was almost a month since we were intimate, and I wasn't going to be the one to give in. The next morning, she seemed tense playing with her food at the breakfast table. "What do you have planned today," I asked, making conversation. She looked at me without saying a word. "Why don't you say something?"

"You're just like my father," she screamed. "There was no talking to him either." Quickly regaining control, she spoke in a quiet and deliberate voice. "And I'm leaving. I want to use the truck to find a place to live."

Her words tore into me like a thousand daggers. "Where would you go?"

"Probably Oakridge, and I want half the money we made from last year's crop."

The chair beneath me seemed to vibrate after she went outside, and I struggled to breath. I remembered the first year when I came up to the valley alone feeling confident and not needing anyone. But that was long ago, and I couldn't imagine living in the valley without her. If she left, it would be a huge defeat. Hughie and Brad would have won, and what money was left after splitting with her didn't seem like much. I actually shivered when walking out into the hot sun. With her leaving, nothing seemed important not even the crop, and I wandered far up the mountainside and sat under a giant fir for most of the day lost in thought.

I awoke the following morning feeling something terrible was about to happen, and when I remembered that she was leaving, the churning in my stomach returned. We sat silently at the breakfast table each into our own thoughts. "I'd like to load my things into the truck and take them with me this morning."

"Is there any way to convince you not to leave?"

I reached across the table and touched her hand. She looked up at me without emotion and moved her hand away. "Don't go, baby. It'll be mighty lonely here without you."

Without answering, she climbed the ladder up to the deck. I climbed after her and stood behind her as she removed her things from a dresser drawer. "Don't leave, baby," I said.

She ignored me. "I know I've been a jerk, and I'm really sorry. Give me a chance to make it up to you." I stood close, rubbing her arm. "We'll have a new beginning, and I'll make you glad you stayed."

"Don't touch me," she said. "You've been a real asshole, and I don't mean just what happened lately."

"I've been unthinking, and I'll make it up to you." I moved closer pressing against her. She continued gathering her belongings. "We'll be like we were in the beginning." She didn't stop me when I pulled out her shirt from inside her coveralls. Reaching up, I rubbed her bare back. "I'm not taking any more of your crap, and I won't have you making me look bad in front of people."

"I love you, baby. I want to make it up to you." She sat on the bed and looked up at me, her expression deadpan. "Let's have a new beginning, sweetie," I knelt on the floor in front of her. She didn't stop me when I unbuckled the straps of her coveralls, but when I tried kissing her, she turned her head. "I'll never let you treat me that way again."

"I'll make it up to you, honest."

"I'll never again let you make a fool out of me. You can bet your last buck on that."

"Let me make it up to you, sweetie."

She looked at me with contempt but allowed me to pull her coveralls down and remove them. She wore nothing beneath, and even her loose-fitting blouse barely covered the tops of her breasts. "All I can say is I'm sorry. Let me make it up to you."

When I caressed her long legs and kissed her inner thighs, she wiggled into position. Sliding my hands beneath her bare bottom, I pulled her close. "You have a lot of making up to … Ooooh! You bastard! There's going to be changes around here."

ALL NONESSENTIAL CHORES AROUND THE HOMESTEAD CEASED BY
the middle of July with all my energy going into the marijuana.
Each day, I dragged myself up the path under a blazing sun and
made countless trips to the creek, but no matter how much water
I carried, it wasn't enough. Growing on the hillside became a
disadvantage, as water drained away more rapidly than on level
ground. "You're looking gaunt," she said at breakfast a few days
later. You're overdoing it."

"I didn't realize how much the rains helped water the plants
last season, and I went and doubled the crop."

"I asked if you'd be able to handle all of them, and you said
it'd be a snap. You never listen to me. It's up to you if you want to
kill yourself."

"I hope you're not implying I pull some of the plants. There's
no way I'd pull any."

"You sacrifice a few to save many."

"There might be another way." I said, pausing and feeling pain
throughout my body that became worse each day. "But it'll take
energy I don't have."

Although it hadn't rained in over four months, the small creek
that watered the plants and was fed by springs continued to produce
four to five gallons a minute. I determined there were millions of
gallons stored in the porous rocks of that that huge mountain and
water would continue flowing for months, maybe even years.

With the hot summer sun beating down, I diverted the flow
in the stream bed above where the plants grew. Digging in slow
motion, I felt excruciating pain with each thrust of the shovel
and swing of the pick. Where I dug was mostly rocks and roots
that needed chiseling out. On the second day, I uncovered a huge
boulder that took two days to remove. I was able to roll it out
only because my hole was still shallow enough. After five days of
exhausting labor, the hole measured four feet deep and fifteen feet

in diameter. At a farm store in Medford, I purchased enough black plastic sheeting to line the bottom and several hundred feet of four-inch diameter black plastic flexible piping. It took five hours for my holding pond to fill with an estimated fifteen hundred gallons, and with hoses inserted into the pond and leading to each of the four growing areas, my new irrigation system was ready to test. Meg came up for the occasion. "How do you get it started," she asked.

"Just like siphoning gasoline out of a tank, and if I get a mouthful, it won't kill me."

After sucking hard on the hose, a gurgling sound came from deep within, and in seconds, water gushed out. "Necessity is the mother of invention," she said, turning to leave.

My days carrying buckets were over. All I had to do was walk around the hillside and let gravity do the work. With enough water to give each plant as much as it needed, I cut watering down to every second or third day. But regardless, they remained stunted and would never achieve their full potential. With the new watering system, my heavy labor eased, and most afternoons as the heat set in, we stayed cool swimming in the waters of the South Umpqua River.

On a sweltering afternoon while Meg and I worked in the garden, Hughie slowly drove past. Even though we were only a few feet from the road, he looked straight ahead and ignored us. "He bad vibes me every time he drives by," I said, "and the son of a bitch is pissing me off."

"He waves to me when I'm alone. Maybe someday you'll learn to get along with your neighbors."

With the temperature over a hundred degrees, I was hot and sweaty and in an ugly mood. Since the spring when she threatened to leave, our relationship deteriorated even further, and it seemed to get worse each day. "He better be careful," I added.

"Forget about Hughie. You need to do something about the fence. The deer are hitting the garden and it's not just the strawberries. The drought's dried up their normal browse, and they like our juicy plants."

"I don't dare go into the woods with a chainsaw. The forest is closed and is a tinderbox. One spark and this whole place goes up in flames."

Giving me her look of disapproval, she walked off leaving me alone with my crappy mood. Within minutes, I spotted Hughie's red pickup returning. Moving quickly up to the road, I stood a few feet up from the front door of the barn where he had to see me when he passed. He approached driving slowly and looking straight ahead pretending I wasn't there. As his truck was about to pass, I reached out my hand in front of his windshield and put a middle finger in his face. He stopped next to me and rolled down his window. Standing close to his truck, I faced him unflinching. "You bad vibe me every time you drive by," I said, "and I'm not going to ask you twice to stop."

"Snotty kid," he said and raised his hand as if to brush me away.

Almost as a reflex, I hit him. Blood gushed out from the corner of his mouth. He quickly exited his truck. I backed up and prepared for the fight. "Come on, you son of a bitch."

Instead of coming at me, he reached behind his seat for his rifle. I quickly slipped inside the barn and grabbed the 30-30 off the rack. I watched through the peephole as he milled around behind his truck holding his gun. "Two can play this game," I shouted.

He quickly put the weapon back behind the seat and drove off. "What was that all about?" asked Meg, after she heard me calling out. I told her what happened.

"You were lucky, Jack. He could have shot you through the door."

"I don't think he wanted to do that. The gun was a bluff, but I didn't bluff."

After evaluating the reason Hughie reached for his rifle, I concluded his action wasn't aggressive, although at first, it appeared to be. The weapon was to be used as a defensive against having to fight me. For weeks, I expected retaliation and remained vigilant, but nothing ever came. Thereafter, I no longer felt Hughie's negative vibes and in fact experienced an improvement in everyone's vibe.

The difficulties with Hughie and Brad were diminishing, but the battlefield came in much closer.

———— ⁓⁓⁓ ————

IN SEPTEMBER, WE TRUCKED WEST OF INTERSTATE-5 TO A U-PICK grape vineyard. Oregon's wine industry was in its infancy, and several U-pick vineyards sprung up along with two growers who were already producing wine. We purchased a hundred pounds of Cabernet Sauvignon wine grapes. The new wine would be in addition to what was left of the pear wine Meg made last season. While visiting one of the wine producers and standing in the vineyard among rows of beautiful grape vines, their leaves turning with the season, I pictured myself growing grapes and making wine. The owner was a short fellow wearing a beret. He seemed to know everything about growing grapes and making wine. I questioned him about the possibility of growing grapes up in the valley. "How high are you?" he asked. When I replied over two thousand feet, he shook his head negatively. "Just too high. You'd be frozen out most years."

Deer continued to raid the garden for the remainder of the summer and fall. I set traps and strung wire, but nothing helped. After losing all patience, I waited in ambush with the rifle. At last light, two deer appeared. I fired at the nearest dropping it instantly. I shook for hours after seeing the bullet strike and blood gush out. It reminded me how much I disliked guns. To add to the unpleasantness, it was a female. She was larger and older than last year's spike, and the meat was tough.

By summer's end, I weighed a hundred and sixty pounds. Never in my adult life did I weigh as little and without an ounce of fat on my six-foot two-inch frame. Meg never let me forget the spring episode and threatened to leave several more times. For most of the summer, I lived in a state of anxiety and confusion and with a loss of my sense of self. I harvested the plants at the end of October, and I was disappointed with the quality. But mostly, I was dissatisfied that the sixty to forty female plants over male plants ratio of last year was reversed. The buds were smaller and less potent, and I would have trouble finding buyers for the less desirable males. But at least, I had a crop.

Cleaning the marijuana became a ritual. We sat cross-legged on the floor with two naked bulbs for light and music playing to keep us in the mood. As we began working, Meg selected an album by a British folk group called, The Fair Port Convention. It was one she chose many times since threatening to leave that spring. One song told a story of a young woman married to an aristocrat who controlled her with his wealth. The young wife had an affair, and her rich husband caught her in bed with her lover. In a dual, he killed the lover and asked who she preferred. In a last act of defiance, she stated: "I prefer young laddie to you and your finery," whereupon he drove his sword through her heart and killed her. As the story unfolded, I watched Meg's expression change to one of indignation. In her mind, she equated me with the rich husband. Feeling mentally and emotionally exhausted, I sat quietly unable to act. With the exception of sex, most meaningful communication between us ceased. Our relationship degenerated into a game of one-upmanship, and I was in the one-down position. "I don't want to go to the city yet," she said, after we finished cleaning the plants. "We have money left from last year's crop. Let's take a trip."

"Where?" I asked.

"Mexico," she answered.

We reached the border at Nogales, Arizona a week later. The day before in Phoenix, I phoned Marshal, an old high school friend. Years earlier, on another trip into Mexico, Isabel and I stayed with him and his wife for several days. After I told him I divorced and remarried, he refused to speak with me and hung up. It was just as well. In the years since our last meeting, my life went through a major transformation. I was much more a dope-smoking hippie now than I was then, and we had little left in common.

We were not taking weed with us into Mexico. We heard they gave long prison sentences for simple possession. In a motel room on the border on our last night in the States, we smoked the last of our stash. "This is it until we get back," she said and flashed a challenging look. "Can you handle it?"

The facts were, she smoked considerably more than I did. "I can," I said. "The question is, are you able to?"

At the border the next morning, the Mexican authorities refused to issue us a travel visa until I bribed them. Once across, it seemed unusual to see soldiers everywhere dressed in full combat gear and carrying M-16 rifles.

My intentions were to drive the Pan American Highway. I was disappointed to learn the famous thoroughfare was as a narrow two-lane road without shoulders, instead of a modern four-lane highway as I expected. Anyone changing a tire had to park on the road surface blocking traffic. Many Mexicans didn't believe in mufflers, and the noise of passing vehicles was deafening. I drove with extra caution after passing numerous small crosses decorated with artificial flowers marking the spot where someone died in an accident. The newness and uncertainty of travel drew us closer, and for the first time in months, the feelings between us was more loving.

The only places available to camp in Mexico were in RV parks. The first night near the town of Guaymas, we camped in a park filled with large American RVs. With daytime temperatures in the mid-eighties, we headed quickly for the pool. While in our tent changing, Meg wondered out loud what would happen if she swam nude as she did in the river. "You love to be seen without clothes, don't you?" She smiled. "If you swim in the nude, we'll be asked to leave."

The pool was large and the water warm. Meg splashed around in the shallow end while I practiced backward somersaults off the diving board. I must admit, I was showing off my lean, hard body in front of the mostly plump, sedentary, middle-aged Americans. Afterward, we sat at a small, round table in the crowded pool area. A woman and two muscular guys sat at a table next to us and looked different from the other RV people. They were drinking beer and responded with a friendly wave when I nodded. "Where are you guys from?" I asked.

"I'm from Kansas City," replied the larger of the two, " and my friends are from California."

"We're from Oregon. Where did you get the beer?"

"We have a cooler full. Come over and visit with us."

We moved our chairs and sat at their small table getting acquainted. Kansas City went to the edge of the grass where he kept his cooler and returned with a beer for each of us. "Groovy man," I responded

"How are you folks traveling?" he asked. I pointed to our little truck. "Oh! You're the people with the tent."

"What do you guys do?" I asked.

"We travel in a caravan. The company we work for puts together trips for people who believe it's dangerous traveling alone in Mexico. On the first leg, the RVs are shipped across the border on railcars. I'm the mechanic, Bill is security, and Karen is the nurse."

After drinking several beers and with all of us a little high on a warm, star-filled evening, Kansas City challenged his friend to an arm wrestle. By then, most of the RV people retired for the night. We moved back and made room at the table. The two muscular guys battled it out until Kansas City won. "Do you want a piece of me, too?" he asked, pointing at me.

"Sure, why not."

It must have been the alcohol talking, because I immediately regretted accepting his challenge. Winning was a long shot. His muscles bulged out from beneath his T-shirt and he looked like a weight-lifter. He grinned confidently as we locked hands, and at the count of three, my arm slowly moved back towards the table. Determined not to let him win in a cakewalk, I held, at least for the moment. My arm moved back again when he grunted and pushed with all his strength. Surprisingly, I held again. Now sweat appeared on his brow. With each passing minute, he seemed to grow weaker and I stronger, and until that moment, I hadn't entertained the idea of winning. Without giving him time to recoup, I adjusted my grip and pushed with all my strength. I couldn't budge him. We sat looking at each other eye-to-eye. When I pushed again, in a sudden collapse, the back of his hand hit the table in a loud thump. I was stunned. "I can't believe I lost," he exclaimed loudly, breathing hard, and looking dismayed. "I'm the champ! Nobody beats me!"

I was as surprised as he was, but the psychology changed. I was now the champ and defeated his partner easily. "I want a rematch," Kansas City demanded. "You're just a skinny guy. I must outweigh you fifty pounds. There's no way you can beat me."

He gave in almost without a struggle and walked away shaking his head and mumbling to himself. My display of strength must have turned Meg on. She hardly gave me time to get my suit off when back in the tent and screamed loudly when she came.

Driving south the next day, we passed what was obviously a shootout. Several bodies lay on the road surrounded by soldiers. A bullet-riddled pickup sat partially off the road. Continuing south, we arrived in the town of Las Mochas in the middle of a demonstration against the government. People carried signs reading, *alto repression*, (halt repression). Soldiers carrying automatic weapons watched the demonstration closely and set up a barrier several blocks up the street to prevent it from going any further. I spotted a couple who looked American. We picked our way toward them through the crowd. "We're from Oregon," I said; "where are you guys from?"

They were young and hip-looking and dressed mod. "We're from LA," he said.

"It's exciting, but we're not sure what's happening. We live isolated in the mountains and don't hear the news. Why all the soldiers and automatic weapons?"

"Mexico is experiencing a minor revolution. For the last couple of years, the Mexican government using American military helicopters have sprayed the marijuana fields with paraquat herbicide, and the campesinos are fighting back."

"I'm sure all this is at the request of the American government," I interjected.

"No doubt," he agreed, "and after the Mexican Government devalued the peso from six per dollar to fifteen, they are bracing for a general uprising."

"Sounds like something good for Americans but bad for Mexicans," Meg responded.

"After the devaluation," he added, "many people can afford to eat only corn and beans."

That afternoon, we entered Mazatlan, a modern tourist town on the Pacific Coast. Several colorful parachutes floated above the blue Pacific holding people strapped in harnesses and pulled by motorboats, and the beautiful beaches were filled with sunbathers. Loud music came from bars and discos, and radio announcers shouted at their audience. Mexican men stared at Meg fascinated by her blonde beauty. I couldn't remember her looking more lovely, and although the town vibrated with excitement, our limited finances required we spend money frugally. Jose was the hotel clerk where we stayed. He invited us to his home to meet his family and experience a home-cooked Mexican meal. We enjoyed visiting with his gracious family. Later that evening after overindulging in tequila, he claimed he loved Meg and couldn't live without her. He didn't turn her on, but that wasn't so for the Alaskan fisherman we met in Guadalajara several days later.

Bernard lived in the RV Park where we set up our tent and was one of many gringos we met who spent their winters in Mexico. Wearing a traditional Greek Fisherman's cap and small goatee, he looked rugged as you would expect of someone who earned his living catching fish in the far northern waters of the Bering Sea. He was in his fifties, slim, and in excellent physical shape. With a long off-season, he spent his days reading and was more literate than I expected. When I returned early from shopping one afternoon and drove past, Meg stood at his door ready to enter. I didn't know if she acted on her own or if Bernard invited her. I may have imagined it, but I thought I saw disappointment on his face when we entered together. Feeling more in control, I challenged her when alone. "I see that you were going to see our fisherman friend without me. Couldn't you wait until I got back?"

"Stop being a jerk. I'll do as I please."

Her arrogance ended our new closeness, and the trapped feeling I experienced all summer returned.

We began the drive home after six weeks in Mexico. While driving through rolling hills filled with blue agave plants used in making tequila, the Mexican Federal Police stopped us. Their leader was a short, slim man with a squeaky voice who spoke good English. Dressed in civilian clothes, they milled around inspecting the bed of the truck. We watched carefully to make sure they didn't plant any contraband to extract a bribe. When I announced boldly we were being hassled, he apologized, and they quickly departed. Meg was already sitting in the truck with the glove compartment open. "That was a close call, Jack. Look what I found."

She held a pipe filled with marijuana that we didn't know was in there. For the first time in six weeks in a motel room on the border, we had sex high on marijuana.

With traffic on I-5 bumper-to-bumper, we reached the City of Angels the next evening around midnight. The infamous LA smog made everything look purple and turned my stomach. I had to force myself to stop for gas. The sky cleared once out of the LA Basin, and we spent the remainder of the night at a rest stop. After driving five thousand miles, we re-entered the valley late the following night and sat in the truck taking long, deep breaths of cool, clean, Oregon air, my insides finally quiet after dancing throughout the trip. It was winter in the northern latitudes, and the cold soon pushed us inside to the warmth of a blazing fire.

I awoke the following morning thinking of the marijuana hidden in the cellar. I wasn't as excited to go to the city and sell bud inferior to last year's and the less desirable males. After a few days rest, we were back on the road heading for San Francisco and hoping for the best.

John-Paul Cernak

CHAPTER 11

———⟨∘⟩———

ONLY AFTER REACHING THE CITY DID I BECOME AWARE HOW emotionally and physically exhausted I was. We stayed with Brandy at her Mill Valley home. Each afternoon, I sat out in her marvelous garden for the few hours the low winter sun warmed the area. A round of social events kept Meg and me from spending much time alone, and the tensions between us never got out of hand. I gave Rick and Reggie their supply and after six weeks sold all the bud. No one seemed to notice the quality was less than last year, but no one wanted the marijuana males. Although they were potent, folks in upscale Marin wanted to smoke only the best whatever the price and rejected the idea whenever I suggested they try them. No one associated getting high smoking males. Marijuana is Maryjane, after all, and not Mike or Joe. On the positive side, the price of bud went up again helping offset the smaller bud crop with pounds selling for twelve hundred and ounces at a hundred twenty-five, but the pressure was on.

Brandy's son, Don lived with her that year, and although I met him before, I knew him only slightly. He loved our ganja and helped by selling to his friends. Since he related better with Meg, I stayed out of the way. One day when I was alone in the house or thought I was, he appeared out of nowhere and confronted me. "You're a miserable son of a bitch," he said, his voice filled with anger and scorn.

His attack surprised me, and before I could react, he quickly left the house. I experienced his confrontation more as a temper tantrum and never told Meg or Brandy about it. It wasn't until I returned to Oregon that I understood the reason for his rant, and it took me back to the San Francisco days when Isabel and I were involved with Debra and Gene, an attractive middle-aged couple who wanted to expand their sexual horizons.

I met the couple while volunteering on the phones with San Francisco Sex Information. After a month of training, I was in the second graduating class. SFSI was the only sex hot line in the country. Our first date together as a foursome was at a Sexual Freedom League Party. Debra was a beautiful, voluptuous blonde and insatiable in bed, and Isabel found Gene exciting. For a year or more, the four of us were inseparable. At times we'd spend the night all four together in one room and in one bed and at other times couples alone.

One day, everything changed for me, and I wanted out of the foursome. At first, my reason was unexplainable, and I questioned why I wanted to end a situation that seemed ideal. It wasn't that I found Debra less desirable, and I loved the sex. But it wasn't enough. Regardless of how much I enjoyed her beautiful, sensuous body or our pleasurable, intimate, mutual exchanges, what I craved was a more meaningful connection. There was another reason I left the foursome that I wasn't fully conscious of at the time, although not less important. I was hoping to open a dialog with Isabel about our marriage. It never happened and we separated. She was involved with Gene and spending more time with him than with me. My intentions were to give Isabel her freedom. He would take care of her physically and emotionally and buffer any pain of a breakup.

A fact I hardly remembered was that Brandy's son Don took my place in the foursome. Debra was a tall, statuesque woman. He was shorter, skinny and had a squeaky voice. Their relating sexually seemed almost comical, but as it turned out, the new arrangement was short lived. After Isabel and I separated, the dynamic changed. As married couples, it was all fun and games. But as a single woman, Isabel became a threat to Debra. After twenty years of marriage, she feared Isabel would somehow get a hold of Gene's resources she believed belonged to her. In the hope of derailing their liaison, she dropped Don and ended the foursome. He saw me as the villain, and when I showed up where he lived flouting a beautiful new mate, it added fuel to his smoldering resentment.

On the long twelve-hour drive back to the valley, we hardly spoke. While in the city, I went through a transformation and was feeling differently about her. I believe reconnecting with people I knew turned me around and helped me realize I wasn't as dependent on her as I thought I was. As my attitude changed, her position also changed, possibly in response to my new mindset. Her arrogance diminished, and she stopped threatening to leave if I didn't submit to her every demand. But after suffering with her for most of the year, I could barely stand the sight of her. As much as I wanted to, I was unable to take the drastic step and end the marriage even after the old intuitive voice came back even stronger warning me that to be with her would lead to disaster. I would have been glad had she left and made the decision for me.

After the stimulating trip to Mexico and the invigorating stay in San Francisco, my energy level hit the floor with a thud on our return to the placid mountains in the dead of winter. At that time of year, the low winter sun stayed hidden behind the mountain until after ten, and the light was gone shortly after three. The lack of sunlight had a depressing effect.

To make matters worse, heavy rain mixed with snow greeted us on our return to the valley, and each day, it seemed to get worse. The drought was over and lasted only one season, as storms roared in off the Pacific one after the other with vengeance. It snowed only a few times on the valley floor, but it didn't melt off the surrounding mountain tops by noon as it usually did. I couldn't remember the weather being as awful since moving to Oregon. As a boy, I read accounts of Lewis and Clark stranded at Fort Clatsop on the Oregon Coast near Astoria in the winter of 1805, because of the cold and rain, and until that winter in the valley with Meg, I never fully appreciated how miserable they were.

For most of the day, I sat huddled next to the woodstove feeling numb. There was no arguing. We had no energy for fighting; our conversations consisted mostly of grunts, and just feeling her presence irritated me. I tried avoiding her as much as possible, but that wasn't a good strategy in a one-room dwelling. Going outside into the cold and rain wasn't an alternative either. The only solution was to get away by going back to the city, and I had the perfect excuse.

She sat huddled next to the woodstove when I told her my plans. I added firewood to the stove and avoided looking at her. "We've been back three weeks," I said, "and I don't think I've seen more than two cars drive past. Where the hell's everyone?"

She responded lethargically, sniffling and fighting a cold, her voice scratchy. "Its winter and everyone's hibernating."

"What's wrong with this stove," I said. "It's not putting out much heat."

"The wood's probably wet."

"As you know, the money we made off the bud will barely get us through the year, and if I don't sell the marijuana males, I'll probably need to find another outside job."

"You're in charge of sales. I don't know what to tell you."

She looked at me with a blank expression. "It's fine with me if you don't mind spending the summer alone again."

I stoked the fire and added another log. "Sell them to someone local," she added.

"If I knew any local dealers. We've always sold the crop in the city. I don't see any other alternative than to go back and try again, and it would be better if I went alone. I shouldn't be gone more than a couple of weeks." I closed the door on the woodstove and looked her straight in the eye. "Can you handle being alone that long?"

———

UPON MY ARRIVAL IN THE CITY, I HAD NO IDEA WHERE I'D STAY until I remembered Billy Carpenter, an old friend and business associate who I hadn't seen since the Haight-Ashbury days. His number was in the phonebook, and when I called, he said he had a spare bedroom and to come on over. He lived in a rented house south of Market on Valencia Street near the old Levi Strauss jean factory. It was five years since I saw him last, and I was shocked at how he aged. His face was craggy, his hair long, and he gained weight. With drooping eyelids, heavy, untrimmed brows, and his moustache, that he always kept looking dapper, covering his upper lip, he reminded me of a sad-looking hound dog. A cigarette dangled from his upper lip. "Come in," he said. "Man! you've lost weight."

"I feel great. What's happening with you?"

"When you get old it's the same old shit."

What a bummer! His mood was as bad as Meg's. At least the weather was better in the city. I remembered Billy as a suave, good-looking man in his late fifties and always impeccably groomed and dressed. Everyone knew Billy Carpenter; he had a man-about-town personality and was a ladies' man. He once flirted with running for mayor. In lighter moments, we talked about him making his run and with me as his campaign manager. When I first met Billy, he was in a relationship with Brandy. When it ended, we stayed friends, and he was often a visitor at the Victorian.

We sat at the kitchen table drinking coffee. On the table close to his elbow was a bottle of cheap brandy and a supersized ashtray filled with cigarette butts that gave off an acidy stench. Billy was from the old school and never learned to smoke marijuana. His drugs of choice were alcohol and tobacco. The kitchen looked as if a tornado had come through. With dirty dishes piled in the sink, old newspapers and crap everywhere on the floor, and his stove top covered with grease, food stains, and mouse poop, I hesitated staying but couldn't think of anyone else to call. "I haven't seen you in years," he said, lighting another cigarette from the butt of the one he was smoking, "and you suddenly appear out of nowhere."

"It keeps people guessing."

"After you sold the house, you disappeared. You could have at least called."

"I didn't call anyone. You know how divorces are, Billy. You went through enough of them. It was a time when I didn't know if I was on foot or horseback."

"A while back, I ran into Brandy. She told me you moved into the mountains in Oregon, and you're growing weed. I hear the price of marijuana is going through the roof, and lots of easy money is being made."

"The price has gone up considerably, but there's nothing easy about it. Do you still have the wholesale mail-order business?"

It was the business I had before becoming a printer. It still had value, but selling it seemed too much of a hassle. Billy lost his job as a copywriter with a publishing company, and I gave the business to him. There was no money exchanged, only a vague agreement he would share profits with me at some point in the future, but that I would ever see any money was mostly fantasy like the run for mayor.

"I still have it," he said, "and if I had any brains, I'd dump it. I never did make any money, and I'm too old to start something new. It's the only thing keeping me going. I should give it back to you, but you'd probably turn it into a gold mine. Nothing ever comes easy for me, and you, you bastard, always lived a charmed life."

He wouldn't say that if he knew Meg. "By the way, how's Eddie?"

Billy was raising a son from a second or third marriage, and during a party at the Victorian when Eddie was about twelve, he stole money from a dresser drawer. His thievery angered me, and I barred the kid from the house. Billy thought the penalty was a little severe, and our friendship cooled for a while. That evening, he called his ex-wife to come pick up the boy. Peggy was an attractive older woman with great legs and long hair streaked with silver. A few days later, she called me at the shop. "I want to apologize for what my son did. Let me buy you a drink, so we can bury the hatchet and be friends."

We met that evening at a bar. She was a charming woman and had a way of making me feel I was the most important person in the world. Her warmth drew me into liking her immediately, and we buried the hatchet later that evening in the back seat of the old Rambler. Thereafter, we met for drinks occasionally and renewed our deep friendship. I didn't want Billy to know I was playing around with his ex-wife. He didn't want her but would have complained, as he did that day, that everything came too easily for me.

"Eddie lives with his mother," he said, "when he's not in jail. I kicked his ass outta here."

He refilled our coffee cups and added brandy to his but didn't offer me any and moved the bottle closer protecting it. Billy always had a cynical streak, but now added to the cynicism was anger. When he spoke, he contorted his mouth, and his words had a bitter ring indicative of someone who felt life passed them by. The spare bedroom was a pigsty, and I wouldn't sleep on the bed until after I washed and vacuumed.

I was out of the house early the next day to call on people who were possible customers for the marijuana males. My first visit was to a young guy who previously purchased a small quantity of bud. The city was full of small dealers like Jerry who dealt only to pay for what they used and maybe a little extra. He lived in an upstairs flat way out on Taravel Street in the Sunset District near the Great Highway. As we talked, I watched through his front windows the sun reflecting off the calm, blue waters of the Pacific.

The post Haight-Ashbury era was a confusing time for Jerry and a whole generation growing up in San Francisco. He was a second-generation hippie and different. Times had changed, as they always do. But he was a San Franciscan and had a tradition to uphold. He listened to the Grateful Dead and other rock bands, but they too had changed. The essence and spirit of the Haight-Ashbury and of the 1960s was gone and existed only in the minds of the people who lived it. He and most of his friends wore their hair long, but he looked as if he just stepped out of an advertisement for the Gap. What connected him and his friends to the Woodstock Generation was that they smoked marijuana.

As we talked, I opened my backpack and withdrew an ounce of males. "I called you," he said, "but some lady said that you already went back to Oregon."

"Why did you call?"

"I wanted to buy more bud. I wasn't sure it would sell it at the higher price, but it sold quickly."

"I'm sorry to report I'm out of bud." He twisted his mouth in a look of disappointment. "But I have something that might interest you. I have male flowers and small leaves that grow with the bud called super shake."

"I've never smoked males. I don't think I'd be interested."

"I understand how you feel. Most people haven't smoked males. Why I came is to have you try them."

When I showed him an ounce of males, he made an unpleasant face. "They don't look anything like bud."

"Don't judge until you've smoked."

I rolled a joint, and as he toked, his expression changed from skeptical to believer. He liked the high, as I knew he would, and he liked the reduced price even more. Jerry purchased a pound, and after contacting other small dealers, I had everything sold within a week.

A feeling of freedom came with the last sale signifying the end of a difficult year. To celebrate, I treated myself to an ice cream cone from my favorite parlor on Twenty-Fourth street in Noe Valley. As the clerk handed me my reward, the door opened and an old girlfriend walked in. "Oh My God! It's Jessica." She looks startled when she saw me and screamed: "Jack!" Several customers turned to look. "I can't believe what I'm seeing. Is it really you? How are you?"

"Hi, Jessica," I said, taking a long, slow lick of my double chocolate, ice cream cone and feeling a tingle deep inside.

"Let's go for coffee and talk," she said. "I know a good coffee shop a few blocks up the street."

We talked walking along Twenty-Fourth street past Victorian houses filled with upscale shops in what was once a working-class neighborhood. Delicious smells of coffee and pastries greeted us when we entered a European-style deli and sat at a table off to the side drinking coffee.

Jessica was a pretty lady with a bubbly personality and a high, squeaky voice. Since I saw her last, she looked even better. She was busty and wore her dark hair in a semi-afro that gave her a wild, untamed look. She taught high school biology, and I imagined all the young guys at the school where she worked lusted after her, especially when she wore miniskirts, which was usually. There was something exciting about her in the way she approached life with all systems set at full blast. I was falling madly in love with her until I learned she was an outrageous groupie. She lusted after famous athletes, especially those with great bodies, which were most of them. She wasn't interested in forming relationships. Her only desire was to give them oral sex and the more renowned the athlete the better. Her special talent was deep throat. She and her friends compared notes on how many celebrated sports guys they blew. But it was a little much for me, and I faded away. "It's good to see you," she said. "I wondered what happened to you. You just disappeared out of my life."

"It was such an unsettled time. I didn't know which end was up."

"You're such a rogue, Jack. You knew I considered you a special person. Now you've got yourself married."

"I don't know how that happened either."

"And living in the mountains and growing weed. Goodness! What some people will do. But I must say, country life agrees with you. You're in such great shape. Your body is so hard. Where're you staying?"

"I'm crashing at a friend's house."

Catching me off guard, she brushed her hand over mine and stirred more than just memories of when we were together. Jessica was warm and affectionate and so different from Meg's cold and judgmental attitude. I wondered how life would be different had I married her instead. "Remember the great times we had?"

"How could I forget?"

"How long are you in town?"

"Just till tomorrow."

"Stay with me tonight, and we'll go out for a drink this evening like we used to."

"I don't know, Jessica. I'm leaving early in the morning."

"Jack! I haven't seen you in years, and you appear out of nowhere. There's Divine Providence at work here. I know you won't believe me, but I thought of you just this morning."

Jessica was soft and yielding, and I desired her desperately. I could smell her wonderful bouquet and felt the great ego boost that pretty lady's proposition gave me after so many negative encounters with Meg. But something in me changed. I squeezed her hand. "It was great seeing you again too, Jessica, but I don't think so."

1978

Meg seemed glad to see me. My absence may have given us both the space we needed, and it seemed possible she even missed me. The weather improved, and with longer days and the prospect of spring in the air, I hoped for a new beginning. Lisa and David stopped by several times to chat, and for the first time since the cow incident, both Hughie and Brad began to acknowledge us. Hughie would nod, and Brad raised his finger off the steering wheel in a gesture of hello. To ease the tension, we stayed high and went visiting to Ginger and Bob's or explored up river into the mountains when the rains let up.

On one outing under light showers, we visited a Forest Service campground called Camp Comfort. It was so far up into the mountains that of all the times we visited, only once was anyone camping there, and it was during hunting season. The weather was still too cold and wet for camping, and I was certain it would be deserted.

The road entering was downhill, and for some reason, I cut the engine and coasted into the first campsite. To our surprise, a mother deer and her newborn fawn browsed a few feet away. We sat spellbound watching. The fawn fidgeted nervously, but the doe never looked up. They slowly moved off browsing as they went. "Interesting," said Meg. "What do you make of that?"

"I did have the engine off, but they had to see the truck pull in; we're not invisible. They showed no fear, and it makes me even more convinced this campground has magical powers. Something unusual happens each time we visit. I somehow feel she was showing off her newborn baby."

A light rain was falling, and the smell of wet forest filled my nostrils. The Forest Service built the campground high on a knoll in a grove of towering Western Red Cedars and Douglas Firs. There was no running water, except the river fifty feet down a steep embankment, and with heavy rain and snow melt, it ran fast and deep. We followed a path to where two large creeks cascading out of the mountains came together in a Y pattern and spilled into a deep channel in a loud roar. The two creeks coming together formed the headwaters of the South Umpqua River. Standing at the edge, I looked down into the raging water absorbing its energy. As a fine spray drifted toward us, we sat upriver on a step-like rock formation watching the turbulent water.

Within minutes, the clouds parted and the sun's rays beamed down. "This is truly an enchanting place," I said. "It feels so good here."

"How nice that Old Saul came out," she added. "It's probably raining in the valley."

With her head resting on my shoulder, we sat silently basking in each other's warmth. I watched what looked like a small log floating in the river towards us. As it came close, I saw what it really was, and as it passed a few feet below, I stood and shouted: "Look! Otter!"

Floating on its back and unaware of us until I shouted, the small marine animal dove instantly and disappeared beneath the turbulent water, but his facial expression of surprise and dread sent us into hysterics. Our laughter boomed and echoed loudly down the river and between the walls of the narrow canyon. Surprisingly, I saw our laughter as well as heard it. The flashes occurred much to rapidly for me to describe them, but because it didn't seem possible to see sound, I never mentioned it to Meg.

On the return trip, our humor quickly subsided after falling behind an armada of five or six log trucks loaded with huge old-growth timber heading to the sawmills. Laboring under the heavy loads, their diesel engines belched billows of dirty black exhaust into the pristine mountain air. "This forest will soon become a desert at the rate they are logging," I complained.

I wasn't the only one concerned with over-logging in our national forests. When visiting Ginger a week later, she revealed some relevant news: "The Sierra Club and other conservation groups have proposed to Congress that the remaining old-growth trees in road-less areas remain off limits."

"Finally, someone's taking notice of the carnage going on here," I added.

"Don't hold your breath, Jack," she retorted. "Lumber companies have big bucks to help Congress see it their way, and you know the folks representing us can't resist the money. It's like holding candy in front of a baby. They'll fall over each other reaching for it, and they don't much care the loot comes from the destruction of our national forests."

At dawn a week later, loud noises awakened us. We sat up in bed and looked at each other. "What the hell's that?" I asked. She shrugged her shoulders.

Dressing quickly, we stood outside on the road in front of the barn hearing loud squeaks and groans coming from over the mountain in the next watershed, and it sounded like heavy equipment moving in. Before conservation efforts could get under way, the Forest Service launched a massive road-building program. Early the next morning, the first of many powerful explosions shook and jiggled the barn. As the days went by, the blasts seemed to get stronger. I was afraid one of them would take out the big picture window I installed on the north side of the barn, rattling it each time, and I didn't want to be sitting beneath it when it happened.

A letter from the Forest Service informed us the road building and blasting would last most of the summer. The worst part was they were linking the new road with our valley road and eliminating the dead end. Meg was upset: "Logging begins as soon as it's light enough to see, and in summer that's as early as 5AM."

She feared a trucker jacked up on caffeine or speed rumbling past on our narrow valley road would take out the barn the way a log truck took out the bridge on the River Road near Centerville last summer and closed it to traffic for several months.

In early April, I was surprised when United Parcel Service delivered a package to our door. Until then, I was still under the illusion our valley was somehow inaccessible to the outside world. The knowledge the driver easily found where we lived destroyed my fantasy. "Have any trouble finding us?" I asked.

"None! I stopped at the Tiller Ranger station, and they gave me directions. Never been this far into the mountains before. Lovely valley you have here."

He delivered a package of jerusalem artichoke starts. Meg read how they were to become the next vegetable sensation. They are a tuber like potatoes but more knobby and belong to the sunflower family. A small, yellow bloom grew at the end of each stem. Our plan was to grow a large crop, advertise in different magazines, and become a supplier of starts. Growing another crop was to help us become less dependent on the marijuana. "They're supposed to taste like artichokes," she said, "if you have a good imagination. Growing them is a beginning, but that's still not enough. Look at this ad."

She showed me an advertisement for a greenhouse from a gardening and farming magazine. It was a large walk-in and all glass. "With one like that," she said, "we could grow vegetables all year."

"They're plenty expensive," I retorted. "I'll bet that one's ten grand. More than we can afford. I wonder if we could get them to give us one for free."

She looked at me curiously. "And how would we accomplish that?"

"What would stop us from creating a mythical business and pretend we're a distributor. We'd be delighted to sell their greenhouses but need a sample for our customers to see."

"You think it'd work? And wouldn't we need a letterhead and other stuff when we communicate?"

"Remember, I was a printer. I'll create one."

"What will we call this mythical business?"

"How about simply, The Greenhouse?"

My copy for the letterhead was finished in time for our next supply run, and a printer in Medford ran off a hundred letterheads along with matching envelopes in green ink. She inspected our new stationary the next day and said, 'they looked official.' I reminded her the idea is to have manufacturers believe we're a legitimate distributor of greenhouses headquartered in the metropolis of Tiller, Oregon. "Our next step," I added, "is to compose a letter asking to become a distributor and to send us a sample. Could there be anything simpler?"

She typed out the letters on her portable typewriter, and we scoured ads in old magazines for names and addresses of manufacturing companies. A month later, replies started arriving at our post office box but no greenhouses. Most companies asked for financial statements and letters of introduction from our bank as criteria for becoming involved. Two companies mentioned they would have representatives at the Home Show in Chicago that summer and would be glad to discuss the issue with us there. "Do you think it's worth going to Chicago?" she asked. "If nothing came of it, at least you could visit your family."

"It might be worth a try. I'd need new clothes though, and my hair has grown long again."

On our next visit to Medford, I went to the mall to try on straight clothes while Meg checked out flights to the Windy City.

Men's fashions changed since the 1960's. All the sport jackets had pointed lapels, and pants made from polyester didn't feel good on my skin. My going to Chicago was still uncertain.

I received a rambling, incoherent letter from Billy Carpenter the man I stayed with in San Francisco who believed I lived a charmed life. He rehashed the past about how angry he was for banishing his son from the Victorian and again grumbled that everything came too easily for me. He complained that nobody appreciated him, and he was mostly alone and broke. When Meg asked about it, I related what he said. While holding it, I could feel his bitter vibe. The next morning when starting a fire in the woodstove, I burned it.

———◊◊◊———

BEFORE DAWN ON A SPRING MORNING, THE SOUND OF PITTER-PAT-ter on the metal roof above my bed awakened me. As I lay listening, I heard scraping sounds in the corner across from where we slept. Quietly opening the drawer of my nightstand, I felt around for my flashlight. The beam illuminated a small animal walking along a rafter. While holding the light on the critter, I threw my slipper at him and yelled: "OUT WILLIE!" The slipper didn't come close to hitting him, but my yell sent him scurrying back out the hole from which it came. "What the hell's going on?" cried Meg.

"Go back to sleep. I'll tell you about it in the morning."

"You sure scared the crap out of me last night," she said at breakfast. "What kind of animal was it, and how did it get in?"

From our bookshelf, I found a nature guide describing animals of the Pacific Northwest Forests. "You're not going to like it," I said. "It was a rat. They're sometimes called pack rats."

"Yuck! Aren't they dangerous?"

"They could be but remember we're in the country. Our late night visitor lives in a more natural environment and is not the city guy who hangs out in sewers and has a naked tail. His was hairy, and he used it to hang on to a rafter the way a monkey uses his to hold on to a branch. You've probably heard stories of people finding nests containing diamond rings and other valuables. Shiny objects attract them. He was pretty big though, almost as large as Sammy."

"What I've been wondering all morning," she asked, "is how did you know his name was Willie?"

I slept soundly each night, but my subconscious must have been listening, because a few nights later the pitter-patter on the roof awakened me again. I must have been in deep sleep, because I didn't get down the ladder fast enough, and Willie escaped after taking a bite out of three different apples in a bowl on the table. "So, what are you going to do?" she asked.

"The one thing I know about him is he likes to be high off the ground. There are holes on each corner of the barn just below the roof and even if I block them there are other ways for him to get in. This barn has more holes than a sieve. The easiest way to stop him is to finish him off."

"You're not going to shoot him are you?"

The next time I awakened after hearing the patter-patter, I quickly made my way down the ladder. As expected, Willie entered at the corner where he first made his entrance and that I left purposely unblocked. He walked along a ledge below the deck, and when he saw my light, he sprinted for the opening on the opposite side. After finding the hole blocked, he backtracked towards where he entered. When he came close enough, I would hit him with my club. But he faked me out and slid down to the floor. To my surprise, our tabby cat, Geraldine, shot between my legs and grabbed him by the throat. "Way to go, girl."

As she held him against the floor with her paw, he struggled to free himself screaming in an ungodly, high-pitched wail that sent shivers through me. He was large, and he started to wiggle himself free. To get a better grip, she released him momentarily, and in that split-second, he broke free and scooted out through the hole between the floor and stud. She looked up at me with a forlorn look that seemed to say: I did my best. "Nice try, Geraldine. He would have been a good meal."

All through spring, Willie raided our kitchen at will, and I couldn't stop him. He was smart and eluded all my traps including those I purchased at the feed store that looked like large mouse traps, which I doubted would have held him. Besides, it was planting time, and I didn't have time to spend on the problem. As planting ended, Reggie and his friend Barry visited. Meg prepared a place for them to sleep on mats on the floor near the wood stove.

From the beginning, Reggie was intrigued with our country lifestyle, and I could tell he fell in love with the valley, as almost everyone did. He wanted to help with the marijuana, but since I installed the new watering system, there wasn't much to do except watch them grow. The rains ended early, and the weather warmed. Each morning, we hiked to the back of the valley or explored along the river and ate our meals outside using our newly purchased wood burning cook stove. Reggie couldn't get enough of backcountry Oregon and was reluctant to leave when it came time to return home.

In the predawn darkness on the second morning of their visit, I awakened to the pitter-patter on the roof and quickly slid down the ladder. My light caught Willie walking along a ledge under the deck, and as the cats were out for the night, Geraldine wouldn't rush in and grab him as she had before. When he saw my light, he sprinted to the opposite corner, only to find it blocked. He was smart but didn't have a long memory. As he headed back, I held the light in his eyes. He stopped midway, his eyes shining brilliantly like the headlights of a car. This time he wouldn't get away. To see the light in his eyes dimming and his life draining away bothered me. Even though he was a rat and raided our kitchen, I had to admire his audacity.

With all the excitement, I forgot about our two guests sleeping behind me. Both were sitting up looking startled. "Hey, mate! Was that a rat?"

Our cats feasted on Willie's plump remains for days.

OREGON'S WINTERS ARE LONG AND SLOW TO GO. IT'S NOT THAT it is so cold, but the long months of rain makes it seem so. It's always different, of course, but it wasn't unusual for clouds to block the sun over two hundred and fifty days a year and not shine regularly until July. I looked forward to spending those sunny days outside, even if it meant long hours of hard work digging in the soil. Unlike modern framers who sit in motorized, air-conditioned tractors high off the ground listening to music and separate from the land they till, I dug into it with my hands, smelled its wonderful bouquet, and even tasted it. To my surprise and gratification, I formed a spiritual bond with the land that was a source of satisfaction I hadn't anticipated. Although I was still against the use of gasoline, I purchased a rototiller and had the easiest spring since moving into the valley. The ease in preparing the soil for planting up in the growing area and in the garden using the tiller opened a new era but broke the spiritual bond. After three years, the bloom and freshness of living on the land ended, and like Adam, I was cast out of paradise.

ON A WARM LATE SPRING AFTERNOON WITH THE SUN'S RAYS HIT- ting the tall sugar pines on the hill and bringing in the first shadows of the day, we stopped working and went inside to practice yoga. The wind was still all day, and even the birds up in the canopy stopped singing. It was quiet outside, but inside, it was total silence. While sitting on my mat meditating, an almost imperceptible movement of air rushed past me and made a soft, whooshing sound. I perked up and glanced at Meg. With a nod, she indicated she too experienced it. When the air whooshed past a second time, a metal clothes hanger that hung on a doorknob across the room pinged softly breaking the silence. Without comment, we practiced yoga and at dinner agreed a spirit visited. "A spirit was the first thing that crossed my mind,"

John-Paul Cernak

I said, "but if you weren't here, I would have thought I imagined it."

"Do you have any idea who it was?" she asked.

I paused and reflected on what she said. "Are you implying the spirit was someone we knew who maybe just died?"

"That's the hit I received."

"I can't imagine who it could be.

"Somehow, I feel," she announced after a long contemplation, "it was more your visit than mine."

<hr />

AFTER TAKING A HIT ON THE PIPE ON A BEAUTIFUL, SUMMER MORN-ing, I left Meg puttering around in the barn and walked up towards the growing area dressed only in shorts. Feeling sensuous from a warm summer breeze caressing my body, I paused at the entrance, but instead of going to work, I continued up into the big trees. It just seemed like a good idea. Although I saw no one in the valley below, I played a game of hide and seek concealing myself as I walked along the tree line. Heat waves shimmered off the road, and everything glared in the high summer sun. When I stopped to admire white trilliums growing at the base of a giant fir, I was suddenly surrounded by a flock of chickadees that landed in the nearby shrubbery. After hearing their familiar chick-a-dee-dee calls and seeing their swoop-ing flight, I playfully followed them up into the woods and entered a small clearing. I experienced a momentary confusion when I saw Lisa standing there in the nude. She was beautiful, and I desired her immediately, captivated by the small stars pasted over her nip-ples and a larger one between her legs. More mysteriously, I had the impression she was waiting for me. She beckoned me to follow, and although we never talked, her gestures were unmistakable. In a vision, I saw us making love on a soft bed of leaves next to a stream. I followed her a short distance but turned. I don't remember walking back. Throughout the day, I replayed the incident a thousand times until it felt like a dream. What stopped me was that my sexual con-nection with Meg was back on track.

A REFLECTION ON THE HILL NEAR THE OUTHOUSE CAUGHT MY EYE as I worked alone in the garden on a hot summer day. Standing my shovel upright in the soil, I trekked uphill to investigate. To keep the hot sun off, I wore my straw cowboy hat and sleeveless coveralls but with nothing on beneath to allow the breeze to circulate. The reflection came from an old tin can a hippie dropped long ago next to an old log, and the land was reclaiming both. But the instant I nudged the log with my foot, I knew I made a mistake, as yellow jackets swarmed out from beneath the rotting wood buzzing angrily. My first impulse was to run. I froze instead. Quickly, six or seven wasps landed on the front of my coveralls, but because it ballooned in the breeze, air was all they received when they stung. I swatted them calmly as they landed.

When a second wave emerged, they buzzed around confused and didn't know where to strike. Having remained motionless, I became invisible to them. Slowly, imperceptibly, like a statue, I backed away until out of range and escaped without receiving even one sting.

———∽∽∽———

THE LONGER WE LIVED IN THE MOUNTAINS, THE MORE PEOPLE visited, and Meg greeted most of them in the nude. She loved shocking people, and the greater the jolt she delivered, the more she liked it. She greeted Marge and her girlfriend Martha in the nude, but it was mild in comparison to the devastating wallop she administered to the three college students who visited earlier in the month.

We met them in the city the previous winter when selling our marijuana. Molly was a robust blonde who went to San Francisco State College, played fiddle and was open for most anything. Pamela was a bookish brunette and attended the University of California at Berkeley. Anthony was an athlete and runner and the son of the president of a large corporation. He went to a prestigious college in the east. They drove up in what looked like a "Pop Art Car," that seemed to be held together with spit and bailing wire. I worked in the garden as they sputtered in, parked next to the barn, and quickly jumped out dazzled by the beauty of the forest and mountains surrounding them. "Hi, Guys," I said.

They gathered around asking questions similar to those I asked when I first arrived. "And we're smack dab in the middle of the national forest," I said, ending the session.

We stopped next to the stairs leading up to the side door to look at the garden. Like a Jack in the Box, Meg popped out the door totally nude pushing her nakedness into their faces. "Hello everybody," she said, nonchalantly. "I hope you had a good trip up from the city. Welcome to Ash Valley."

Staring in stunned disbelief, they moved backward in unison when she moved forward, their faces showing acute distress. I would have laughed had I not felt embarrassed for them. After a long moment, they regained a degree of composure and responded with weak hellos. "You came at the right time," she said, in an authoritative voice. "Tomorrow I'm going blackberry picking, and you ladies are coming with me. Anthony can stay and help Jack."

"I was just telling them about..." but she cut me off before I had a chance to finish.

"Drop your stuff inside, and let's go for a walk."

They walked stiffly like robots following her in single file. I settled in at the back of the line enjoying every moment and giggling as she led them down the road like a nude, Pied Piper.

When Martha and Marge arrived, the weather was hot, and for most of their stay they wore skimpy bathing suits. In the past, Marge was rather subdued but not anymore. She ended her relationship with Tim, and it seemed everything about her changed. She laughed and acted crazy in her new sexy fire-red hairdo and had slimmed down and was tanned. Martha was a statuesque blond, and I thought their visit might be a fun time.

On the second day, they brought lunch up to the growing area, and while Meg went nude the first day, she wore a short dress. We toked on the pipe and drank wine in the shade of the maple tree at the top of section four, and in a short time everyone was flying high laughing and teasing each other. Unless I was imagining it, our guests were acting provocatively toward me and their conversation was filled with sexual innuendos. I watched to see if Meg would react, but she seemed not to notice. Marge said something that confused me. "You know we have you outnumbered, Jack. Let's get him."

All three jumped on top of me and pinned me before I could react. "Hey! What's going on," I said, at first thinking they were just fooling around.

Meg sat on my legs, while the other two each held an arm. In the next instant, a rope appeared they hid in the lunch basket. They were going to tie me up. "You're all going to regret this," I said, panicked.

They had no idea how strong someone becomes living wild and free in the mountains. When my warning fell on deaf ears, I effortlessly broke the grip of the two holding my arms, and bringing their arms together in front holding them with one hand. With the other, I grabbed Meg's arm and brought all three together. The maneuver quickly ended their silly, little rebellion, and their looks changed from amusement to shock. Their startled and surprised expressions made me laugh, but it wasn't until later that I regretted what I did. I've always wondered what would've happened had I let them tie me up.

FEW PEOPLE NOTICED ME WHEN I BOARDED MY FLIGHT AT MEDford Airport dressed in straight clothes, my hair and beard trimmed short. At San Francisco, I transferred to a second flight that took me into O'Hare Field on Chicago's far north side. My mother was outside watering her flowers when the Checker Cab dropped me off on a warm, summer evening.

A block north of her house was a busy commercial street and

John-Paul Cernak

the hubbub of the city. I meditated each morning in a large park several blocks to the south where the natural setting helped in my transition from tranquil mountains to bustling metropolis, and although my psyche knew I was in alien territory, I remained focused my entire stay.

Invitations rolled in throughout the week as friends and relatives learned I was in town. My sister, Anna, invited me to dinner as did Gary an old friend who married after I left and wanted me to meet his wife. Neither asked about my life living in the mountains. It was against my sister's principles to pry. Gary was simply more interested in telling me about his life and not much interested in mine.

As young guys, we shared many adventures playing sports and chasing women, but since, our lives had taken divergent paths. With many ups and downs, my worldview and philosophy changed, but Gary's remained the same. He believed in mom, apple pie, and my country, right or wrong. If he knew I participated in anti-war demonstrations, taken LSD, and smoked marijuana, he would have refused to talk with me. For all the years I knew him, he was an incorrigible womanizer and vowed never to marry and allow a woman to tie him down. At dinner, I couldn't count the times he said, "yes dear" or "whatever you say, hon." I had to excuse myself and go into the bathroom to stifle laughter. Later that evening, as we sat talking in the living room after his wife went to bed, she began calling him in from the bedroom. "Come to bed, Gary."

"I'll be right there, hon."

We hadn't seen each other in years and had many things to say, but after the third time she called out, I felt uncomfortable and left.

Most of my old friends scattered to the four winds, and on Friday evening, I met with the few who remained for a small reunion, minus Gary, whose wife wouldn't let him out.

My other sister, Millie, held an open house on Saturday afternoon. Her small parlor was filled with people, knickknacks, and cigarette smoke. Unlike my friends who asked few questions, everyone who came to meet the Oregon Mountain Man was curious about my life in the woods, especially Mary, my sister's mother-in-law. A stylish woman with never a hair out of place, she was married to an executive from a large corporation and lived in a prestigious part of town. What I remembered most about her was that she loved being center stage. I felt she considered her son to have married below his station, although my limited association with her was always cordial. Mary sat across from me on an over-stuffed easy chair. I sat uncomfortably on a couch covered in clear plastic that stuck to my bottom. She began holding court by asking questions, and the room quieted. "Is it true you live in a barn?"

I paused before answering sipping at my vodka and orange juice. "It's true," I said, "but we moved the animals out before moving in."

She didn't laugh at my attempt at humor, and suddenly I felt a little uncomfortable, "And I understand you have no electricity or telephone."

She must have heard from my sister about our lives living in the mountains but was unsure how much she knew. "That's true, also," I answered, "but we have plenty of sunshine and rain."

"And how do you keep yourself so slim? I hope you're not undernourished."

"We live an active lifestyle, and we're mostly vegetarian. Not eating meat usually means dropping ten pounds."

A portly cousin who could have been her sister and she flashed guilty looks. "How do you earn money so far from civilization?"

I hesitated. A hush came over the room. My first inclination was to avoid answering truthfully. But she probably already knew. I looked around at the people in the room. I knew most of them for years, and like Gary, they hadn't changed much, except now they were fifteen years older. I would be gone in a few days. It was doubtful I would ever see any of them again, so I answered truthfully, "We grow marijuana."

"Oh! Those poor children!" She put her hand on her forehead to emphasize her repugnance.

232   *John-Paul Cernak*

Under most circumstances, I would have been diplomatic in handling her charge about how harmful and dangerous marijuana was spread by the government and aided by the media. She cared little for children, and her theatrical display of revulsion was an attempt to humiliate me and to make her look good in front of friends and family. It surprised me how much anger her pomposity generated in me. She never saw my unrepentant counterattack coming, and it almost knocked her off her overstuffed chair. "The facts are, we don't sell to children, only to adults, and some of our customers are doctors and lawyers. And you're the last person to judge me holding a cigarette in one hand and a glass of booze in the other."

I heard gasps and muffled laughter. She turned red and looked at the two items in her hands with horror as if they betrayed her and hoping they would somehow disappear. She quickly looked around.for support. An embarrassing quiet fell over the room, and even her son looked away. The party ended early that afternoon.

On Monday morning at McCormick Place, a huge underground facility near Lake Michigan off the Loop, I weaved through hundreds of exhibitors at the Home Show to find the two greenhouse manufactures we contacted. One company was American and the other a British firm. At both booths, the only people available were sales people without authority to give me a sample greenhouse.

———✦✦✦———

ON THE FIRST MAIL RUN AFTER I RETURNED TO OREGON, MEG received a letter from her brother informing her that her father was dying from cancer. She called her sibling from the pay phone in front of the Tiller Tavern. Immediately afterwards, she called her father. They talked for over an hour. On the drive back, she looked pale and sat pressed against the door. "How long does he have?"

"My brother said that he has six months to a year."

"How did he sound?"

There were tears in her eyes. "How does anyone sound who's dying?"

"You talked for a long time. Did you clear the air between you?"

She moved around uncomfortably. "He said he was sorry for all the things that kept us apart. We talked about the years after my mother died, and he admitted he was wrong in cutting himself off from his kids. He just couldn't help himself, but his being sorry doesn't alleviate all the pain. After my mother died, he abandoned us. I felt discarded all my life." She was crying, something Meg didn't do often. "When he married my stepmother, he was around more, but it was her kids that got everything and his kids nothing. And he was okay with that. He never stuck up for us never looked out for us. When he asked me if there was anything I needed, I remembered you talked about wanting to build a new house. So, I asked if he'd lend us the money."

"Really? What did he say?"

"He said he would. He owes me that much."

"How much did you ask for?"

"You said that you could build us a nice house for around ten thousand. Was that enough?"

"It's enough to frame up a house. We can finish the inside later."

Feeling a tremor of excitement, the next week, I drove to a town near Medford to speak with a builder. Albert gave me an estimate over a year ago from sketches I drew up. He lived in Shady Cove, a small community on the Rogue River. The waterway was a major river system that flows out of the Cascade Mountains, and fishermen told me it had one of the best salmon and steelhead runs in Oregon. Albert was a rugged outdoors guy, big and strong, but with an artistic flair. He painted landscapes in oil, and building houses was his day job until he could earn enough from his art. Most of his paintings were scenes of the forest that surrounded him and of the river that flowed just a few yards from his deck where we sat drinking beer and shearing a joint on a sunny, summer afternoon. I loved his paintings and would have liked to have owned a few. His prices were high, but if he built me a house that looked as good as his art, I would be satisfied. "Are you finally ready to build that house?" he asked.

"I am, but only if you are ready to build a masterpiece."

I'm not a builder, dude; I'm an artist, and every house I build is a work of art. If you have those sketches, leave them with me so I can calculate what lumber we'll need."

A check from Meg's father arrived on schedule, and on my next trip to see Albert, we purchased lumber. Several days later, he drove up to the valley to inspect the building site. "The lumber is coming on Wednesday morning," he said. "Bruce and I will be here early. You haven't met Bruce."

An orange truck with a black cat painted on the door, its back arched, dumped lumber on the shoulder of the road shortly after the two carpenters arrived. I started the generator, and the construction of the new house began. It would have two stories and be built parallel to the road and perpendicular to the barn. The arrangement would create a small courtyard between the two structures. It would have a great view of the valley from the upper story and have over twenty windows to let in light on the dark, Oregon winter days. While Albert and Bruce hammered, I sawed and carried lumber. I chose western red cedar to side the house and would let it weather naturally without paint. Albert and Bruce stayed overnight, and it was a riotous time having the two dope-smoking, whisky-drinking, and cocaine-snorting carpenters staying with us.

On the sixth day of construction, it began to rain. Albert and Bruce went home. It upset me to see rain pouring into the interior through the unfinished roof, and although I was hesitant to admit it, I felt it was a bad omen. After four days of rain, they returned, and the job was completed on the tenth day of construction. It was the most beautiful house in the valley, by a long shot, and I saw envious stares whenever anyone passed.

CHAPTER 12

WITH MEG AT GINGER AND BOB'S FOR THE NIGHT, I EASILY MADE my way up to the growing area in the dark on a moonless night. I hesitated using a light so as to not pinpoint where the marijuana was growing if someone was watching from the road up in the clear cut. With Meg gone, I must have felt restless, because there was no specific reason to go up the hill. Everything was fine in the growing area. But the hair on the back of my neck stood up when I jumped over the creek going down. I paused and looked at the big trees up in the ancient forest. Although everything was black and saw nothing, I felt something threatening. Was a big cat stalking me? Yet I somehow understood that what I felt was not within the realm of humans. There was no way I would go up in the dark to investigate and hurriedly descended into the valley feeling something shadowy following close behind.

Down in the valley, my apprehension persisted, and instead of going inside, there seemed to be a compelling reason to walk a short way up the road. I will never understand why I did that, because I felt comfortable everywhere in the valley at night except on the road just opposite the orchard. A scary vibe came from the forest above, and whenever I walked past the area after dark, I experienced fear and had no explanation for it. Several times I explored the woods in daylight and found nothing unusual, except that my focus was extra sharp. When I looked at plants or rocks, their colors seemed extra deep and their shapes and textures more intriguing. But it didn't have any connection with the problem. I was aware that during the day, I used my eyes and at night relied mostly on feeling. Was I feeling something my eyes couldn't see?

When I walked past the orchard and looked up at the blackness above the road, goose bumps covered me from head to toe. Before I could retreat to the barn, a blast of wind hit me in the face, and I went into trance. Regaining awareness, I felt calm and remembered something similar happened on my first night in the valley.

Sleep wouldn't come when I snuggled into my sleeping bag up on the deck and tried shrugging off my unsettled feelings. I lay listening unsure of what I was trying to hear. But when the first howl resounded from out of the darkness, I knew immediately. How I loved hearing their howls that seemed to come from right outside the front door. In the silence afterward, I understood the wind in my face was how the spirits announced their presence. On the first night in the valley, I was tested to determine if I was worthy of living in their domain. I remembered the large coyote who came calling the first summer while digging planting holes and disappear into the woods above the orchard. He must have been a spirit coyote. I then recalled other times they came but until that night was unable to remember. They came visiting before the cow incident and before Larry and Carolyn ripped off the marijuana and several other times and each was to warn me of an impending problem or danger. I wondered what was in store for me this time.

"I'm feeling locked-in," said Meg over breakfast several days later. "You went to Chicago and were gone over a week. I've been stuck here all summer. I need to get away for awhile, too."

"OK! So what do you wanna do?"

"I'm taking the truck and leaving for a while."

"Where are you going, and how long will you be gone?"

"I don't know where I'm going, and I'll come back when I'm ready."

With a sinking feeling, I watched the truck disappear into the distance. I kept busy for the remainder of the day and tried not to think about her abrupt departure. The first morning alone, I slept in longer than usual, but the sinking feeling returned at seeing her empty bed. Determined not to let it bother me, I prepared a special breakfast of vegetables and eggs. After watering, I hiked to the back of the valley to the mountain with the clear-cut. When I crossed the cattle guard and entered the national forest, I discovered everything changed. I avoided the area until all the earthmoving equipment used in building the new road had departed. Now I had to figure out which road led where. The new road coming from over the mountain bypassed the road up to the mountain with the clear-cut and was blocked with large rocks preventing anyone from using it. After walking up the old road only a short distance, I discovered the vibe changed, and the land was already reverting into wilderness.

Looking up from the base of the mountain, I estimated the top to be seven to eight hundred feet. Trees regenerated on the east and north slopes, but only shrubs grew on the south and southwestern exposures. The Forest Service replanted and reseeded the clear-cut many times, but trees failed to regenerate due to the angle of the slope to the hot summer sun that cooked the young seedlings. For some reason, I had an urge to climb and nearly started up.

For the next two days, my mood was a repeat of the first day. On the fourth day, everything changed when I saw flashes of Meg with people my psyche didn't like, and my apprehension level spiked. The following day, I lost all focus wandering around aimlessly and sleeping little that night. In the morning, I felt emotionally and physically exhausted similar to when she ran off with Bruce, and I was in a quandary. If she were being unfaithful, I would have to make a decision whether or not to stay with her in the relationship. If I chose to stay, I would again have to live with her infidelity. The difference was that this time we were married and lived together for five years. If I chose to end the marriage, it would be difficult living alone until I found a new mate, and I wasn't looking forward to the pain and hassle of a divorce. I wondered what was in her psyche that needed to shake things up when we were doing so well together—and kick me in the teeth for remaining faithful.

On the afternoon of the sixth day, I lost all faith she would return, and I would have to search for her to retrieve the truck. Since I didn't know where she went, I had no idea where to begin looking. With my mind in turmoil and in a fit of desperation, I walked rapidly towards the back of the valley and reaching the mountain with the clear-cut started climbing. At lower levels, loose soil.prevented me from gaining a foothold, and the going was slow. With their branches pointing downward like daggers, shrubs grew close together and prevented me from walking through them. I backtracked several times and started up using different routes. Although it was mid-afternoon and the hottest time of the day, I was oblivious of the heat.

Halfway to the top, I reached a series of ledges or outcroppings and scaled the mountainside like a wall climbing from foothold to foothold. I stopped fifty feet short from the top when I could go no higher without a rope. The view was spectacular. Mountains and forest stretched to the horizon in all directions. At that moment, I didn't care if she were cheating. All I could think of was that I loved her and wanted her back. Standing on the narrow ledge, I shouted at the top of my voice into the vastness: "MEG!! WHERE ARE YOU? COME HOME!" My voice bounced off the surrounding cliffs and echoed back after a short delay. I was afraid people in the valley would hear me, but I didn't care. I just wanted her back and yelled several more times. Feeling total dejection, I sat with my back against the mountain and cried angry and bitter tears. Abruptly, I stopped feeling a deep calm. All the emotional turmoil and pain I experienced for the last six days was gone and replaced with indifference. Now I didn't care if she never came back.

I slept soundly that night and awakened refreshed. I began my day working in the garden, and as the sun crossed the zenith, I heard a vehicle enter the valley. The truck pulled into the parking space under the maple tree across the road, and the door slowly opened. I stood in the road casually leaning against my shovel. She slowly climbed out from behind the wheel, and I saw apprehension written across her face. "Hi, Meg. Did you have a good time?" I didn't hug her.

She smiled nervously. "Hi, Jack. I'm glad to be home. Something scary happened yesterday."

"Really?"

I was on the beach at Newport when suddenly I'm waist deep in water. A rogue wave hit the beach and almost swept me out to sea."

"When did that happen?"

"Yesterday afternoon."

"What time was it?"

She looked at me as if to question why I wanted to know the precise time but answered. "I think it was around three."

"That's interesting." I didn't tell her about climbing the mountain and calling out her name. "Who were you with?"

My direct question caught her off guard, and she hesitated, a twitch in her expression. "A couple of guys I met."

"Did you sleep with them?"

"Just a couple of times. I told them to come-by sometime."

"Was that wise considering what we grow here?" She didn't answer.

History repeated itself. Along with the old message that to be with her would lead to disaster came a new and more ominous warning that she would bolt and abandon me at the first sign of trouble, and I knew our marriage was over. We would go on for a time as if this hadn't happened, but I wasn't building any castles in the air that included her and lifted all restraints I placed upon myself to remain faithful.

While having dinner several days later, a car pulled up, and there was a knock at the door. I answered. The visitor was a middle-aged, official-looking woman holding a briefcase. "Does Meg Cernak live here?" she asked.

"Who are you?" I inquired. Meg stood behind me.

"I'm Judy Wilson with the Jackson County Health Department. I drove out from Medford. I work in the communicable disease control division. A patient who came in with gonorrhea for treatment gave us Meg's name as a contact. She must come into the clinic in Medford for testing. It's the law. If she fails to come in, I'd have to report her to the county sheriff."

The next morning, I drove her to the clinic. She tested positive for gonorrhea and was immediately given several injections of an antibiotic. "Gee! Aren't you lucky," I said, on the drive home.

"Screw you, Jack," she replied.

A friend of Meg's brother visited the following week and took some of the pressure off between us. I wasn't about to hang out our dirty laundry during his visit, and everything went back to normal, at least temporarily. Roger was a lot of fun, and after spending several days in the valley, we drove to Crater Lake. I looked forward to renting a room at the lodge. There was no room at the inn. To rent one, I would have needed to make reservations a year earlier. Luckily, we brought our camping gear, but it gets cold at night at seventy-three hundred feet above sea level.

———❧❧❧———

IT WAS A LONG, HOT AND DRY SUMMER, THE KIND OF WEATHER that produces the best marijuana. I harvested the males in the third week of August and eased back on watering to encourage the females to bloom. Ten females quickly blossomed, and unexpectedly, it started raining. Surely, a brief summer shower won't hurt them, but after a week of heavy downpours, it showed no sign of stopping. Still, I didn't worry and felt assured it would soon stop. It was only the first of September, and they could possibly have six more weeks to mature before harvest. During that period, no other females flowered.

The following week, dressed in winter rain gear, I walked around inspecting plants and came upon one of the ten females that flowered before the deluge began. Instead of growing flowers, she grew seedpods. A male must have pollinated her before I pulled them. She was an experimental plant and grew from seeds that came from Thailand and was a different genus. All plants before her came from Colombian seed. If she produced seeds, next year's crop would be a combination of Thai and Colombian.

When the storm continued into the third week, a little voice in the back of my head sounded an alarm. The rain couldn't continue forever, and I did my best to remain detached. With all the water, the plants grew large, but it wasn't leaves I wanted. It was the buds I was after. After twenty-one days, the sun finally came out, but the days were shorter and the nights cooler. Almost overnight all the females bloomed but were three weeks late. I wasn't sure they had time to grow large enough and to produce the high quality of previous years. Nonetheless, I remained resigned to my fate.

As the days moved into October, the buds took on a purplish color, and although they were small, there were more of them because of the large size of the plants. Although the weather remained clear, I harvested the plants in the third week of October. The buds grew as large as they would, and the quality would only deteriorate out in the cold.

Sitting cross-legged on the floor, we began the yearly ritual of cleaning plants. I could hear the steady hum of the generator in the shed outside. We smoked some of the buds the day before to test their quality. "I was very stoned," I said, "but the buds aren't that large."

Let's weigh a few," Meg countered, "and find out how much we're getting from each plant."

After cleaning and weighing six plants, the average was five ounces. "Disappointing," she said. "I'm sure we'll get more from the ten plants that bloomed before the rain started?"

"Yes!" I exclaimed excitedly and feeling a bit of hope. "I almost forgot about them."

I hung all ten together in a corner, so I knew where they were, and I was especially interested in the female that grew from seed that came from Thailand. I called her "Lady Thai." She was larger and her color a darker green. The pods she grew looked like tiny arrowheads and were empty, but not all of them. "Here's another seed," she said. "That makes over two hundred and enough to grow next year's crop, and they're plump and round."

When weighing the buds from Lady Thai, the triple beam scale balanced at over a pound and a half. "I don't think we'll get that much from the other nine," I said, "but surely a lot more than a quarter pound."

After smoking some Lady Thai that afternoon, she proved to be some of the most potent marijuana I ever smoked. As we began working the next afternoon, a pile of buds on the floor in front of us, Meg's face showed alarm at the sound of an approaching vehicle. It slowed and stopped in front of the barn. I ran to the front door and looked out through the peephole. A familiar yellow Camaro pulled in behind the truck. "Jake sure has a knack for visiting at the right time," I said.

As he approached, I opened the door before he could knock and quickly closed it behind him. He gave me a strange look. "What's going on?"

"Guess what we're doing."

He looked around at the hanging plants and the piles of buds on the floor. "Couldn't have timed my visit any better, could I? Hope you guys want me to be a tester again."

"That's exactly what we want. Take a look at this."

I showed him the Lady Thai and explained what she was. "I'm at your service ladies and gentleman."

His eyes instantly widened after taking a hit, and he started to laugh. "Tiller Killer," he said, emphasizing and elongating each syllable. "Holy Cow, I can't believe this stuff."

"Jake just gave us a name for our new product. Let's keep an ounce for ourselves and create a new category of super bud and sell it at a premium."

We packaged the bud in half ounce and quarter ounce baggies, and, as in previous years, I stored the large leaves in the cellar.

There were now six bags filled with leaves that I planned to take to the city sometime soon.

⸺ ❦ ⸺

AFTER DRIVING FIVE MILES ON OUR LAST SUPPLY RUN TO TOWN before going to the city, Meg discovered she forgot something, and I pulled into a deserted campground next to the river to turn around and drive back. It was already mid-morning after a late start. We quarreled, and the mood between us was sullen. "I have an idea," I said, exiting the truck. "You drive back yourself. I'll wait for you here." She flashed a venomousness look getting in behind the wheel and drove off.

Although I made concessions and stayed with her after her infidelity, our relationship continued to erode and had reached the point of no return. The real reason I stayed with her was from fear I wouldn't find another woman to live with me in the valley. The new warning that she would bolt at the first sign of trouble and abandon me was giving me the willies. It felt as if I was running out of time and could no longer justify staying with her for any reason. I made a mistake the first time taking her back. I won't make the same mistake again. This time, I would end the marriage before it was too late.

San Francisco was where our relationship began, and it would end there. In less than a week, we would leave for the city. After arriving, I would announce to her I wanted out of the marriage. The city was a power place for me, and over the next month or two, as I called on customers, I would again be in the midst of people I knew and was more likely to connect with another woman. It would also give her time to find another place to live. In the past, whenever I tried ending the marriage, something always inter-ceded to change my mind. Living in the wild and solitude of the mountains created uncertainties and muddled my thinking and decision-making processes concerning her. This time, there was no going back. This time, I would not allow anything to influence me.

I was determined to leave her even if I had to live in the valley alone.

I awakened that morning feeling anger as I had each morning since her infidelity. I made several attempts to speak with her about it, but she either cut me off with a caustic remark or stonewalled me. Her refusal to discuss it only made me angrier. I was the eternal optimist perhaps hoping for a miracle, or maybe I just wanted to hear her admit she regretted her betrayal. I was skeptical that even an open and frank discussion would accomplish anything positive. Since awakening, I hadn't said a word to her and felt the tension building between us. Throughout breakfast, I sat silently at the table refusing to speak or even to look at her. "Oh! For Christ sakes, Jack; just let it go. What I did is what I did. There's nothing to talk about."

As she washed the breakfast dishes, I collected items in the kitchen we'd need on our trip into town. With an angry scowl, she turned and glared at me, her body tight like the spring of a wound-up clock. "I told you I don't want to talk about it, and I mean it, Jack. I don't care if you never speak to me again."

I remained silent ignoring her. As far as I was concerned, the marriage was already over, and I would remain voiceless forever if necessary. "You son of a bitch," she screamed and spinning around threw a cup at me. My hand automatically shot up deflecting it and sent it crashing into a thousand pieces against the wall behind me.

"You bitch," I screamed back. "You fuck a bunch of guys and you want me to just let it go. On top of that, with your whoring, you bring home a disease and jeopardize my health."

"Fuck you, Jack. I don't have to give you or anyone else an excuse for what I do. I said it once and I'll say it again, I don't intend talking about it."

Watching the truck disappear into the distance, I suddenly felt a shock at finding myself alone and quickly became aware I was in a bummer mood. In her presence, I felt anger, but alone, I couldn't mask my feelings of resentment and bitterness and was choking on negative thoughts and emotions.

Pacing nervously, I threw rocks into the river trying to shake out the tenseness I felt throughout my body. Tall trees, growing thick along the river blocked out much of the light on an already dark and cloudy day and intensified my depressed mood. Across the road, a large, gray basalt outcropping protruded from the ground, a hundred feet high, and reminded me of a huge tombstone. Since leaving the valley, I hadn't seen or heard another vehicle, and the silence felt oppressive. Growing more tense by the minute, I began feeling pain.

At first, it was slight, and I experienced it as physical, although I couldn't pinpoint from where on my body it came. It seemed to come from everywhere and yet from nowhere and quickly became excruciating. I launched into deep breathing and walking fast, and the more pain I felt, the more rapidly I moved. Soon, I was running. After circling the campground several times, I discovered a path leading past the outcropping across the road to more campsites in the forest. Tightness in my chest was making it hard to breath, and I thought I was going to die. With panic welling up inside, I struggled to keep myself together. When as mysteriously as it started the throbbing suddenly ebbed, I walked slower and slower reaching the road just as she arrived to pick me up.

A few days later, as I headed out to the garden to pick carrots for the dinner I was cooking and opened the side door, a deer was raiding the garden. He must have come in through the small section of fence still incomplete. Ducking back inside, I pulled the 30-30 rifle down off the rack. Meg was sitting next to the large picture window on the north side of the barn looking out into the fading light and saw me take down the gun. "What's happening?" she asked.

"There's a deer raiding the garden. Get ready to do some canning."

I exited through the front door and circled around to approach it from downwind. Holding the rifle against the side of the barn, it would be an easy shot. Remembering the repulsion I felt last season after shooting the female, I lowered the gun and chased after him on foot. It was a young male, and he raced along the fence looking for the way out. In his confusion, he ran in the wrong direction. After a long chase, he stopped and reversed himself and ran towards the opening. As he approached the hole in the fence and freedom, he stopped and changed direction a third time. After another long run, I pinned him against the fence, and when he tried edging past, I hit him in the head with the barrel of the gun. He went down. I stood over him, and when he didn't move for several minutes, I knew he was dead.

With the deer laying at my feet, I thought about the transitory nature of our existence and wondered how much time I had left on the planet. An incident from my youth suddenly came to mind. After I made my first slingshot and was practicing hitting tin cans, a bird landed on a fence nearby. Unthinking, I fired, and the shot killed it. I felt guilty for weeks. As my awareness returned to the present, I noticed all the action occurred on the north side of the barn where Meg sat looking out the window. With a thin line of light on the western horizon giving just enough light to see, I could feel her watching and sensed there was more to this kill than my conscious mind perceived.

The winter rains arrived, and Thanksgiving Day was dark and gray with persistent showers keeping us inside, although we didn't argue. As we prepared to leave for the city, the mood between us settled into a tense calm. I bided my time until the day in San Francisco when I would end the marriage. Several weeks before the holiday, Meg announced she wasn't going to eat turkey. "Who knows what chemicals are injected into those birds?"

"If you're concerned, we can get an organic one at the natural food store."

"You can eat meat if you want; I'll stay vegetarian."

As I didn't want to purchase a whole turkey only for myself, I ate the vegetables with tofu and brown rice that she ate on Thanksgiving day. It was a very unsatisfying meal.

As daylight faded, I sat on the couch in the dark and watched a blazing fire in the new woodstove I recently installed. The heater had large double doors in front and became a fireplace when opened. Everything surrounding reflected in a warm reddish glow. After an early dinner, I toked on the pipe and retreated into a pleasant reverie blocking out any thoughts of her, although earlier I saw her light up on the sleeping deck. To my surprise, she came up behind me and massaged my neck and shoulders. I couldn't remember her ever doing that before. We didn't speak. After a few minutes, she left but quickly returned and sat on the far end of the couch. "Jack!"

At hearing her voice, I turned. She was reaching a glass of wine out to me. When our hands touched, I received an electrical shock. Attempting to ignore her, I sat quietly feeling irritated by her sudden arrival, and my pleasant mood quickly evaporated. As hard as I tried not to, I glanced towards her again. She changed into a long, loose-fitting, flannel nightgown, and her blonde hair shimmered in the glow from the woodstove. When I added fresh wood, the fire lowered, and she moved closer to stay warm. As the new wood ignited, waves of radiant heat flowed into the room. Feeling her move, I glanced towards her again. She was lifting her nightgown up over her.head and removing it. When she saw me looking, she sat straight regally displaying her naked body.

Since meeting the gawky, plump girl in San Francisco, she blossomed into a beautiful woman, and although I saw her naked many times, my desire to have her never reached the intensity I felt for her at that moment. I would have killed to have her. She sat calmly looking at me with a knowing smile. "Come to me baby," she said. "I know what you need."

Our kisses had such passion that it took my breath away, and we devoured each other for what seemed like hours, our bodies merging together into one and becoming indistinguishable from each other until the final explosion that sent us into deep space.

With our passions spent, we lay locked in each other's arms, and I dozed after closing the doors of the woodstove and covered us with a blanket. As we made love, I perceived a warm, pinkish glow surrounding us. The light felt soothing and comforting, and it broke though into my consciousness once or twice. I attributed it coming from the woodstove, but after the doors were closed, it was still there. A little later, her voice coming out of the darkness brought me back to awareness. "Jack! Can you hear me? I have something to tell you."

I felt a pleasant afterglow. "I hear you."

"Do you remember when we went to town last week, and I went to the clinic to make sure there were no ill effects from the disease?"

"I remember."

"While there, I had them remove my IUD."

"What? You did what?" I was suddenly wide awake.

"I want children, Jack."

"Damn it, Meg! Don't I have anything to say about this?"

"I thought you wanted kids, too."

Without another word, I climbed up to the deck and crawled into bed. I rarely thought about having children and was glad we had none, as I knew with certainty our marriage was over. Our divorce would affect only her and me. Children would change the equation and inextricably link us together. Furthermore, I heard horror stories of how the system treated estranged fathers. I was almost asleep when she got into her bed next to me. Like a bomb going off in my head, I suddenly understood the meaning of the pinkish glow that surrounded us as we made love, and I sat up startled, fully awake. "Meg! Can you hear me?" I said in the dark.

"I hear you."

"You're already pregnant," and I remembered the deer on the Mendocino Coast and her prophesy that Meg would give me children.

———— ∞ ————

I DROVE TO CALIFORNIA ENOUGH TIMES TO TAKE I-5 ALL THE WAY and feel comfortable transporting the marijuana. It felt good to be in California's sunshine again even though the freeways seemed more crowded than usual. We stayed again with Marge. She lived in a modern two-bedroom apartment in San Rafael near the freeway. A week later, Meg announced her period was late. "Could it be because of having your IUD removed? Don't you have to be late a couple of weeks?"

"I don't think so. I felt nauseous this morning."

She saw a doctor that week who confirmed her pregnancy. The doctor had a reputation as one of the best in Marin County, and he traded marijuana for his service. After Marge left for work, we lingered over breakfast and talked about the upcoming child. "While I'm pregnant," she said, "I won't use any drugs, not even aspirin."

"Can you stop smoking weed for nine months?"

"I'm stopping everything. I won't even drink coffee. Another thing, Jack, I don't want to stay here. It doesn't feel good. I want to go back to the valley."

"You want to be alone in the valley a month or more in winter?"

"I'll be fine. There's plenty of firewood, and the pantry is full. The quietness of the valley in winter appeals to me now."

"What are we naming our little girl?" I said to her back as she started walking towards the door.

She turned and faced me. "How do you know it's a girl?"

"I don't know how, I just know."

"How about Annie?" she said.

The next day, I drove across the Golden Gate Bridge into San Francisco, and on that morning in early December, 1978, it was the first time in memory it didn't feel good being there. The feeling was similar to how it felt in November 1963 after the assassination of President Kennedy. Traffic on the bridge was light and the streets half empty giving the day an eerie feeling. In November of that year, two calamities struck the city of San Francisco, and people suffered from shock and bereavement. In Jonestown, Guyana on November 18, over nine hundred people died in a murder, suicide, including Congressman Leo Ryan and five people in his party.

He and his group were in the small, South American country to investigate, The People's Temple led by Jim Jones, and many of the people who died were from San Francisco.

The second incident hit the people even harder. On November 27, as we drove toward the city, Dan White, a former supervisor on the City Council, shot and killed Mayor George Moscone and Supervisor Harvey Milk in their offices at City Hall. Milk was targeted for execution because he was the first openly gay supervisor. I never met the mayor or the supervisor. I did meet Jim Jones. Before their move to Guyana, his church was in the Haight-Ashbury. He came into the print shop seeking free printing. When I refused, he gave me a look of hatred that still haunts me whenever I remember it. As I drove through the city that morning feeling the confused and grieving energy, I wanted to believed it had no effect on me, but I would be lying. Although I hadn't lived there for over four years, I still considered myself a San Franciscan and probably always would.

My first visit was to Isabel at her office. Her back was turned when I entered. "I'll be right with you," she said and spoke without looking to see who entered. When I looked around and saw all her familiar belongings, it brought back memories of when we were together. It was a time when life seemed easier. "Hi, Isabel," I said.

Hearing my voice, she spun around. "Jack, I haven't seen you in so long. How are you?"

I forgot how beautiful she was and had a momentary regret we divorced now that my marriage with Meg had soured. "I'm fine, and still living in the woods. How about you?"

"I have bad news. Mom died."

"Oh, no! What happened?"

The heaviness I felt in my head and chest all morning seemed to compound after hearing the bad news. Each time I visited Isabel, she'd announced someone close had died. "When did it happen?"

"It was June 13. I'll never forget that day."

When she told me the date, my mind went spinning back to a spring day when a spirit visited the barn as we meditated. Isabel's mother was a caring and supportive friend throughout our marriage, and I remembered our unusual relationship. While very different, she was intrigued by how I saw the world but didn't understand my using marijuana. There was also something different about Isabel. Whenever she had bad news, she'd want a comforting hug. Now she remained standing at her light table. The change made me aware that each time I visited, I reverted into the person I was when we were married and she probably did too. Moreover, since our divorce, I maintained an illusion we still had a connection. I was jolted into the realization we were total strangers.

With memories of Isabel's mother spinning around in my head, I could see Market Street from the second floor landing on my way out, and everything looked familiar; yet I felt disconnected and separate from everything. Nothing was going as it should, and a deep discontent and longing filled my life. On the trip down to Pacifica, my disillusionment and pain intensified. I felt alone in the world and as if nothing mattered, not even Meg's pregnancy. Dark storm clouds moving in fast from the west intensified my gloom. As I drove south, strong gusts of wind blew sand across the Coast Highway. With my mental state deteriorating and feeling nauseous, I stopped for some air along a deserted stretch of beach. Parking along the road, I walked up a short dune. The wind blew in my face in a gale, and large, angry waves crashed against the shore. The heavy, dark overcast turned the day into night, and feeling an unbearable anguish, I screamed at the sky: "Fuuuccck!!"

Drowned out by the howling wind and churning sea, no one heard my torment. But the universe did. As if in acknowledgment of my agony, a long, jagged flash of lighting snaked across the sky. It struck nearby in a deafening thunder clasp shaking the ground and stopped the world for a fleeting instant. As it started up again, huge raindrops splattered in my face, and everything was turned around. Instead of seeing my life as tragic and cause for regret, I saw humor in my predicament. Dancing around in the soaking rain, I laughed hysterically until I exhausted myself.

LATER THAT AFTERNOON, I CAUGHT UP WITH RICK AT A TAVERN where he and his band were playing. The sun shined brightly from a clear, blue sky after the storm. I stood in the low light near the door several minutes before I could see him sitting at the far end of the bar with two friends. "Well! If it isn't my friend from Oregon. This man grows some of the best weed on the West Coast. Good to see you Jack. How's Oregon?"

The bartender set a tall, cool one in front of me. "It's wet but not any wetter than the storm that came through here a few hours ago. I thought it was a hurricane."

"It was a bad one. Dropped a couple of trees on the street where I live. How was the crop this year?"

I took out a doobie rolled from Lady Thai. "I'd like you guys to try some of this."

Taking our drinks with us, the bartender gave us a key to a back room. With cases of beer and liquor stacked against the wall, we sat at a table where employees took their breaks. After we toked, it became quiet. "What are we smoking?" Rick finally asked.

"It's a Thai, Colombian blend I call Lady Thai."

From my backpack, I removed a half ounce for him to try. He smiled and tucked the baggie into his shirt. "What's the price of good bud these days?" I asked.

"Ounces are selling for a hundred and fifty, and pounds for fifteen hundred, if you can get any."

"Amazing! I'll leave the usual amount with you, but Lady Thai is special order."

I gave him one of the business cards I printed up the first winter with the phone number of the apartment in San Rafael written in. "We're playing tonight," he reminded me. "Stick around and listen to some good music."

"What a great idea!"

There were strings attached to Meg's announcement she would

stop smoking and drinking during her pregnancy. Beneath her proclamation was an unspoken edict that I do the same. I didn't quite but abstained when we were together. I knew she'd be pissed as hell when I came in late knowing I was smoking and drinking and having a good time without her. Two other band members arrived and started the musical evening. Immediately, a good-looking chick asked me to dance. I was hot that night, and it seemed all the ladies wanted to dance with me. I danced my best while high on marijuana. I didn't just hear the music, I felt the rhythm in my bones.

I realized how much I missed living in California. Partying with Rick and his friends was easy and fun. By nine o'clock, the establishment was packed standing three deep at the bar talking and digging the music. It was like a big party. By the end of the evening, I knew almost everyone there. They were my kind of people and with an ethos different from the unfriendly and judgmental Oregonians. When I arrived back at the San Rafael apartment sometime after two AM, she was asleep and never awakened when I carefully slipped under the covers next to her. For the moment, at least, there'd be peace between us.

The next day, I visited Reggie at his shop in Mill Valley. After yesterday's dark mood in the city, spending the day in sunny Marin put me into a better headspace. It was early, and the gallery was empty. Reggie appeared from behind a screen. "Hey, Matey! Good to see ya. Come on back."

Before we smoked, he closed the shop for lunch so we wouldn't be disturbed. I rolled a doobie from Lady Thai, and we spaced out. "I want some of this," he said, suddenly, after a long silence, "not to sell but to take with me when I head out to the Caribbean in a few weeks."

"Sounds like a nice trip. How long are you planning to be gone?"

"About six weeks, but if I hadn't already paid me airfare and all, I'd probably cancel the trip."

"Really! Why?"

"I flew home to London for six weeks to see me mum and just got back. She'd been ill, and I wanted to make sure she didn't slip away without me seein' her again. If the shop's closed for a second six weeks, folks'll think I'm out of business."

"I'll be in town for most of the winter. Hire me to take over while you're gone."

He gave me a long, slow look. "That's a mighty good idea, laddie, but you don't know anything about the framin' business."

"Didn't you say that you'd be here until after the holidays? Teach me."

Without a word, he began cutting a mat. After he finished, he handed me a shop apron. "Here mate put this on. We haven't got any time to lose."

Since I already possessed many of the skills needed, there wasn't much I had to learn. I wasn't an expert when he left but with sufficient skill to take over.

During the holiday's, Meg and I went to a round of house parties. Beards and long hair hadn't gone completely out of style, but we stood out and looked different from city folks. Everyone asked where we were from. "We're from Oregon," I said, "and in town selling the marijuana we grow, and it's the best around."

During the festivities, I sold product to many people who bought on the spot. Marge left to visit her family for the holidays, and we had the apartment to ourselves. A few days after New Year, Meg went back to the valley and Reggie departed for the Caribbean. Each morning, I hitchhiked and walked part way to arrive at the shop by eleven. Working with art appealed to me, and it was fun pretending I owned the gallery. Coming home evenings, I caught a ride with the woman who owned the dry cleaners up the block. She was a big, busty blonde and single. She hinted that she was available and wanted me to date her. "You really shouldn't spend so much time alone, Dearie," she said. "Drop by for lunch, anytime."

In another incident, two women came in looking for Reggie. When I told them he was gone, they asked if I would take them out drinking that night. As payment, I could have either one or both. I wasn't interested in connecting with anyone and spent days at the shop and evenings at home mostly alone in my room reading or vegetating and not turning on. Like Meg, I suspected my need for solitude had something to do with the approaching birth of my child.

No one talks about the male experience during childbearing. Motherhood is so powerful, and the father's contribution remains unsung. Women give birth and are the primary nurturers. What else is there? But there are always two people involved, and I was going through profound psychological changes. In one episode, I experienced hallucinatory visions of hunting game and fighting off wild beasts. I suspected I was experiencing remembrances from past lives when I actually did pursue game and did fight off wild animals. I was bringing a new human into the world, and my psyche wasn't taking it lightly.

Before I knew it, Reggie returned from his holiday pleased I did such a good job running his frame shop. During the six weeks, I easily sold the remainder of the marijuana, although I wasn't looking forward to Meg's return. Just thinking about her made me irritable. Several days later, the inevitable happened. She was back, and I found boxes stacked against the wall in my room. Meg never treaded lightly and left deep footprints in her wake. During my time alone, I felt peaceful and calm and lived a simple and orderly life. At her return, my peacefulness was in shreds. Feeling intense frustration, I yelled at her instead of welcoming her back. During the long twelve-hour drive into the valley, it took six hours before I realized something changed. Instead of quarrelsome and contentious, she was relaxed almost mellow.

John-Paul Cernak

CHAPTER 13

1979

IN EARLY MARCH, A COLD FRONT DROPPED DOWN OUT OF CANADA, and temperatures tumbled into the single digits and almost depleted our firewood supply. "Jump into bed with me," she said, holding up the covers. "I'm freezing and you can keep me warm."

Although we were out of the habit of sleeping together, we cuddled, made love, and slept in her queen bed to stay warm and experienced a renaissance in our marriage. Mornings, after building a fire, I jumped back into bed until the barn warmed. With time and with the expected arrival of our child, I pushed her infidelity out of my mind.

In late March on a supply run into Medford, Meg dropped me off at a Kubota tractor dealer while she went to speak with a midwife. That evening, I showed her brochures the salesman gave me. "They're not cheap, are they?" she remarked. "Remember, we're having a baby."

"This was the best money year we ever had."

"Well, if you think we can afford it."

The following week, I purchased a mid-size tractor with a sixteen-horsepower diesel engine and with all the bells and whistles. I finally had the power tool I needed to cut the grass and till the soil. When Brandy learned Meg was pregnant, she became a regular visitor and usually brought her sister and a group of friends. On one visit, she brought news that Billy Carpenter died. He was the man I stayed with in San Francisco who believed I lived a charmed life. With Meg not smoking, I rarely did either, and for the first time in years, I witnessed the world straight.

On a mail run in April, Meg received a letter from her father. She held it unopened on her lap on the drive back. "Open it." I said. "How else are you going to find out what he says?"

"I'll open it later."

Her curiosity won out, and she tore it open. As my curiosity mounted, she sat quietly looking out the window. "Well! What does he say?"

"He wants to visit before he's too weak to travel."

The news gave me the jitters. We both sat quietly with our own thoughts until I pulled into the parking space across from the barn. "Wait," I said.

Quickly running around to the passenger side, I helped her out of the truck. Taking my arm, she stood up and looked at me unemotionally. "What are you going to tell him we grow here," I asked. Are you going to tell him we grow marijuana?

"If he comes, I don't see how we can hide it from him."

"If he's as straight as you say, how will he react?"

"He doesn't have much choice, does he? He'll just have to accept it."

After I brought her a cup of tea, we sat on the old leather couch in front of the woodstove. "I was thinking," she said, "that while he's here we'll repay more of the money we owe him."

"We've already sent him half, I thought we were going to spread the payments over several years."

"I don't want him thinking that we'll wait until he dies and not pay him. Even if we pay him everything and pay off the tractor, too, we'll still have plenty of money to get us through the year. But regardless of how much we have, it's not enough. We need to generate more income."

"We have more money now than we've had since moving here. How much do we need?"

Her mood softened. "We're going to have a family now, Jack."

"And how would you suggest we generate more cash?"

"Open a business in town."

"Are you suggesting we leave after building the new house?"

"Jack! I'm tired of living in the wilderness away from people, and I'll have a baby to care for."

"What kind of business can we open that would give us income?"

"When we came back from California, you said how much fun you had running Reggie's frame shop. The last time we were in Centerville, I checked, and there's only one other. With the watering system and the new tractor, there's no reason we couldn't do both, and with all the Californians moving in, the town's growing and everyone's prospering. The mills are running full blast, and with the high price of marijuana, everyone has lots of cash to spend."

Feeling ambivalent, I drove to Centerville to look for a place to open a frame shop after I finished planting the crop. I loved living in the valley. On the other hand, having a business in town could be fun, too. I also understood how Meg felt with a new baby coming, and I consented to explore the possibilities only because I saw myself as living both in the valley and in town and having the best of both worlds.

The first place I looked was in the downtown where there were several vacancies. As I walked up the street looking in at all the fancy window displays, I nixed the idea. It was to glitzy for me, and I'd have difficulty relating with all the straight business people. Moreover, I wasn't quite ready to jump feet first into the business world after living for so long in an unstructured environment. The area that appealed to me more was several blocks north of the downtown across from the courthouse where a sandwich restaurant and natural food store were located and owned by counterculture people. A new restaurant was coming in on one end of the block, and near the other end was a space for rent next to a creek. Two doors up was the Happy Hour Tavern. I went in looking for a payphone.

It was a funky, old saloon filled with loggers having their morning beer. I looked hippie and out-of-place among all of the plaid shirts and suspenders. Nobody paid any attention to me. Two pool tables next to the front windows had games going and with people gathered around. There was a sign above the bar with the bartender's name. "Hey Woody! Is there a payphone around?"

"We don't believe in paying for calls. Sit yourself down on that corner stool," and he handed me the house phone. "As long as the calls are local."

"That's mighty friendly. Why not pour me a draft while I'm here?" (If I remembered correctly, the beer cost thirty-five cents.)

I picked up a key to the empty space and let myself in. A musty odor told me it was vacant for some time, and although the size was about right, the old building was in disrepair and in need of a renovation. The landlord agreed to discount the rent if I fixed it up. I related my days adventures to Meg that evening and remembered Bruce lived in Centerville. He was the carpenters who helped build the new house. I called him when I returned to town the following day. He was between jobs and consented to help. The best part was he would accept payment for his work half in cash and half in marijuana. I gave him a key and drove back to the valley.

Meg was six months pregnant, and I was concerned about leaving her alone isolated in the valley. When I returned to town after three days, I dropped her at Ginger and Bob's. Bruce began to cover the old cracked plaster walls with pegboard, and the next job was to install a shower and a small kitchen in the back. When he was in the valley to help build the new house, we never had a chance to talk. Now with just the two of us working side by side, he told me his story.

Bruce was a short hair, born again, Christian hippie from Santa Cruz, California. He was tall, blonde, and in his early thirties. He met Albert while attending San Jose State College, and they were smugglers. "That was before I became a Christian and was reborn," he said.

"Really! And from where did you smuggle?"

"Brother Albert and I started going down to Mexico to bring

John-Paul Cernak

back snort to support our habit, and the next thing I knew, we were making tons of cash and couldn't stop. I was using a lot of coke and burning out my nose. Cocaine'll do that you know. To give my proboscis a rest, I'd roll up a little crystal in some hashish and stick it up my butt. It always made me laugh to see a bunch of guys sitting around with their hands in their pants getting high."

"Whatever works," I said.

"If we knew we'd score big, we'd take friends down with us, strap on seventy-five to a hundred pounds of marijuana and cocaine, and walk most of the night through the desert high on snort and across the border where a vehicle was waiting. We could make a hundred grand each trip."

"I'm in the wrong business," I said.

"Listen bro, I knew you guys were marijuana growers as soon as I saw your place."

"What gave it away?"

"Just how isolated your valley is. If I owned land there, that's what I'd be doing."

When Bruce went home at five, I made myself a quick dinner, but the excitement wouldn't let me stop. Going into the country was easy. Coming out was excruciatingly difficult. Although we spent winters in the city, I never noticed everything changed. My psyche still remembered how it was six years ago. Each evening, I walked off my nervous tension exploring the town. On a side street off the downtown, I discovered a vegetarian restaurant and a western bar with live music. Several blocks up from the shop was a disco. When passing, the beat of syncopated music floated out. Several carloads of young women dressed in high fashions, high heels, and with high makeup just arrived. I only recently heard disco for the first time, and it made me aware how much I was missing living isolated in the mountains.

With my energy spent late in the evening, I'd sit in the dark with my back against the wall listening to music on the radio. Everything moved too fast during the day to integrate the changes until along at night. So far I was having fun, and it seemed a good thing to have a break from Meg after living together so intensely for six years. Nonetheless, I couldn't help seeing the irony. She wanted out, but it was me who was in town experiencing the new environment and having adventures.

During the first night sleeping on my mat on the floor, sounds coming from the dog-grooming parlor next door awakened me periodically. The owner was a slim, blonde woman who stayed awake all night and must have been on speed. I spoke with her briefly the next day. She owned land a hundred miles south and stayed in town the days her shop was open. She wasn't the warm, friendly type, and that was fine with me. I was grateful for her parlor providing a buffer between my shop and the tavern. I named the new business "Deer Creek Custom Framing and Gallery" after the creek that flowed alongside.

I was flying high. Everything was coming together smoothly. Life felt good with a new daughter coming and my relationship with Meg the best it had been in a long time. Although I became involved with starting the business reluctantly, the momentum carried me along. On Wednesday of the following week, Bruce and I spent the afternoon driving in the last few nails and vacuuming the sawdust. The following week, Meg came to see the shop and to help with painting. With her large belly sticking out, she worked standing on the low rung of the ladder. We both enjoyed living in civilization and having hot showers and meals at the vegetarian restaurant. For the first time in years, I shaved my beard and cut my hair and made plans for the grand opening, but it would have to wait until after Meg's father's and stepmother's visit.

We picked up Tim and Claudia at the Medford Airport. Tim was tall as I knew he would be, possibly six feet five or six, and he looked only in his middle fifties. He was once strong and muscular. Now he was thin and frail and walked stooped over. I never spent time with anyone before who was dying. He was peaceful as if he'd accepted his fate. He was understanding and non-judgmental even when we showed him the marijuana growing on the hill. His attitude was child-like in a desire to understand and learn new things, as if the approach of death shook him out of some old and ridged lethargy. I liked him and could see he cared about his daughter and especially about the unborn child.

Meg's stepmother, Claudia, was about his age and a little portly. Throughout their stay, she wore a dress. Her mood was upbeat, but she was there only to care for Tim. The following day, we drove to Medford, rented an RV, and for the next several days showed them the beauty of Oregon. We drove in a circle and ended back in Medford to drop Tim and Claudia at the airport and the RV at the dealer.

Only the hippies working at the businesses along the street and a college guy named Bob from the record store next to the tavern came the first day. He offered to share a joint. I took a rain check. Late Friday afternoon, people began coming in mostly for the free wine and goodies. Saturday was busy with people coming in all day. A woman named Wanda came in late that evening. Her sister was opening the restaurant up the street. She helped herself to wine and went off to look at the art. "Here's a list of the paintings I want. I'll give you a deposit and pick them up next week."

"You're my first customer, and I'd like to do something nice for you. I'm not sure how to do that."

"I'll be helping my sister at the restaurant part time, and I've always loved art. If you want to do something nice, give me a job working in the gallery and teach me picture framing."

Feeling strangely apprehensive that evening when locking up, I hurriedly drove to pick up Meg. It was late when I arrived. Ginger answered my knock. "I've been looking out for you," she said. "Meg's asleep," but she immediately walked out from her room. "Would you like to stay over until morning?"

"I'd love to stay and have a leisurely breakfast with you guys, but I have so much work waiting for me tomorrow, it's best we get going."

Meg was quiet on the trip back to the valley, and it wasn't until I pulled into the parking space across from the barn and turned off the key that I suspected a problem. With everything quiet, I could feel her tenseness. "Aren't you interested on how the grand opening went?"

"You don't give a shit about me, Jack, and you never have."

I took a deep breath before I responded and felt the churning already beginning in my stomach. "What brought this on?"

"You haven't touched me in weeks."

"I guess I haven't with all that's been happening, but it doesn't mean that I don't care."

"You think I'm ugly because I'm no longer slim."

"No! That's not true. For the last six weeks I've been opening a business in town."

"I don't want to hear your fucking excuses," she screamed and quickly exited the truck slamming the door behind her.

The honeymoon was over. I sat alone feeling exhausted the night somehow comforting and tried to reconcile myself to the new reality while saying a prayer for my unborn daughter growing in Meg's womb.

She was calmer the following morning but not more receptive. When I dropped her off on Wednesday, the feeling between us was warm and loving. Four days later, everything changed. I was familiar with her Jekyll and Hyde shifts from past episodes and wasn't totally surprised. Once she fell into that state of mind, she locked me out with no possibility of reaching her and with no way to give her what she needed, the perceived offence becoming a self-fulfilling prophecy. I cooked breakfast in the hope of turning her around. She sat sullen at the table. I spoke in a cheerful voice and set a plate of food in front of her. "I sold three paintings," I said.

"Didn't I tell you that you'd have lots of business, but you never listen to me."

"Who bought them?" she asked tersely, her brow furrowed.

"Remember the new restaurant coming in down the block?

The sale was to the sister of the owner, and she asked me for a job."

She looked at me suspiciously. "Did you hire her?"

"I did and I didn't. I told her that I'd have to get the shop paying for itself first, but if she wanted to come in on her own time, I'd teach her how to frame."

"You bastard!" she screamed and sent her plate crashing to the floor. "I'm stuck here with a fat belly carrying your kid, and you're fucking every bitch in town."

I swept up the mess feeling detached. Yes! I had a business in town and was no longer dependent on her for all my needs. Since starting the project, I felt more liberated than in years. I moved into the valley to be free and lost it in a way I least suspected. The worst part was that I hardly recognized it until that moment.

—◦◦◦—

I FELT CONSIDERABLE TREPIDATION WHEN HANGING OUT MY 'Open' sign the following Wednesday. My three days in the valley with Meg unnerved me more than I realized. The confidence that came from the success of running Reggie's shop in California seven months earlier had long since faded, and all my insecurities and doubts surfaced. Did I really know enough about picture framing to run a successful business? With a wall full of sample molding corners and a rack filled with a variety of colored mats, everything was ready for my first customer. For the first three days, a few people came in to look at the art but no framing orders. While I waited, I framed several pictures for myself to keep busy. On Saturday morning, a man entered carrying a folder. I saw him before and knew he worked in one of the government offices across the street. He dropped the folder on the desk. "My wife wants these framed," he said.

He turned and walked towards the door. "Wait! Wait! How do you want them framed?"

His face was a big blank. "I don't know a thing about this stuff. Do what you want."

In the folder were six watercolors ranging in size from a few inches to a twelve by fourteen. All the customers at Reggie's shop knew what they wanted. They selected the frames and mats, and I created what they ordered. My insecurities nagged me as I began matching different colored mats and frame profiles to the art. There were hundreds of mat colors and as many moldings corners. All afternoon I tried different combinations unsuccessfully. Several looked okay, but some innate understanding told me it wasn't quite right. Feeling frustrated, I began to chafe under the demands of my first job. At closing, I was still back where I started. Feeling pressured and stressed when picking up Meg that evening, I blew up when she did an accusatory act. During my three days in the valley, we hardly spoke, and I worried about the unborn child.

The following Wednesday, I threw myself into working on the six watercolors determined to get them right. After closing at six and a quick dinner, I worked until ten or later. It helped block out thinking about Meg and the valley. It was July, and the days were long and hot. At night, I'd lay on my mat sweating and listening to the radio before falling asleep. During those early days, I neither smoked marijuana nor drank alcohol and longed to be back in the valley experiencing the peacefulness of the forest, working with my plants, and staying cool swimming in the waters of the South Umpqua River.

When I first received the watercolors, I considered them a curse. Later, I recognized they were a blessing. With them, I learned different techniques and aspects of picture framing that would have otherwise taken months or even years to acquire. They brought out and polished an innate color harmony I didn't know I had. Thereafter, all I needed was to look at an artwork, and I quickly visualized which frame and what color mat would display it the best. I stopped calling myself a picture framer. I displayed art. To appreciate my first creations, I hung the finished framed pictures on the wall behind my workbench before contacting my customer. He picked them up and paid the.bill without looking at them, and

I received no feedback. The nice part was that he returned several weeks later with four more watercolors. That first job launched my framing career, and thereafter, business increased each month with always a two-week wait.

Wanda started coming in, and I began teaching her picture framing. As in Reggie's shop, regulars dropped in to spend a little time discussing world affairs. One of them was a middle-aged guy named Patrick. He recently returned to Oregon from Sitka, Alaska where he lived for twenty years and had a dry cleaning business. Another was Jeff the mailman and Bob from the record store. They didn't stand around smoking marijuana and drinking beer as they did at Reggie's shop. My workbench was out front and visible to everyone walking past, and none of them knew I was a grower.

A few weekend later, as I watered plants on a hot humid day, Meg entered the growing area and walked unsteadily towards me looking uncomfortable. "It's time," she said.

I helped her down the hill and drove to the payphone at Crooked Creek where she called, Debbie, her midwife. She lived in the Applegate Valley and wouldn't arrive until the following day. Meg then called her father who was near death to let him know she was in labor. I called Wanda to open the shop on Wednesday morning. "How often are the contractions coming?" I asked.

"Just once in a while."

"Let's drive up to Camp Comfort."

We sat close on the bench seat of a picnic table overlooking the river in the deserted campground and talked quietly letting the big trees and rushing water sooth the pain that existed between us for the last six weeks. It was difficult feeling close to her after she bombarded me with caustic remarks and a hostile attitude for so long. I gave her as much love and comfort as possible. I didn't want to think about the conflicts that divided us but to experience the joys of becoming a father. "What does it feel like when you have a contraction?"

"Something like when you have to go to the bathroom really bad."

The Odyssey of a Hippie Marijuana Grower   267

That evening, I moved her mattress down to the floor near the woodstove. It was summer, but I could always add more warmth in the morning if necessary. I made her a light supper, and she rested comfortably for most of the night. By morning, her contractions were coming more frequently. Around eight, her water broke.

The day started bright and clear with the sun coming up over the mountain. Out of nowhere, towering thunderheads formed above the valley, and it rained in a drenching downpour. Long, jagged flashes of lightning snaked across the sky followed by loud thunder claps. When one struck somewhere up on the mountainside and a giant fell in a loud thundering roar that shook the barn, I refused to think about what omen the incident held. By then, my nerves were well jangled, and Debbie was late adding to my apprehension. She was unfamiliar with the area, and I worried she took a wrong turn and was lost

Meg told me Debbie had a good reputation and delivered many babies. When Meg first became pregnant, we talked about her having the baby in the hospital. Her reply was that hospitals were for sick people. She wasn't sick but having a baby. She considered hospitals unsafe and wanted to have the child at home with the help of a midwife. When she made her decision, I wasn't worried but concerned. If anything went wrong, the nearest hospital was in Centerville over seventy-five miles away. Moments later, my tensions eased as Debbie's car pulled into the parking space behind my truck. I held the door open as she dashed through the downpour holding a large medicine bag. What I remembered most about her was her clear, blue, intelligent eyes that seemed to take in everything at once. She wore sandals, a long skirt, and a white, loose-fitting blouse. She had a gentle demeanor but oozed confidence and assumed control without any fanfare.

Meg was in labor for twenty-four hours, and stress lines appeared on her face looking like shadows. Quickly, she dilated to ten centimeters and Debbie urged her to push and get the baby out. Her pain was excruciating, and her pushes were anemic. After a half-hour, the fetus hadn't moved and she was becoming weaker by the minute. She lay back to rest, but the pain was too intense. After another round of pushing, the fetus moved slightly but stalled in the birth canal. Meg moaned in pain and was near exhaustion. During a lull, I slipped outside to get my head back on straight. The rain stopped, and the day turned warm and sunny. In a prayer to the Great Spirit, I asked for help delivering my baby daughter safely.

I had to admire Debbie's skill and focus. She did her job calmly and efficiently throughout the chaos and never hinted there was a problem even when the situation seemed dire. Finally, after many pushes and with Meg on the verge of collapse, the baby's head and face showed. Vocally, she was already letting us know of her discomfort. "Get me out of here," she screamed.

Moments later, Little Annie was born, and Meg immediately passed out. After Debbie put drops in the babies eyes and tied the umbilical cord, she wrapped her in a blanket and gave her to me. I never experienced anything as exhilarating or humbling as when I held my daughter those first moments after her birth. Sitting on the wood box next to the stove, I cradled her singing songs, and we became acquainted. I told her how much we loved her and how glad we were she came to live with us. In return, she cooed and made loving sounds of approval and was soon asleep. When Meg awakened, I gave her the sleeping infant. I bonded with my baby daughter before her mother even held her.

A few days later, when Meg felt strong enough to travel, we drove down to the telephone at Crooked Creek, and she called her father. He died several days later after learning she delivered a healthy baby girl. With the birth, the hostilities between us lessened but never completely ended. Still, it felt as if we turned a corner. I cast aside any doubts and merged my energies into the communal pool and committed myself to the cause. The little girl was a joy, and I never experienced as many emotions of love and protection.

In mid-October, I harvested the marijuana. It was the largest and best crop yet. We went through our yearly ritual of cleaning the plants with the baby next to us in her bassinet smiling and giggling and enjoying the music and activity. As usual, we weighed and bagged the bud for immediate sale and stored the large leaves in the cellar. There were now eight bags full.

CHAPTER 14

WITH WANDA RUNNING THE FRAME SHOP, THE THREE OF US headed for San Francisco. We stayed with Brandy. I was relieved her son Don no longer lived with her. The little girl charmed everyone who visited. They couldn't resist her blue eyes and smiles she gave away to everyone. But Meg was struggling. She was unprepared for the difficulties of traveling with an infant as young and insisted on returning to the valley after two weeks.

Once again, the price of marijuana increased as it had every year with bud selling for a ridiculous two thousand dollars a pound and ounces selling for two hundred. I returned to the city alone after several weeks, but it wasn't as much fun as in the past. I felt pressured, and after living in town, going to San Francisco no longer had the impact it once had after being cloistered ten months in the mountains. In bygone years, I spent time leisurely calling on customers, socializing, and getting stoned, but those days were gone forever.

After the epiphany I experienced last year that Isabel and I no longer had a connection, I wasn't going to see her again but talked myself into one last visit to say goodbye and wish her well. After I climbed the stairs to the second floor, her office was vacant. The scraped off outline of Cernak & Associates was still visible on the glass. I remembered standing in that very spot years earlier and experiencing a premonition that one day I would find her gone and never see her again. I called information, but there was no listing for her or for a brother who lived in Santa Rosa. It seemed they fell off the face of the earth.

Isabel had a close relationship with her brother and after thinking about it perhaps too close. After her father died, he became the strong, dominant, male figure in her life. He was very different from me and was a keep your nose to the grindstone type, taking himself very seriously. He never approved of my more freewheeling personality. He traveled two hours in each direction to his teaching job each day, and there didn't seem to be any joy or humor in his life. Throughout the years of our marriage, he and his wife never visited, even after we purchased the Victorian and had a house-warming. Isabel often compared me to him, and I never quite measured up. It wasn't the reason our marriage ended. The reason was we never talked about the things that really mattered. It wasn't just her, of course; it takes two to make a marriage, but she never inquired why I turned off.

<hr />

1980

I TRAVELED ALL DAY ON MY RETURN AND ENTERED THE VALLEY at nightfall. The barn was barely visible in the distance and everything was dark. Could she be asleep already? I let myself in, and before I could light a lantern, Meg's voice rang out from the darkness. "Is that you, Jack?"

"It's me. How's the baby?"

I was concerned. Debbie warned me that she might go into depression after giving birth, and her father's death might contribute. "She's fine!"

"You're in bed early."

"I was feeling tired."

"Have you eaten anything today?"

"I didn't feel much like eating."

"Come down and keep me company while I fix us something to eat."

She hugged me warmly. "It's good to have you home. It's hard when there's no one to talk with."

During the next few days, her depression lifted, but on Wednesday morning, as I prepared to leave for town, she looked downcast, her clothes disheveled and her hair uncombed. She sat heavily in a chair gripping the arms and her face showing strain. "Jack! I need to get out of here. I'm locked up with an infant four days each week, and I don't know how much longer I can do it."

"It's only for a short time longer. I know how you feel, and I wish we could change places for a while. I'm sure the money will come in soon. Just hang in a little longer."

We made a decision to buy a house in town, and each week, I checked the classifieds to see what was for sale even though there wasn't enough money for a down payment. What I hoped for was that the money received from Rick and Reggie would make a down payment large enough that I wouldn't need to prove our income when applying for a loan from a bank. The shop hadn't been open long enough to have established credit. I didn't think that it would be wise to tell a loan officer we were marijuana growers.

To ease the pressure, Meg came to town and stayed with me at the shop the following week and again the following month, but it wasn't set up to accommodate the three of us. During her stay, I felt she was encroaching on my territory similar to when she came to the valley the first year when I was getting the barn ready. While I worked, she drove around looking at houses for sale. It was a cold and rainy March, and each afternoon she'd come into the shop shivering and wet holding the baby and stand next to the wood heater getting warm. "Damn! There are so many lovely old houses in this town, but they're expensive. The one I looked at today was big and had lots of built-in cabinets and all the woodwork was natural without paint. I want one, Jack!"

"I hope we can afford what you want."

The days seemed to move more slowly at that time of year waiting for spring. As the cold and wet weather lingered, her frustration increased, and she became more demanding. "I want you to take more of responsibility in caring for your daughter."

To keep things peaceful, I did as she asked, or rather, as she demanded. On my days in the valley, I'd mind the baby, changed diapers, cooked meals, plus all the other things that needed doing. I gave it my all, but it was never enough. And each week, she demanded more. With the truck packed and ready to leave on Wednesday morning, she stood blocking the doorway. "You don't want me moving to town, do you?"

"Don't be ridiculous." I said, trying to edge my way past her. "You know there isn't anything I can do until the money comes in."

"You're lying, Jack. I can feel it. You're getting a perverse pleasure from seeing me suffer.

"You're delusional."

Once on the road and with time to ponder her statement, I had to admit that there was some truth in her accusation, and the reason went all the way back to her infidelity with Bruce. From the beginning and even after contracting gonorrhea, she never showed contrition. On the contrary, she wore her infidelity like a badge of honor rubbing my nose in it, and I couldn't help feeling pleased her karma finally caught up with her. It looked as if she would have to stay in the valley.

Fate intervened on her side. Reggie called to let me know he had money for us. I made a quick trip to the city and collected a portion from him and from Rick giving us enough for a large down payment. As luck would have it, almost immediately afterwards, a man who was retiring sold me his beautiful house in a great part of town at well below its market value. The best part was he carried the loan on a land sales contract, and I didn't have to ask the bank for a loan after all. Additionally, the money we had on hand originally was sufficient for the down payment. But there was a hitch: "I'm seventy-two," he said, "so I can't give you a thirty-year mortgage. I won't be around that long. I need the money as soon as possible. Since I'm giving you such a good price, I want two balloon payments one in six months and the other in twelve months after that for the balance."

"It's a deal," I said.

Instantly feeling pressured, I knew I would have to come up with large amounts of cash in a short time. With the money from the marijuana already in the pipeline, I felt reasonably sure I could make the first balloon payment. For next year's larger installment, I would need to harvest and successfully market the next crop that I was already starting in the greenhouse. On the way to the valley to tell Meg the good news, I actually felt glad she was finally coming out. When she heard me driving.up, she came out and stood by the front door. "What are you doing back? It's only Friday. Are you ill?"

I smiled teasing her. "I have a surprise for you."

"Well! Tell me; don't just stand there with a stupid grin."

"I bought a house."

"What are you talking about, Jack? Have you flipped out?"

"Get the baby ready, and let's drive to town; I'll tell you about it on the way." We were almost halfway to town before she was finally convinced it wasn't a joke. As I drove, the stress that showed on her face was already lifting. "OK! Jack, tell me about the house."

"It's a fine old house, the kind you've been wanting, with five bedrooms, high on a hill, and in a neighborhood of fine old houses."

With an air of respectability, we settled into our new home on upper Jefferson Street and assumed the life of a middle class family—Meg a mother and I the proprietor of a local business. To all the neighbors who watched us closely, we were the All-American Family, and when they learned we spent a few days each week at our country place, it added to our status. We still smoked marijuana, but more carefully now hiding it from our straight neighbors.

My one regret about moving into town was our cats. They were part of the family, and they seemed bewildered. I held each and gave them love, while trying to convince them how happy they would be living in town. I lied. I knew they would never adjust to living in civilization after dwelling free in the beauty and wild of the national forest.

Meg must have really been pleased that I bought the house, because she bought me a bicycle for my birthday, a ten-speed Peugeot racer with narrow tires. And what a joy it was to ride a bike again. While I mostly adjusted to living in town, I still longed for the unstructured freedom of my life in the valley. With the sun and wind in my face and oblivious of time, I never felt freer. I always loved riding a bicycle and remembered as a kid taking off for hours and disappearing into the Chicago neighborhoods looking for new places to explore, as I must have searched the wilderness on my horse in my past life.

I learned early that riding while high on marijuana was forbidden. Ignoring my inner warnings, I toked on the pipe one afternoon before riding off. I hadn't lost my physical edge, and riding up hills was effortless. While pedaling up a steep incline—totally stoned and marveling at my own stamina—I failed to notice that once past the crest, the street shot down steeply. Holding on with both hands and riding over lawns and through flowerbeds at forty miles an hour and totally out of control, I used all my will and concentration to stay upright. To reach for the brakes even for an instant, which were only inches from my hands, would have been disastrous. After hitting a rock, the bike went flying, and I somehow landed back on the seat. For a moment, I thought I was going to.die, but in the next instant, I was safe back on the street and amazed at my good luck. Maybe it was true that I lived a charmed life, but I didn't take my luck for granted. There were no second chances. I never rode stoned again.

Patrick, one of the regulars at the shop, stopped in one morning looking miserable. He was usually all smiles and had a sunny disposition. With his forehead creased and his shoulders slumped, his vibe could have curdled milk. "Why so down, Patrick?"

"It's my wife. We just don't have anything in common anymore."

He talked about his life in Alaska with such fondness, I wondered why he returned to Oregon leaving all his friends behind. "It wasn't me that wanted to come back. It was her. I don't want to be here."

"Do you argue much?"

"Hell no! We have nothing to say to each other and live in separate worlds. She spends most days with her mother and doesn't cook or clean any more. It seems, I'm totally on my own."

"Maybe that's not so bad. At least your house is peaceful. You should live in mine. Meg and I are at each other's throats constantly. Have you ever thought of leaving her?"

With a painful look on his face, he stood quietly for a long moment before answering. "Then what?"

"I know what you mean. I've asked myself that same question."

Almost without noticing, Meg took over, and I found myself marching to the beat of her drummer. The worst part was her cavalier attitude about my needs and that somehow they didn't matter. "We have a family now and the baby comes first," she replied, when I tried talking about my concern.

While living in the valley, she gardened, hiked, hauled firewood, and spent active days outside in nature. She looked radiant, and her skin glowed with health and vitality. Immediately after moving to town, she cut her hair short and began wearing matronly dresses that gave her a stern severe look. She stopped doing all the things that made her beautiful. Within months, her healthy glow disappeared, and she rarely smiled. After living an unstructured lifestyle for years, she scripted every moment of her day and gave up yoga. In its place, she became a Chanting Buddhist. Each morning and evening for a half hour, she sat cross-legged on the floor in front of her altar, which was a crate covered with an old tablecloth, burning incense and chanted in Japanese: "Nam-myoho-renge-kyo, Hoben-pon, Dai ni "

I actually enjoyed listening to the rhythmic beat of her mantra, except now she considered anyone who didn't chant as inferior and insisted that unless I did also nothing good would happen in my life. "People who chant will change the world, and all others will be left behind. We are influencing destiny through sound."

Rather than helping, her incantations made it harder to communicate. Somehow, I wasn't speaking her language anymore, and if I suggested we give ourselves time together, she looked down her nose at me as if I were no longer good enough for her. Finally, my patience ran out. One evening after putting the little girl to bed, I let her know I wanted to talk. She sat in her chair upstairs in the TV room leafing through a magazine. I sat on the couch opposite her. "It's been a long time since we've been close," I said, trying to keep my tone pleasant, although feeling frustrated and a little irritated.

"So! We have a family now," and she went back to browsing in her magazine and ignored me.

"This is important, Meg. Before the baby was born, I know everything wasn't always smooth sailing between us, but we somehow managed to stay close. We haven't had sex in over six weeks."

"Taking care of Annie, cooking, and this big house takes all my energy."

She didn't take anything I said seriously and continued leafing through her magazine. "Damn it! Listen to me. You've not only cut me out and relegated me to the outer edge of the family, but your vibe towards me sucks. You walk around with an air of superiority. We don't have sex anymore, and we don't talk anymore either. Are we ever going to return to something more normal?"

She turned towards me with her eyes flashing daggers. "Oh! Come on, Jack! It's not just about you anymore. When are you going to grow up? You're just a selfish little boy. I'll go to the store tomorrow and buy you an all day sucker."

Calmly, I walked out. The town was full of beautiful woman. I'll find someone else to play with and immediately thought of several women who came into the shop and were extra friendly. One was a married woman named Jamie. She was in her forties and with a pleasant personality. She stopped in to talk a few times after having a picture framed, and it was obvious she was lonely. She came in one afternoon shortly after my talk with Meg, and we sat in chairs out in the gallery. "How long have you been married?" she asked.

All our previous conversations were about art, and when she asked about my marriage, I concluded she wanted to talk about hers. "I've been married five years," I said. "How long have you been married?"

"Over twenty years," she replied with a grimace.

"What does your husband do for a living?"

"Bob works at the mill when he's not riding his bicycle, but he's always riding and never home. The only time I see him is when eating dinner. In fact, we have separate bedrooms."

Although I sympathized with her husband on the bicycle part, I identified with her on the sex and knew it wouldn't take much to woo her into a bed. Feeling her repressed sexual energy so strongly, I became aroused and was tempted to close the shop early and begin her therapy immediately in the backroom. That was why I had no idea what compelled me to say what I said next: "I'll bet you'd get along with my wife. Come by the house, and I'll introduce you."

Several weeks later as I watched the late news up in the TV room, I was surprised when Meg joined me. She wore what looked like a man's shirt that came down halfway to her knees. Lately, it seemed her mood improved, and she even looked better. She smiled and sat next to me on the couch instead of alone in her chair where she usually sat. "It was nice of you to bring Jamie home to meet me. She's such a dear."

She leaned over and kissed me on my cheek. "I do my best," I said.

"For being so sweet," she kissed me passionately.

She hadn't kissed me with as much passion in months, and I kissed her back. When she leaned forwards, her shirt flared and exposed her breasts. When she saw me looking, she smiled and unbuttoned her shirt all the way open. Feeling intense passion and desiring her desperately, I switched off the lights and dropped my pants to the floor vaguely aware she was manipulating me. From the beginning, when I first met Meg in San Francisco and through-out the years of our marriage, I was never able to resist her even

The Odyssey of a Hippie Marijuana Grower   279

when she cheated on me. Many times, I told myself never again, but in the next moment, I was melting in her arms and feeling my usual lust for her.

To prolong the rapture after the long abstinence, I moved in and out slowly. When I felt her nearing, I purposely slowed and removed the urgency. Now I was struggling to hold back and wasn't sure how much longer I could last. With her breathing accelerated, I felt her bliss knowing she wanted to come, but this time, I wouldn't be able to stop it. When I felt her grip tightly with her legs, thrust hard, and explode, she took me over the edge with her. During that moment of peak pleasure, I perceived a light coming through the drawn shades bathing our nude bodies in a soft, pinkish glow.

———⊙/⊙/⊙———

SIX WEEKS LATER, REGGIE PAID US A SURPRISE VISIT. HE CAME to bring the remainder of the money and to see the new house. We discussed him becoming a partner for next year's crop. Meg was pregnant again and would give birth in the spring. I'm sure it happened the night she came up to the TV room. She wasn't approachable afterwards, and I remembered the pinkish glow that filled the room similar to the one that surrounded us when we conceived our little girl. I didn't give it much thought believing it came from the street outside. After learning she was pregnant, I accepted the outcome and decided a second child was desirable, and I knew it was a boy. We named him Paul.

On Saturday, Reggie and I drove up to the valley in his red MG, a two-seater sports car, my long hair becoming tangled blowing in the wind. "Do you have a top for these wheels?" I shouted loudly.

"No, just the way it is."

"I don't think this would be a good vehicle for around here in winter."

"The birds love this car mate."

I was lost in thought for most of the drive up to the valley. When Meg told me she was expecting, we talked about next year's crop. We just finished breakfast on a bright, Sunday morning and lingered over a second cup of coffee. Little Annie sat in her high-chair making a mess, and the Sunday paper was scattered around. It seemed Sunday mornings were the only times we could talk without arguing. "Next year will be our seventh crop," she said, "and each was better than the one before."

With the money from this one," I said, "I hope to pay off the house, and maybe this should be the last."

"That's your choice, but the last time Reggie visited, he dropped hints he'd like to be a partner. One more would give us a little nest egg."

To my surprise, Reggie knocked on our door the next day. It set me wondering if the timing of his visit was coincidental, or was his becoming a partner predestined. Reggie had qualities I desired. He had good energy, and I trusted him. Where I saw a source of conflict was that we were both fiercely independent and each needed to be in charge. Between the two of us, I was the easier going one. If compared to an element, I was wood, but he was metal. There was something unrelenting about him, and when he announced he wasn't the marrying type, which he did often, I sensed he wasn't rejecting marriage as much as refusing to compromise. Although he never grew a crop commercially, he sounded as if he knew about plants. The question was, could he grow marijuana?

Like other flora, Maryjane needs sun, water, and nutrients. But she is not an ordinary plant. She's like a beautiful woman you wish to possess. If you give a woman what she desires, she'll reward you with her favors. With Maryjane, you desire the high she gives you, and since she and sex are intoxicants and both euphoric, they are similar. Once you possess a beautiful woman, you want to be her only lover. That's only your daydream, because she desires many lovers. It is then the relationship changes to one similar to a pimp and his whore. She'll spread her favors around to those who have the money to pay. It was an exchange I gladly made but with a word of warning. She's narcissistic and demands total devotion. If the grower makes the mistake of seeing her only as a source of profit—she cares little about proceeds—she will turn on him and create havoc. Reggie thinks only of himself, and I understood how important it was that I maintained a high level of involvement in growing the crop, as Maryjane and I have had a long and beautiful love affair.

———◦∕∕◦———

IN THE VALLEY THE NEXT MORNING, REGGIE AND I STOOD AT THE top of the growing area looking down at the sea of giants gently swaying in the breeze. The plants were close to the end of their growing cycle, and although I lived in town and didn't give them as much attention as usual, it looked like another record crop. During the weekend, we pulled flowering males. Reggie loved the valley and was in seventh heaven the whole time, hiking in the cool of the morning and swimming and exploring by the river in the heat of the afternoon. "Next year," he said, "I'll turn the shop over to Amanda and move up in April, but I'll be giving up all the profit from the shop for almost eight months. That's a big hit, mate. I better make some good cash here."

Another reason Meg wouldn't be able to help with the crop was that she started an in-home business boarding veterans who were patients at a nearby V.A. hospital. Some vets preferred living in private homes out in the community for which the government paid a monthly rent. Two vets moved in immediately. The first was Grandpa John. He served in World War Two and was wounded in a battle somewhere in Europe. But his greatest disability was his alcoholism. He was a gentle old soul and loved Little Annie. He told us about his life after the war driving a cab in a big city and always during the night shift. His only reason for working was to earn enough money to purchase a quart of gin each morning. Because of his drinking, he went through several marriages, and his children refused to speak with him. Somehow, the gin didn't kill him, but it left him with brain damage and tremors in both legs. It was difficult watching his legs vibrate uncontrollably.

John-Paul Cernak

The second was also a veteran of the European campaign but with mental problems. Before he moved in, the director at the hospital told Meg he was schizophrenic, although not dangerous. He also told her he relapsed before. I worried about my little Annie's safety. I wanted to talk with Meg about it, but she would only regard anything I said as criticism. I felt so strongly that I had to speak, regardless. With the little one at a friend's house for the night, the opportunity came at dinner the following evening. As usual, our conversation was strained. "I'm having some concerns about the vet with schizophrenia," I said. "Are you sure you want to take the chance?" She looked at me coldly but didn't say anything. "When you're dealing with people with mental problems," I continued, "there could be unforeseen circumstances."

She went to the stove for more food and didn't reply until sitting back down. "I want to get this business off the ground, and he's the only one available."

"I understand your impatience, but you don't want to put our daughter in danger."

"Damn it, Jack," she said, throwing her fork forcefully on the table. "I know what I'm doing. This is my business, so stay out of it."

Her reaction wasn't totally unexpected. From her facial expression and the language she used, I detected jealousy. Was she envious of my thriving picture framing business? I couldn't imagine a wife being offended by her husband's success. Yet the evidence pointed in that direction and added another daunting item to the growing list of Meg's irrationality. To my relief, the vet relapsed immediately after moving in. For the two days he lived with us, he stayed in his room and urinated on the rug. The hospital staff quickly came and took him away. Afterward, two or three others lived with us briefly for a month or two and left. The business of boarding veterans became competitive with many households available. The more her business declined, the more resentful, disagreeable, and irrational she became.

CHAPTER 15

Now that I lived in town, I fully reintegrated into society and kept myself informed nationally and internationally by
listening to the news on the radio, reading newspapers and magazines, and watching informative TV programs. In the summer
of 1980, the country was experiencing high inflation and another
gasoline shortage similar to the one when I was leaving society in
1974. The followers of the Ayatollah Khomeini in Iran were holding fifty-two American hostages, and President Carter's approval
rating was in the cellar. The worst news was that Ronald Reagan
won the Republican nomination for president. We listened to his
radio show each Saturday morning where he expressed open hostility towards the counterculture. He hated anyone who looked or
thought differently and especially anyone who smoked marijuana.
After he said: "If you've seen one redwood tree you've seen them
all," it was easy to understand he cared little for the environment.
I perceived him as dangerous and with little regard for civil rights
or human rights, for that matter, especially after he stated, "Let the
bloodbath begin," when as Governor of California, he advocated
violence in dealing with the student protests at the University of
California at Berkeley and at San Francisco State. It worried me
that someone with his Machiavellian mindset and methods would
be elected President of our country.

On the home front, southern Oregon's economy continued to
expand. Centerville's downtown had no vacancies, and on the other
side of town, ground was broken for a new shopping mall. Huge
piles of old-growth logs filled the yards of lumber mills running

three shifts, and with the lumber industry booming and with marijuana selling at two thousand dollars a pound, money flowed into the economy and kept the cash registers ringing happily in the towns along Interstate-5. Once called Appalachia of the West, Southern Oregon was poor no more.

Bob from the record store stopped in at the shop one afternoon in September filled with enthusiasm. He attended the local junior college and was a drama major. A semi-professional theater group was presenting a play at the school, and students in the drama department received credit for helping stage it. Bob was stage manager for the new production scheduled to open in late winter and run through spring. He rested a stack of textbooks on the counter and sat in the director's chair I had for customers in front of my workbench. "Hey, man!" he said, "You wanna be in a play?"

"Sounds interesting. What's the play?"

"Inherit the Wind. It's about the Scopes Monkey Trial, and several parts would be just right for you. I'll get you a script and give you a head start. Auditions begin in a couple of months followed by eight weeks of rehearsals. It's a commitment though. This theatre group puts on professional productions."

"It's something that I'd love to do, but with Meg close to delivery, I don't think there's much of a chance."

"There's really nothing like working in front of a live audience," he continued, trying to convince me. "I had a leading part last season, and it was one of the few times in my life I really felt alive."

"Let me run it by her."

"By the way, Mom wants you guys over for dinner on Friday."

After framing several pictures for Bob's mother, Sally, we became friends, and she often invited Meg and me to her house on the river for dinner and drinks. Sally was middle-aged and was married to a high official with the DEA. They lived in Washington where all the action was. She talked excitedly about the undercover work and living the highlife with the Washington crowd, but after their divorce with regrets, she lived a secluded life back in the boonies. She didn't smoke weed but knew her son did and that we were growers.

While watching the Tonight Show on TV with Johnny Carson that evening, Meg laughed at several jokes, and it seemed the right moment to tell her about the play, aware of the storm I was about to unleash. As usual, she sat alone in her chair. "Bob stopped in today and Sally invited us to dinner on Friday."

"That's nice. I haven't seen her in a while."

She never looked at me and continued watching the tube. "Bob told me about a play they're presenting at the college. He feels several parts would be just right for me, and I'm thinking of trying out."

She swung around in her chair her lips pressed tightly against her teeth and anger written across her face. "You just don't give a shit about me or your family, do you? How could you even consider it with me pregnant and having all this work taking care of Annie and this big house? You're so inconsiderate, Jack, and I'm sorry I bought you that bike. I know you go for rides just to get out of helping around here."

She reacted as I anticipated, and without another word, I went to bed.

As business at the frame shop increased, I often rode my bike down to the shop after dinner to work a few extra hours. Since both the shop and house were on Jefferson Street, my bike ride was a straight shot down the hill through the downtown and past the courthouse. Going was easy, but returning was all uphill. A long block down from the house, Jefferson became a one-way street coming up. On Thursday evenings, the downtown shops were open, and the area bustled with customers and traffic. All other evenings after six, it was a ghost town, and I could ride down the middle of the street and never see another person or vehicle.

One evening, as I rode the wrong way down the deserted street, a policeman appeared out of nowhere and flagged me down. He was someone I saw before. I remembered him because he was taller, slimmer, and in better shape than the other cops on the town's police force and didn't have the big, fat belly many of the others did. Wearing high boots, a trim uniform, and a strap coming off his shoulder, he looked more military than police. Since I shaved my beard and cut my hair shorter, I thought I removed myself from their hit list. I didn't look hippie anymore, although maybe a little. "Where are you headed?" he asked.

It was none of his business, but I answered his question. "I'm on my way to my business on Jefferson across from the courthouse."

I flashed back to when I hitchhiked in New Mexico and remembered the sheriff who wore a ten-gallon hat and was going to arrest me until he learned I owned a print shop. Police are very status conscious, and owning a business gave me status. Homeless people, minorities, and hippies have little prominence and never do well in dealing with those representing law enforcement. His tone was stern and uncompromising, and to avoid a confrontation, I played his game and acknowledged his authority letting him believe I was intimidated, although thinking he must have more important police work than to harass a citizen for riding a bicycle on an empty street even if it was the wrong way. I considered riding my bicycle more akin to walking than driving a car. Would I be harassed if I walked the wrong way? "Riding the wrong way on a one-way street is against the law," he said.

"Gee officer, I didn't realize."

"I want to see your driver's license."

"I'm not driving a car. Why do you want to see my driver's license?"

"Any tickets will go against your driving record."

"I don't think that's fair."

He gave me a long slow look. "You probably don't deserve a second chance, but I'll let you go this time. If I ever catch you again, I'll write you up."

Pretending to adjust the chain on my bicycle, I waited until his car disappeared around the corner and continued my descent riding down deserted Jefferson Street the wrong way. Once past the downtown, I experienced light traffic and rode up on the sidewalk. About a block from the shop, a squad car with its lights flashing and siren blaring followed closely behind. Pedaling the short distance to the shop, I leaned my bike against the wall and turned to face him. To my surprise, it was a different cop. He was someone I never saw before and was younger, shorter, and seemed unsure of himself. The military guy must have radioed ahead, and the rookie waited in ambush. "I want to see your license," he said.

When I handed it to him, the loathing and disgust I felt for the Centerville police spilled over. "I'm beginning to understand you guys," I said. "You must be hard-up for action. Now you can brag you caught someone bicycling the wrong way on a one-way street. Wow! You are certainly brave. I'm sure they'll put a plaque up for you at city hall and create a holiday each year on this day. Hey! Maybe they'll change the name of the town and rename it after you."

When he finished writing, he was shaking with rage, and the madder the better I liked it. "The bail is seventy-seven dollars," he said when handing me the ticket.

"See you in court," I shot back. He turned and glared at me before getting into his vehicle.

You would have thought I committed murder the way they came after me, and a seventy-seven dollar fine for riding my bike the wrong way was legal extortion. It was the police and the establishment who were illegal and unconstitutional in their harassment and were detrimental to life, liberty, and the pursuit of happiness. When I told Meg about the ticket that evening, she gave me her look of disapproval, and I could see she was pleased I received it. In her logic, my trouble with the cops proved I was a bad person. "You'll learn," she said.

Feeling anger all evening, I tried finding a way to avoid paying a large fine for such an absurd offence. My first solution was to ignore the ticket, but I nixed the idea after remembering they had my license number. To give it breathing room, I let the problem percolate overnight. In the morning, I awoke with the solution. That afternoon I went to the courthouse to schedule a court date. "You must pay the fine first," said the clerk, "before you can appear."

"Have you ever read the Constitution that says people are innocent until proven guilty?"

She gave me a blank stare. "If you win, we'll refund your money, and we accept only cash."

I wasn't surprised at the barriers erected to prevent me from having my day in court. I'm sure they would have made it impossible to appear in court at all and would not have hesitated to suppress people's rights if they thought they could get away with it. They knew once the fines are paid, most people will skip the court appearance and forfeit the money, and working people are reluctant to take a day off. I refused to be deterred, however.

On the morning of my court appearance, I arrived early to learn how the judge operated, and what I learned made me cringe. Most defendants were big logger guys. They stood in front of the judge looking down at the floor thoroughly intimidated and stuttering: Yes Sir, when he asked if they knew why they were there. In each instance, he found them guilty, and most never had a chance to tell their story. The worst part was the huge fines the court levied that were outrageously out of proportion to their misdeeds. In just an hour, the Town's, "Greed Machine," imposed several thousands of dollars in fines, and I began to understand the boys in blue would enforce any law that brought in money regardless of how senseless. "Jack Cernak!" the bailiff called out.

I stood boldly in front of the judge. The young cop stood off to the side. "Are you, Jack Cernak?"

"I am, your honor," I said in a clear, loud voice.

"You are charged with riding a bicycle the wrong way on a one-way street."

When he read the charge, I almost laughed. It sounded almost burlesque, like a comedy routine. You're charged with stepping on a crack and breaking your mother's back, but he wasn't playing a game. This was for real. "How do you plead?"

"Not guilty!"

From his skeptical look, I saw he considered my contesting the citation foolish. He didn't need to hear my side of the story. In his mind, I was guilty, and only by a long stretch of the imagination could I call him a judge. He was a money-changer in the temple.

"The police don't write these citations unless someone's broken the law," he said and turned towards the young policemen. "Explain to the court why you wrote the ticket."

"After he was stopped on upper Jefferson Street by officer Beal and given a warning, he continued to break the law by proceeding to ride the wrong way all the way down Jefferson past the court-house."

"How can you claim that you're innocent?" he asked, turning towards me. "Both officers saw you."

"Because I wasn't on the street. I rode on the sidewalk."

"Riding on the sidewalk is against the law."

"Your Honor!" I said, in a harsh and scolding tone that surprised even me. "I wasn't cited for riding on the sidewalk."

He recoiled from my censure and seemed confused. He was unaccustomed to anyone fighting back, and I pressed my advantage. "I am charged with riding a bicycle the wrong way on a one-way street, but your Honor, how can I be charged with riding the wrong way when the street's a two-way street. The citation has the address of my shop, and as you know, Jefferson becomes a two-way street at Taylor." I held it up above my head and pointed to it. "This ticket is invalid."

He turned white and stammered something unintelligible about law-abiding citizens in an attempt to make me feel guilty. I wasn't buying any of it. He didn't have any choice and dismissed the citation. After I was issued papers for my refund, I exited the courtroom through a side door into a small courtyard. Standing on a balcony across the walkway was the young cop. No one else was around. "I'll get you!" he said, in a loud, threatening voice.

I smiled. He compounded his defeat. Instead of just losing in court, he made a fool of himself and added icing to my victory cake. When I reclaimed my money, the same clerk waited on me and frowned when she handed me the check. How they hated to give my money back.

I felt jubilant. It was a small but satisfying victory for me and for the people of Centerville, although the win was short-lived. Ronald Reagan won the presidency in November, and I could feel the gathering clouds and the coming storm. When I told Meg about my victory, I could see disappointment on her face she couldn't conceal. She actually hoped I would lose. The old warning that to be with her would lead to disaster had mostly stopped. On that day, it came back even stronger, and the new warning—that she would bolt and abandon me in a crisis—was already happening. With a daughter and another child on the way, I was even more deeply committed. Seeing no way to extricate myself, I felt trapped and had trouble sleeping that night.

———⟨ೲ⟩———

THE AUTUMN OF 1980 WAS AN OREGON CLASSIC, WITH WARM temperatures and sunny days. I harvested the marijuana in late October, and from the size and quality of the crop, I felt optimistic I could easily make the final payment on the house. As soon as the plants dried, I launched into cleaning and bagging. If I finished early, I intended to make a quick trip to the city to give Reggie and Rick their supply and call on a few customers. The pressure was on for me to return before the start of the busy holiday season at the frame shop. I worked alone in the valley for two days.

Now that I no longer lived there full-time, I saw everything with fresh eyes. The days were clear with an autumn crispness. The leaves of the ash, maple, and alder trees lining the valley displayed reds and golds. I loved the smells of drying marijuana, the radiant warmth from the woodstove, and the way the October late afternoon sun bathed the barn in a soft, golden glow and highlighted the natural wood tones. But the feeling of contentment I sought eluded me.

Meg came up the last day to help finish. As daylight faded, we sat cross-legged on the floor and cleaned plants. It felt like old times but with a sad feeling in knowing this was the last year we'd share this experience. Little Annie sat on the floor behind us surrounded by her favorite toys and near the woodstove—in almost the place where she was born fifteen months earlier. As usual, we packaged the buds and stored the large leaves in plastic bags in the cellar. Along with those from previous years, they now totaled ten.

We hadn't seen Jake in some time and knew he wouldn't visit unexpectedly as he always managed to do at harvest times. The Forest Service transferred him to another ranger district, and living mostly in town severed what little connection we had with the people in the valley. I never saw anyone, except Hughie, and he was looking old and tired. He drove up and down the valley road each morning as he always had, but now he waved as if there never was a problem between us. Ginger went back to LA to find a new mate after her marriage to Bob ended.

In the first week of November, I made a quick trip to San Francisco and stayed with Rick at his house in Pacifica. Autumns were the sunniest and warmest time of the year on the California Coast. As temperatures in the central valley cooled, the fog strayed out to sea. Rick visited Oregon the previous year and remembered what it was like when I talked about growing the marijuana. His eyes drifted up and off to the left remembering what it was like when I talked about spending time in that beautiful valley deep in the mountains.

I was out of the house early, and my first call was to see Candice an old girlfriend. For the past several years, she was in a relationship with Roger and a partner in his painting business in Marin County, where they painted houses for the well-to-do people living in the upscale towns surrounding the city. Their rented house was on Spring Street high above the town where it was always warm and sunny and in a neighborhood of large houses built far apart among giant eucalyptus trees that always seemed to be shedding their bark. It was Tuesday, and I didn't expect to find anyone home. Surprisingly, Candice answered the door. She gave me a strange look. "Holy Cow, Jack! Where the hell've you been? What happened to you last year? I put cash away to buy some weed, and you're a no-show."

She was tall, slim, and athletic and had a strong, deep voice. Yet she was feminine. We were born the same year, and it must have been a generational thing, because we saw the world similarly. What I liked about her was she always told me what she thought and held nothing back. I took a deep breath before I spoke. "It's a long story, Candice, but hell, I'm here now. How come you're home? Don't you guys work anymore?"

"We're between jobs, and business is slow. California's in recession."

Roger sat in the kitchen finishing breakfast and gave me a surprised look. He was a no-nonsense guy who worked hard and had his trip together running his business in the underground economy and taking all the money for his painting in cash under the table. After sharing a joint over coffee, he went into the bedroom and came out with money for two ounces, while Candice made calls to friends asking if any were interested in purchasing some good smoke. On her second or third call, she spoke with a woman who was a taker.

She lived in a large house in Tiburon and was tall, slim and middle-aged dressed in a business suit. Her hair was tied in a bun. Through an open doorway, I could see an elegant crystal chandelier hanging in her dining room. She led me through a lavishly furnished living room to an office. She was an attorney, and the entire wall behind her desk was a bookcase filled with leather-bound law books. Candice said she could be trusted. After taking a hit from a joint, she sat back silently. Suddenly, she perked up. "I like it," she said. "It might be some of the best I've smoked. It's very stony. Yet

I feel mellow and uplifted. Candice says you have a goodly amount. Could you sell me three pounds?"

Wow! Feeling excited I hit pay dirt, I reminded myself to ask top dollar and not give it away. It was the best weed to be had anywhere. After we agreed on a price, she said something I didn't want to hear. "For such a large amount, it's not possible to give you cash. I'll have to give you a check."

I must have given her a strange look, because she immediately spoke up. "You can be assured its good."

"It's not the check; cashing it is the problem."

"If you go immediately to my bank, I'm sure there won't be any problem. If there's any question, have them call me."

Her bank, in San Rafael, had a long tradition in California. Employees talked among themselves in the nearly empty branch. I handed the check to a teller, and her eyes widened at seeing the amount. "Do you have any identification?" she asked.

I handed her my Oregon Drivers License.

"Do you have any other identification?"

"How much identification do I need?"

"Usually, when we receive a check this large, we require several pieces. Do you have a credit card or something with your address, like a water or electric bill?"

"I live in Oregon. Why would I carry around a water or electric bill? And I don't have any credit cards."

I remembered why I hated banks. "One moment please."

She walked away and after several long minutes reappeared followed by a man dressed in a white shirt and tie and whose expression I didn't like. "This is Mr. Paulson our branch manager."

Although I was dressed neatly, my hair was longer than average, and my bushy moustache and clothes all screamed counterculture. The look on his face and his vibe said he didn't like people like me. He stood behind a short fence holding my check. I moved in front of him. "I'm sorry, we can't cash this check without additional identification."

"The issuer said that if there's a problem, you should call her, and she'd verify the check is legitimate."

"I'm sorry, I can't do that."

He probably suspected the check was for a drug purchase and felt justified in refusing to cash it. If I was wearing a suit and tie and was dressed more as he was, he would have fallen over himself to cash it even if he knew the money came from robbing the poor. I was finished with tolerating people like him. He was a big guy, and because of his size, he probably felt safe and never expected what a skinny guy like me would say next. I moved closer until our faces were inches apart. "You pompous, hypocrite, son of a bitch," I said, with all the vehemence I could muster.

My extreme insult jolted him, and he drew back in shock. All the blood drained out of his face. He probably discriminated many time before and assumed I would accept it passively. I wanted to punch him, but that wouldn't have been wise with a truck loaded with marijuana. Taking the check out of his hand, I walked out. On my return to Oregon, the bank where I had my shop account cashed it without question. The trip was one of the best financially, and I assigned all the money towards the balloon payment on the house.

In early December, the world was shocked and saddened with the news of Beatle, John Lennon's death. As a memorial, I framed his picture from the White Album and put it in the window of the gallery. For weeks, I listened only to his music and to the Beatles, and although I mourned his death, it rekindled the joys and the spirit of the 1960s.

———

ONE OF THE FEW PLEASURES REMAINING FOR ME WAS GOING INTO the woods to cut firewood. I always felt restored afterwards. I cut wood for the house in town that had a large wood-burning furnace in the basement, and for the shop, and a lesser amount for the barn now that we went to the valley only occasionally. It seemed Meg lost her enthusiasm for living there. I didn't blame her. It was more difficult caring for an infant. When the winter rains began and prevented me from riding my bike, I went to the shop evenings to work and usually stopped at the bar for a beer afterward. The bar people were more satisfying. We hardly spoke, and when we did, it always ended in an argument. That winter, I went to the valley mostly alone. The days were cold, dark, and rainy, and I experienced such longings, I'd want to cry.

Christmas 1980 was really Little Annie's first. She was much too young to understand what it was all about the first year. I can't remember ever feeling such joy at having the little person in my life, and although my relationship with Meg remained bleak, we signed a truce to keep argument-free over the holidays. The treaty was short-lived, however. Over breakfast on New Year's Eve, I asked if she would like to go out for a drink and bring in the New Year together. "You can drink pop, and I'll have a beer."

"I don't want to go out. I'll probably be in bed before midnight."

"As you choose. I'll go by myself and bring in the New Year with friends."

"You can't go out, Jack," she said.

"Why not?"

"Because I don't want you to."

Something inside me snapped, and pushing away from the table, I stood and pointed at her. "Go screw yourself," I said, "and I'm finished. I'm moving out."

I gathered my clothes, threw my mattress into the truck, and moved everything to the shop. All day I felt liberated and questioned why I hadn't done it sooner. I brought in the New Year at the bar, danced my ass off until closing, and staggered back to the shop after drinking too many beers. Early the next morning, a banging aroused me from a deep sleep. As my consciousness drifted up from what seemed like miles below, it was light when I opened my eyes, and I was still a little drunk. The sound was coming from someone banging on the door. It persisted after I pulled the covers over my head. My clock read 8 AM, and it wasn't even fully light yet. Damn! Who could it be at this hour? I crawled to the edge of the partition covering the front windows and peeked around the corner. It was Meg, and my little daughter, Annie, was with her. I unlocked the door letting them in. "I've been knocking for over ten minutes."

"What did you expect? It was New Year's Eve, and I had a few drinks."

I gave Little Annie a hug. "Hi, Sweetie."

"How come you're sleeping at the shop, Papa?"

"It's a long story, sweetheart. What do you want, Meg?"

"Let's go for breakfast. I'll buy."

Although I knew her coming was a ploy to get me to return without making changes, the desire to be with my daughter won me over, and I proved my point. Even though I was gone only one day, the act of leaving sent a message that I no longer accepted the conditions she dictated. "I'll go take a shower," I said.

CHAPTER 16

1981

At the end of February and with months to spare, I made the final balloon payment, and the house was ours free and clear, although I felt no joy as my relationship with Meg continued to.deteriorate. Around that time, I moved out twice more and on one occasion lived at the shop over a week.

One evening as daylight faded, I paced back and forth next to the front windows feeling lonely and frustrated and watched a woman ride past on her bicycle. It surprised me to see anyone on a bike, because it was cold. Nighttime temperatures were expected to dip into the low twenties and my wood stove was cranked up. The woman was someone I saw before, and I knew from the clothes she wore and from her masculine looks that she was a lesbian. She chained her bike to a post and went into the Happy Hour tavern. I had a feeling.

I closed the shop a few minutes early and went to the bar for a drink. It was the Saturday evening crowd loud and rambunctious. Many people were there all afternoon and were already drunk. I walked along the bar greeting a few people I knew until I found an empty stool where I could watch her playing pool with several loggers. She was short and busty, in her early twenties, and dressed in pants and vest her long hair tucked under a cap, and she was lovely. The loggers were straight guys and liked their women more feminine. She was much too different for them to be turned on by her masculine looks no matter how delicious the woman was beneath the façade. When she sat on the stool next to me, everything seemed to be falling into place. "Did you win?" I asked.

She glanced at me but didn't smile or say anything. If my feeling was wrong, I wouldn't waste my time and looked around for another empty bar stool. Then, she turned and looked at me. "Aren't you the guy who runs the picture framing business next door?"

Maybe my feeling was right. "I'm the one. My name's Jack."

"I'm Sylvia. I have some pictures I'd like framed, but I hear it's expensive."

"Well, it is expensive, but not for what you get. What kind of pictures are they?"

"They're color photos of the woman I'll be living with. I'm a lesbian, and I'm moving back east in a couple of months to live with her. I'd like to give her the photos as a gift."

"Where back east?"

"Baltimore."

"That's a long way from Oregon."

"Yeah! It's OK," she said, and turned away, her voice filled with frustration and anger. "People around here don't understand people like me."

"Can I buy you a beer?"

My offer seemed to soften her discontent, and she turned and looked at me with curiosity. "Sure, why not?"

"Two beers, bartender. What size are the photos?"

"They're five by seven's, and I'd like to have all four put into one frame. Can you do that?"

"I can cut four holes in a mat."

"I'll bring them in sometimes."

"How about this evening?"

She turned and gave me a strange look. "What do you mean this evening?"

"I'm living at the shop right now, and if you bring them in this evening, I'll buy you dinner."

My offer surprised her, but she quickly countered. "Howdiya know I was hungry?"

"I can see it in your eyes." She gave me a knowing smile. "Let's get out of here," I said.

We chug-a-lugged our beers the bartender just set before us, and when we got up to leave, several loggers playing pool rested their cue sticks on the floor watching us as we walked out. "Wait," she said. "What about my bike?"

"I'll throw it into the truck and drop it off at your house."

I was unfamiliar with her part of town, and after she put the bike into the garage, we drove off into the night, the pretense of framing pictures already forgotten. To minimize the possibility of running into someone I knew, I drove north on I-5 ten miles to the next town. Neither of us spoke. Our destination loomed ahead after driving over the crest of a mountain, and the lights of Barley Hill appeared. It wasn't actually a town but a cluster of motels, restaurants, and gas stations built along the freeway. I remembered one restaurant served good hamburgers. Afterward, at a western bar featuring live music—where all the guys wore cowboy hats and western boots and the women skirts—we luckily grabbed two stools in the crowded bar when the people sitting there suddenly got up and left. We quickly became the focus of two couples sitting across from us that snickered and laughed among themselves. I ignored them, but I could feel Sylvia's distress from their taunting. It was too noisy to talk, so I sat back and listened to the music. After a couple of beers, she turned and leaned towards me. "Let's get out of here," she said.

Under a canopy of stars, I drove back to Centerville in under ten minutes and stopped in the parking lot behind the shop sitting in the warm truck. I looked for hesitancy but saw none when I said: "Let's go inside."

I didn't turn on any lights. After adding firewood to the stove, it felt cozy in the semi-darkness with enough light to see coming in off the street. We could see out, but no one could see in. Since entering, we hadn't touched each other. Suddenly, like two magnets, our bodies attracted, and we came together locked in a passionate kiss. Hugging and kissing and holding each other tight, we showered together and afterward gave each other the affection, pleasure, and acceptance we sought and needed. Like two souls wandering lost in the wilderness, we somehow found each other. I felt beautiful the next day surprised I could still feel good about myself after feeling ugly all those months living with Meg. A few days later, I moved back into the house, and it seemed she missed me. Quickly her animosity returned even stronger. If it were not for the little girl and the unborn child, I would have packed and left. Pressed against the wall, I could back no further.

⸻ ❧ ⸻

I FELT HIS EXCITEMENT WHEN BOB CAME INTO THE SHOP AND stood next to the woodstove shaking rain off his jacket on a cold, wet, and wintry day in early February. "What's up, man?" I asked.

"Rehearsals started for the play, and a cast member quit. I told Roger about you. He's directing and also teaches drama at the college. You don't have to try out or anything like that. Just come to rehearsal this evening, and you're in. It's not a large part, but it's meaty."

"There's little chance. The baby's due next month."

"Don't make any decision now. Just come tonight and see what it's like."

I went to the college that evening only to observe. Meg believed I was at the shop working. The college was at the outskirts of town and was a complex of five or six large, modern buildings on fifty acres with beautiful landscaping and all paid for from timber revenues. The auditorium was in the main building with seating for around three hundred. Rehearsal was in progress, and the theater was dark, except for the lighted stage. The stage set was a street scene and looked authentic. The director sat in the audience. He had an open notebook on his lap, and was surrounded by several

The Odyssey of a Hippie Marijuana Grower   301

assistants. I observed until the break. "Hi! Are you Roger?"

"I'm Roger. You must be Jack. Bob told me about you," and he handed me a script. "The part's not that long, and you shouldn't have any problem picking it up. I've underlined it for easy identification. Read it over and join the cast after the break. We'll begin on page forty-five." He stood and shouted. "People! I want to introduce Jack Cernak. He's our new Jesse Dunlap."

Everyone applauded.

When he handed me the script, I became aware he assumed I was accepting the part. I guess I let him make the decision for me, and for the next five days, I went to rehearsals with Meg believing I was at the shop working.

In the past, I would have brought home a bottle of wine to mellow her before making such an important announcement, but she wasn't drinking, because of her pregnancy. Saturday evening I thought would be a good time to tell her. All the vets moved out, and Little Annie was asleep. As usual, she sat alone in her chair watching TV.

"Remember," I said, "a couple of months ago, Bob asked if I wanted to be in the play they're putting on at the college. Well, he dropped in and told me that a cast member quit. To make the story short, I was offered the part. For the past week, I wasn't at the shop working but at the college rehearsing. It was something that happened unexpectedly, and it's what I want to do."

She spun around in her chair anger written on her face. "You took a part in a play with me ready to deliver?" She held on to the arms of the chair to steady herself shaking from anger. "I'm the one holding this family together working day and night, and I forbid you from being in that play."

In a hope of avoiding a blow up, I started towards the door, but before I could leave, I turned, and my words came bursting out. Feeling burned out with having my life in constant turmoil, I spoke in a deadly calm. "You've always exaggerated your importance and undervalued mine, and I'm sick of you and your arrogant and manipulative ways. Nothing I do is good enough, and you're right, I've reached a point that I don't care."

She was standing when she spoke. "I knew from the start I made a mistake marrying you."

"You've got it wrong, sweetheart. I'm the one who made the mistake, and you're right; I don't give a shit."

"Get out of my house!" she screamed. "Get out of my house!"

I moved back into the shop that night. I moved there so often that when my marriage finally ended, it seemed anticlimactic, although with a feeling that it was final this time, and I was saving my life. With my days busy at the shop and evenings filled with rehearsals, I had little time to think about the breakup—relieved I was finally free of her and the tension between us over. When I visited my little daughter, I would put her in her walker or on the child seat of my bike and quickly leave. On the morning of March 19, a few hours before the spring equinox, I received a call. Meg was in labor and close to delivery. I remember thinking that he was early. He wasn't supposed to be born until April and would be a child of winter. Closing the shop, I went immediately to the house.

I arrived just before noon on a cold, windless day with a lead-gray, yellowish sky that felt oppressive. Meg's midwife, Debbie, was already there. This time, she was accompanied by two assistants and a high-tech fetal monitoring system with listening devices attached to Meg's stomach. Jamie was there as her coach. They became close friends, and I flashed back to the day I introduced them thinking I was crazy. Now I understood why I did it. With Little Annie on my lap, we took our place on the floor at the foot of the mattress. Meg's contractions were coming at regular intervals, and she quickly dilated to ten centimeters.

As this was her second delivery, I assumed it would be routine and not the ordeal she experienced the first time. She began pushing, and the fetus slowly moved into the birth canal. The process was going smoothly, and her pain was also much less this time. Everything was under control with Debbie there, and I relaxed.

Without warning, my emotions were quickly turned upside down when she suddenly announced the fetus was in distress, and her words to Meg expressed the utmost urgency.

"We're monitoring the heartbeat that should be around a hundred and fifty beats per minute and it's already down to ninety. You better push hard and get that baby out of there fast."

"What's wrong?" I asked.

"We're not sure. My guess is the umbilical cord is wrapped around his neck."

I remembered how calm Debbie was during the first delivery and never indicated there was a problem even when the situation seemed dire. Now I heard alarm in her voice and saw apprehension in her body language, and the promise of an easy delivery quickly evaporated. Meg increased her pushing and moaned in pain. She passed out but quickly regained consciousness. After fifteen minutes, his heart rate dropped below fifty beats. "Push harder," Debbie urged.

With everyone in trance watching as Meg withering in pain fought to save her unborn child, and the scene was somehow reminiscent of a Greek Tragedy play with Jamie kneeling behind her glassy eyed and no help. After many minutes and many pushes, his head finally showed, and Debbie finessed him out. But something was wrong; he looked strange as if he was wearing a mask. "He has his veil," she said.

Reaching under his chin, she lifted off a membrane covering his face. I recoiled in horror when I realized his skin was a hideous blue with splotches of white, and he wasn't breathing. She lifted him by his legs and spanked his bottom. But he didn't respond. I remembered how the little girl was screaming before she was even fully born. There was no response when she spanked his bottom a second time. Even after massaging him and spanking his bottom a third time, his little body remained lifeless lying on the bed.

The tension in the room rose to an unbearable level, and it seemed an eternity had passed since he was born. How long could he last outside the womb without breathing? Did we get him this far only to lose him at the last minute? As I watched in agony, his chance of survival dwindling, I'm not sure what I did next was something that came from my own volition or compelled by an outer force. Without a conscious thought, I climbed up onto the bed next to Debbie, and grabbing his arm, I shook it. "Come on Paul!" I exhorted. Crying and overcome with emotion, I quickly left the room. As I entered the hallway next to the bedroom, I heard his first cries. He was alive and would make it.

Later that afternoon as the frenzy of the birth subsided, I experienced an overwhelming joy that I had a son but with a bittersweet awareness I was shut out from being with him. I saw into the future that Meg would resent any influence I would have with the children and destroy it.

As Debbie stood next to the door ready to leave, I asked her about something I was curious. "What does it mean when someone is born with their veil?"

She smiled. "Some people believe it's a sign of good luck and the person has a special calling."

"What do you believe?"

"I don't know," she replied.

Sitting on the gallery floor in the dark that evening with my back against the wall listening to music and reliving the day's events, I understood Paul's reluctance to enter the world. We argued savagely throughout her pregnancy. It must have injected toxic emotions into his system far worse than any drug. There was no evidence the umbilical cord was wrapped around his neck, or for that matter, any other physical problem. He believed he wasn't wanted and already left his body, His spirit was in the room watching. When I crawled up onto the bed next to Debbie and called out his name, he learned he was wanted. The act of grabbing his arm and shaking it gave him the energy to be born into the physical world.

THE PLAY AT THE COLLEGE WAS A SMASHING SUCCESS, AND I WAS surprised so many people in a small lumbering community appreciated good theater. The local newspaper gave us a five-star review. All performance were a sell-out, along with several added shows. Several ladies in the cast asked me out, and I accepted every offer that helped keep my mind off of the break-up. After a slow start, Paul was gaining weight and was becoming more responsive each day. Thankfully, she didn't prevent me from seeing the children.

Business was brisk at the frame shop through February, and it looked like another financially successful year. With little warning, traffic died in March. The rest of the country was in recession, and I knew it would eventually arrive in Oregon. I was at a loss to explain why it happened so suddenly. I learned that the Federal Reserve raised interest rates to fifteen percent at Ronald Reagan's directive, and housing and other construction throughout the country came to a screeching halt. When the demand for lumber stopped, mills shut down and laid-off their workers plunging the economy into deep recession. The downturn was late arriving in Oregon, but when it came, it was in spades.

With half the stores closed gutting the downtown, I saw fewer shoppers each passing week. On Thursday evenings when the shops were open, I could fire a cannon down the street and not hit anyone. As the recession deepened, people lost their homes to foreclosure, and red tags appeared in windows with as many as five or six empty on each block. Property values plummeted, and as the town emptied, garage sales were everywhere. If you had money, it was a bonanza. A whole house of furniture could be purchased for pennies on the dollar. "Please buy something," they pleaded. "All I need is a few bucks for gas, so I can get my family out of here and go where I can find a job."

Feeling people's pain so intensely, I had trouble sleeping nights, and although the situation was critical after the mills closed, what kept the economy from plunging into total depression was marijuana money. Luckily, I paid off the Jefferson Street house and Meg and the children were safe. She had enough money saved to keep her going for a while, and I pledged money from the next crop so she wouldn't need to find a job. After the initial slowdown, enough business came into the shop that allowed me to stay open and pay my bills. At least I had a place to live, along with five pounds of bud from last year's crop and ten large plastic bags filled with leaf stashed in the cellar of the barn that could be converted into cash. I hoped the next crop with Reggie as my partner would see us through what I felt would be a long and difficult economic downturn.

⸎

Reggie arrived in early April and stayed at the shop a week before moving up to the valley. He.connected with Wanda and promised he would come to town every now and then to be with her. We left for the valley on Saturday evening. I would return Wednesday and leave him isolated in the mountains four days each week without a vehicle. He was an extreme extrovert and needed constant stimulation. It worried me he would have difficulty adjusting to the solitude. With all the other things on my mind, I didn't give it much thought after my initial moment of concern. He would have to work it out for himself.

I was in the valley only a few times that winter, and when we arrived, the barn felt strange and filled with ghosts. When I grabbed an old jacket hanging on a hook, a bat flew out and escaped through a hole I hadn't discovered. He probably lived in it all winter. While inspecting the growing area the first morning, Reggie pointed to an area along section three where I piled brush to keep out deer. "If we open up the area by moving the barrier back," he said, "we'll have room for more plants."

After several hours of work, enough new space was liberated to accommodate twenty-five additional plants.

The next day, while filling paper milk and juice cartons with planting soil and laying them out on the floor of the barn, it was obvious the little greenhouse I used since the first spring was inadequate to hold the additional plants. "We have no choice, mate," he said. "We'll have to build a new one."

I hauled in the lumber the following week, and we launched into constructing it against the south wall of the barn. It was of solar design and was three times larger than the old one. I felt encouraged at how well Reggie and I worked together. We finished work each afternoon around three and enjoyed the remainder of the afternoon smoking and drinking. Reggie liked his beer. "A few beers takes the edge off, mate," he'd say.

<hr />

NOW THAT THE PERFORMANCES OF THE PLAY WERE FINISHED AND with business slow at the shop, I had too much time on my hands and began to dwell on the breakup. I never anticipated having children would affect me as deeply, and I wasn't prepared for the strong feelings of loss. Furthermore, I was convinced Meg was emotionally unstable and worried she would psychologically damage the children unless I somehow maintained a strong influence. It seemed my prayers were answered after a bill passed in the Oregon Legislature to allow joint custody, only to have the governor veto it under pressure from women's groups giving Meg total control. She let me know unequivocally there was little possibility she'd let me have any voice in raising the children. "Give you joint custody? You must be kidding me, Jack!"

After living with Meg for many years and learning who she was and what she was like, I knew I could never live with her again. On the other hand, I also knew my only hope of having any influence on how the children were raised was to reconcile. The dilemma caused me to vacillate and put me into a state of limbo. I was stuck in an in-between place, not in the marriage but not out of it either. After hearing repeatedly from her I was a depraved and unworthy person and the sole cause of the break-up, I began to believe it. After all, I wasn't always the model partner.

Going to the valley each week was a diversion distracting me and helped relieve the pain. Reggie's enthusiasm rekindled my passions. Mornings, we took long walks to the back of the valley or down to the river while having long conversations. In most things, we saw the world similarly, and our partnership was developing into a friendship. He noticed how quiet I was. "You can't let yourself get down, mate. Birds are like streetcars. If you miss one, there's another right behind."

"It isn't the bird I miss. It's the chicks."

I brought Little Annie with me that week, and she rode on my shoulders during our walk. "Giddy-up, Papa," she said, urging me to walk faster. "You're such a slow horsey."

Reggie informed me that morning that one of his girlfriends was coming up from California in two weeks for a visit. We scheduled to begin planting that week, and the timing of her visit didn't feel right. "You think it's a good idea for her to be here while we're planting?"

"It's already set, mate."

When I drove in from town, they were standing outside in front of the barn. I met her before. "Hey! mate! You remember Bonnie."

We didn't hug. "It's nice to see you, I said. "It's been a while."

She was short and slim and wore her short black hair in bangs across her forehead. She was stylishly dressed in two hundred dollars a pair designer jeans and drove a new, black BMW. After seeing her, most people would agree she was hot. What you learned about her immediately was that she was outspoken, and what she said usually made her look good while making others look not so good. Even though she was attractive, I usually avoided her, because of her arrogant and aloof attitude. Since she was Reggie's girlfriend, I tried to keep an open mind, but I sensed I was in for a difficult time. "I see you're still driving that little beat-up pickup," she said. "I thought you were a big-time dope grower."

"I'm sure my little truck feels hurt when you speak about her that way, and by the way, your Beamer is parked in my spot."

When I found my parking space blocked, I drove a short distance past the barn and parked on the shoulder of the road. After greeting her, I walked back to the truck and opened the passenger side door. Little Annie climbed out. She was napping when I pulled in and didn't want to wake her. Taking her hand, we walked back toward where they stood. "Who's that woman, Papa?" she asked, looking up at me.

"She's a friend of Reggie's."

Bonnie's arrival didn't help improve my mood. As I watched them hug and kiss, it increased my pain knowing they would be intimate that night, and I was alone and had no one. Hearing them talk about their busy lives in California, going to the symphony, attending performances of the Russian, Bolshoi Ballet, and seeing the latest movies, they seemed so much more sophisticated than I was. I listened to classical music and went to the opera when I lived in the city, but after eight years isolated in the mountains and residing for a short time in a small lumbering community, the awareness I was a simple country boy amplified my feelings of inadequacy.

That afternoon, I drove the tractor up the hill and rototilled the soil in preparation for planting. The job took less than two hours. It was in contrast to the weeks of hard work using a shovel. As I worked the soil, the little girl dug with her small shovel and pail. Bonnie and Reggie stood around watching. On my second pass, she took a camera out from her purse and snapped a picture of me riding on the tractor. I stopped next to them. "No pictures, please! Remember, what we're doing here is illegal."

"What's the matter, Jack?" she retorted. "Are you paranoid or something? Poor boy's afraid of a few snapshots." They both laughed.

She didn't take any more photos of me riding on the tractor, but the remainder of the afternoon was an avalanche of picture taking. They took shots of the barn, the marijuana growing in the new greenhouse—with greenery covering the floor from wall to wall—and of each other. They voted me down each time I sounded the alarm that taking photographs was asking for trouble. In fact, they rebuked me repeatedly whenever I disagreed with either of them even on minor issues. They had to be right and made sure to let me know I was wrong. At first, I said nothing not wanting to create a hostile environment. I quickly understood they interpreted my silence as weakness and became even more insufferable. I fought back counterattacking fed up with their self-importance. "Your judgment is impaired," said Reggie, "by living isolated too long. The world is no longer the way you see it, mate."

"On the contrary, isolation has given me a clarity of mind unavailable to those living in the noise of society."

There was nothing I said or did they approved of, and I quickly understood from Bonnie's criticisms and from her attitude that she considered herself elite and looked down in contempt at everyone else. I wasn't surprised to learn she thought of herself that way. It was Reggie I felt disillusioned about when I realized he was the same. His demeanor changed, and he turned hostile after she arrived. He was suddenly a person I didn't know. We connected because he successfully moved product. As a more complete picture of who he was surfaced, I realized I made a mistake in choosing him as my partner. For my three days in the valley, the atmosphere was hostile and combative and not the spiritual experience planting marijuana always was. They degraded the sacred with their loud, opinionated arrogance.

The next day, while Reggie and I planted up on the hill, Bonnie minded Little Annie down in the barn. She suddenly appeared looking frazzled. "Jack Cernak," she screamed. "Come down and do something with your daughter. She absolutely won't mind me."

When I entered the barn, the little girl played calmly with her toys. "Bonnie says you won't mind her."

"I don't like her, Papa," she said in a determined voice.

I laughed. I hadn't meant to but couldn't help myself.

In the weeks following, my relationship with Reggie improved, although it never went back to the way it was before Bonnie's visit. That the crop was in and growing was the only good news. The weather warmed, and it looked like another beautiful Oregon summer. What gave me pause was that whenever I came in from town, Reggie had all the work done, and I saw no way of mitigating Bonnie's damaging influence at planting time. Furthermore, I was distressed by how he watered the plants.

Since installing the gravitational watering system, I walked around the hillside moving hoses from plant to plant while giving individual attention to each plant. Without consulting me, he changed everything and dug a shallow trench between plants. All he had to do was run the water at the top, and as it ran down, each plant received water. It was ingenious. I considered doing something similar but rejected the idea aware running water in open trenches caused soil erosion. I agonized and felt sick by what he did. It was my growing spot, and he had no right to change it. The growing area was a sacred place given to me by the Spirits, and I was responsible for its care and protection. He watered the plants quickly and was involved with them only inasmuch as they would give him profit. The summer of 1981 was the low point in my life, and I was having difficulty keeping my life together. To avoid another confrontation, I said nothing.

When I drove in late one day in the middle of August and found the barn empty, I knew Reggie would be up in the growing area. Catching the late afternoon sun, the towering cedars up in the ancient forest cast long shadows down the path, and giant marijuana plants greeted me when I entered the growing area. Instead of feeling elated on how good they looked, I felt like a foreigner. Reggie took over completely, and I was redundant. The effects of losing my children and the place that sustained me spiritually all those years was devastating to my psyche. I drove in late, because I didn't even want to come into the valley and was aware how much I disliked him. His controlling personality making me feel I needed him was similar to Meg's and was sucking the life out of me the way heroin does to an addict. Growing marijuana was more than just a way to earn money. His willingness to log all the trees, catch all the fish, and kill all the buffalo to make a profit was abhorrent to my Indian nature. I quickly blocked out my feelings when he emerged from behind the plants. "Hey, Matey!"

Wearing only shorts his body tanned and his hair bleached from the sun, with a worried look, he told me about a plane that flew over: "It circled a bunch of times and came in so low it almost scraped the top of me head. I hid in the bushes and don't think they saw me. Could it be the authorities?"

"Not to worry," I said, brushing off the incident after I remembered what the sheriff said the first season about not looking for it. "We had planes fly over every year. Probably a fire suppression crew out on a jaunt. If there're no fires, they get bored easily."

He relaxed after I assured him there was no problem. "Some of the plants are flowering," he said.

We harvested fifteen males that afternoon and hung them upside down in the dark on the first floor of the new house. That evening, he suggested we go drinking the next day and hit a few bars. "Business is bad at the shop," I said, being evasive, "and I don't have extra cash these days." I was hardly able to get out of bed mornings, and the last thing I needed was to go drinking. Moreover, he handled liquor far better than I did, and I would pay the price if I went. "Relax, mate, this one's on me."

Instead of being firm, I gave in again. "Where do you want to go?"

"Let's drive to Centerville, hit a few bars, and on the way back stop at the Tiller Tavern."

After drinking at several saloons in Centerville, we headed back in early afternoon. The Tiller Tavern was just past the Ranger Station over the bridge, and when we pulled into the parking lot, I was already feeling pretty good. Dorothy and Chubby had sold, and I was there only once or twice after Glen, the new owner, took over. The day was hot and sunny, and I quickly headed inside for the cool air-conditioning. Something delayed Reggie, and I entered ahead of him.

The new proprietor sat behind the bar talking with two customers. I walked past and pulled out a stool ready to sit. He came out from behind the counter and pointed at me. "You're not allowed in here," he said. "Get out!"

I looked at him as if he was mad. "What the hell have I done?"

He never answered, because when he saw Reggie walking in behind me, he went behind the bar and came out holding a shotgun and pointed it at him. "As for you, you son of a bitch, I'll blow your fucking head off if you ever touch my woman again."

I froze and looked around for something to hide behind if he should start shooting. After a long tense moment, he lowered the gun. I quickly walked past them and out the door. Since his arrival in April, Reggie never talked about the four days he spent alone each week. I assumed he was spending them quietly in the valley; instead, he was on an ego trip that put him, the crop, and me in jeopardy. "The bird said she wanted to play," was all he said about the incident. "Let's stop for a couple of six packs at the Tiller Store and take them back with us."

I awoke the next day with a terrible hangover. After sleeping on the rug, I remembered seeing Reggie passed out on the couch. I lived in a fog for most of the day my head throbbing. It was evening before I could eat. On a warm, sublimely beautiful, summer evening, we ate dinner outside on a small table behind the barn, the air filled with a delightful scent of wild flowers growing up in the woods. We lingered outside until after sunset. As daylight faded, the heavens became a massive blanket of twinkling lights. I learned the Milky Way filled the sky above the valley in late August and early September. Then to my amazement and delight, the sky exploded into torrents of reds, violets, and greens. For the eight years I lived in the valley, I never experienced the aurora borealis or anything else as beautiful.

John-Paul Cernak

CHAPTER 17

In the predawn darkness, the rumble of vehicles far down the valley broke through the haze of my sleep and jolted me awake. Who could that be coming into the valley this early? It isn't even light yet and too early for Hughie. When a caravan of vehicles projected themselves on my mind screen, I sprang from my bed and reached the window just as a white truck stopped on the road below with, POLICE, printed on the roof.

"Oh God!" I said aloud, "it's a raid!"

With my heart pounding and my mind racing, I looked for a place to hide or a way to escape. There wasn't even a closet to conceal myself in when I looked around at the unfinished second floor of the new house where I slept. My only chance was to get across the road and into the woods. With a million acres of wilderness, the forest and mountains would swallow me. But quickly, more vehicles stopped on the road a few yards apart blocking all avenues of escape. Then came the sharp rapping on the door, and I knew from that moment on my life would never be the same.

Each night for the last three weeks that I slept in the new house, I watched a spider sitting in its web outside my second story window. It was large. Its greenish body was the size of a quarter, and its long legs made it much bigger. When it first spun its web, I intended to brush it away. I didn't want it getting inside where I slept, but I heard spiders were good luck. Each night, I made sure it was still there. Last night when I shined my light through the window, the web was empty.

It was dark when they arrived, and I don't remember when

it became light. Sunrises in the valley were spectacular affairs. Somehow, I wasn't there. In the past, other events disappeared from memory. As a boy living in Chicago, I swam out too far in Lake Michigan and didn't have the energy to swim back. After swallowing large amounts of water, I yelled for help. The next thing I remembered was sitting on the beach rescued but by whom I do not know. In a panic, I thrashed around attempting to reach shallow water, except for a small part of my brain that watched and remained detached. I walked down the stairs calmly feeling that same indifference. "Raise your hands in the air," said a tall, red-headed cop pointing a gun at me. "You're under arrest for the manufacture and possession of a controlled substance. Is there anyone else in the building?"

"I'm the only one."

He read me my rights, and the next moments are gone from memory. The tall red-headed cop was Sergeant Kenneth Hall of the Douglas County Sheriff's Department. He and his associate, Deputy Vern Bishop, were in the plane that flew over and saw the growing plants. Their questioning brought me back to awareness. The sun was shining brightly, and I was dressed and uncertain how much time passed. "Where's the boundary of your property?" asked the tall deputy.

Why is he asking about the property line at a time like this? "Up there," I said, pointing up towards the woods, "just above the big water tank." Throughout the difficult months ahead, I would learn why the border of the land was so important.

"I'm just a visitor," said Reggie. "I don't know anything about what's going on here. I didn't know marijuana was grown here, and you should release me. How could I know when I just arrived?"

The tall cop wrote down everything he said but didn't release him. At that moment, Reggie didn't realize his claim to have just arrived would come back to haunt him. When the police moved in, he was asleep on a cot outside between the houses. "They put a gun to me head," he said, "and told me to slowly take my hands out from under the covers. I didn't argue."

Life was coming at me fast. A second crew arrived with weed whackers, the kind with saw blades at the bottom to cut down the plants. The crew chief was tall and slim, and his good looks had a feminine quality. We looked at each other in a long, penetrating stare. Although I never saw him before, I felt I knew him all my life. From the look on his face, he must have felt the same. As he disappeared up the path, I received a flash he was someone I knew in a past life, and in that life, he was a woman.

Representing three policing agencies, the Douglas County Sheriff, Oregon State Police, and the DEA or Federal Drug Enforcement Agency, a lot of high-priced manpower just to bust a couple of farmers, the cops quickly went to work tearing the place apart. After their preliminary questioning, as they demolished everything, we were left alone standing outside next to the barn. The tall redhead or his associate occasionally came around to check on us. After seeing us standing calmly, they went back to work. I briefly flirted with the idea of casually walking across the road and disappearing into the woods. What stopped me was I would then be a fugitive, and I was pissed. After turning a blind eye and giving tacit approval all those years, the bastards suddenly reversed their policy without warning. But what did I expect, a card in the mail telling me that if I grew marijuana they'd bust my ass?

I was aware I lost control of the crop as far back as Bonnie's visit and had no one to blame but myself for not seeing this coming. After bringing in six successful harvests, I was the one with the "Midas Touch." Yet I was never consulted on anything. Reggie had it in his mind after Bonnie's visit that anything I said was irrelevant. Although I sensed trouble after the incident with Glen at the Tiller Tavern, nothing registered. I detached from everything. Had I been involved even to a small degree, my antenna would have picked up that there was something different about this year's flyover.

Do I dare say I had hints? Several weeks before the bust, while in the growing area, I perceived discordant vibrations I never experienced before. They were subtle and on a deep level. While they sounded like a warning, I rejected having any knowledge of what they meant. It was Reggie's crop, so why should I be concerned. As a grower, I listened to the world around me, an important consideration when growing an illegal crop. Now it was his job to listen. Instead, he was getting drunk and chasing women. His dependency on alcohol had a dulling effect, and Reggie wasn't a perceptive person. I never mentioned what I experienced and would be hard-pressed to admit I didn't want him to succeed. As fate grinded onward relentlessly, I felt powerless and did nothing vaguely aware a tsunami was about to sweep everything and everyone away.

Feeling nervous and agitated on the evening before the raid, I went for a short walk up the road before going to bed. At the spot past the orchard where I always experienced fear, I looked up at the blackness, and goose bumps covered me from head to toe. I quickly retreated to the barn. Before I could go inside, a blast of wind hit me in the face, and I went into trance. The Spirits made one last attempt to reach me, but I wasn't listening. I was much too involved in my self-pity to hear.

I had no complaints about how the cops treated us. They were friendly, and it seemed more like a social call then a bust. They handcuffed us in front when they took us to town instead of behind our backs as was usually done, and I sensed uneasiness among the deputies. They were busting folks for doing what everyone was doing including the possibility that some of them were growers themselves. It was no secret almost everyone who owned land was a grower and that included straight people. Growing marijuana was a Southern Oregon cottage industry, and it was understood the money was responsible for the increasing prosperity.

During the last election that catapulted Ronald Reagan into office, a new conservative sheriff was elected in Douglas County. Shame on me for failing to notice his philosophy changed from liberty and freedom to repression and tyranny. I was a political prisoner and a casualty of the despotic new regime. The worst part was they were killing the goose that laid the golden eggs. With the economy already in recession, busting the growers would send it tail-spinning into a deep depression, and the suffering would be doubly deep and pervasive. The folks who voted for the new sheriff to put those dirty, dope growing hippies behind bars will know they shot themselves in the foot when they lose their homes, families, and everything they own.

The deputy who drove us to town apologized all the way and treated us more like passengers.than prisoners. He rendezvoused with a state trooper at a rest stop, and the friendliness of the deputy became the cold suspicion of the trooper. He patted us down before putting us in the back seat. I sat quietly fighting panic and watched the beautiful, green, forest covered hills of Southern Oregon sail past, as the reality of what happened finally hit home.

———❧———

Reggie was booked first and disappeared down a corridor. I called Meg with my one phone call. "The cops raided us," I said, "and I'm in Jail."

After being fingerprinted and mug shot, I entered the holding tank. Reggie was already entertaining three or four guys. A guard suddenly reappeared. "Which of you is Jack Cernak?"

"That's me."

"You've been sprung."

Reggie grabbed my arm as I was about to leave. "Bail me out, mate," and he told me where he hid his money.

I was surprised Meg came as quickly as she did. At first, I thought she wouldn't, until I said I would do my best to keep her out of it. She must have reasoned that it was to her advantage to get me out fast. "There's probably enough evidence in the barn to implicate you," I said, but I was thinking of the children. If she went to prison, they would be motherless. Out in the sunlight, I could see she was frightened. "Am I in danger of getting arrested?" she asked.

"I think you're okay, but nothing is certain at this point."

Wanda was at her sister's restaurant and agreed to drive me back to the valley so I could bail out Reggie. After remaining calm all morning, on the return drive, I began falling apart and vowed never to smoke marijuana again. I entered the barn feeling dread. It looked as if a tornado came through. Every drawer and cabinet was open and all their contents scattered over the floor. I couldn't think, my head ached, and my vision blurred. I filled a glass with water and sat down to survey the carnage. I then saw the trapdoor to the cellar open. "NO!" I screamed. "They found it." Wanda backed away frightened by my sudden outburst.

Even though I knew they would discover it, I, nonetheless, received a demoralizing blow seeing it open. When I lowered myself in and saw all ten bags of leaf were gone, my psyche sank into a deep muddy swamp. All that remained were a few cans of paint and several cardboard boxes. One looked familiar, but I couldn't remember what was in it. I slid it over, and when I pulled the lid open, I stared in disbelief at the contents. Although confused and disorientated, I felt elated. Inside was the five pounds of bud from last year's crop the cops somehow overlooked. Instantly my paranoia returned. What if they come back? I had to hide it somewhere else.

Wanda looked scared and probably thought I was a madman. She didn't know I was broke, and without money to hire a defense attorney, there was little chance of winning a trial using a public defender. The high quality bud was my ticket to freedom. "I need to get back," she said, warily edging toward the door. "I'm working tonight at the restaurant."

After I watched her car disappear into the distance, fighting desperation, I climbed the mountain and buried the box at the base of a large fir under needles and debris. My anguish increased after discovering the tractor was gone and would have cried had I not remembered Reggie's money. With everything ripped apart, I felt certain they found it, but when I entered the barn, the crock-pot sat inconspicuously and undisturbed next to the wall in the kitchen.

Under the lid was Reggie's wallet filled with money. Maybe there was hope after all. How sharp could these people be if they failed to find a box full of bud and Reggie's money?

I had one more thing to do before returning to town. With tear-filled eyes and holding my marijuana pipe, I walked up the path, as I had a thousand times over the years. The growing area looked naked. Short stems protruded from the ground where beautiful plants grew. After digging a hole with my hands, I buried the pipe. Suddenly, the sky darkened. I stood looking around. A small, solitary cloud drifted over the sun and seemed to just sit there. Everywhere else the sun shined brightly from a cloudless, blue sky over the forest covered mountains. The message was clear. My marijuana growing days were over.

—————⟋⟍⟋⟍—————

The news of the bust was on the front page of the town newspaper and showed pictures of the barn and new house. Now all the neighbors on Jefferson Street and everyone else knew we were growers. The story was probably on TV, but I didn't have a television at the shop. After I bailed out Reggie, he went home with Wanda. The next morning, he borrowed the truck. They went to retrieve his things. The Spirits found him unworthy. His time in the valley was over. After they returned, I drove there alone and retrieved the box of bud from up on the mountainside. I didn't want anyone to know where I hid it and was going to protect it all cost. When I returned to the shop that afternoon, I received a call from Sergeant Hall. He requested my presence in his office at the Courthouse the next day.

Deputy Hall and his sidekick, Deputy Vern Bishop, were there when I entered. A pile of photographs lay on his desk next to a large Manila envelope. "Thanks for coming in," he said, his manor friendly and cordial. He held up the picture of me riding the tractor Bonnie took. "We confiscated your tractor because it was used in the cultivation of the marijuana."

I felt anger at both Reggie and Bonnie. It wasn't for disregarding my warning; it was for their arrogant, mocking attitude. Reggie never showed me the photos, possibly because he knew of my objection against taking them. "And one more thing," he said, holding up a picture of Bonnie. "Is this your wife?"

"No," I said, but feeling that it would be fit karma if Bonnie was somehow snared in the net that the cops had cast.

"Would you ask your wife to come down to our office at her earliest convenience?"

When I called Meg and told her that Sergeant Hall wanted to see her, she sounded frightened. I talked with her later that afternoon on the phone after her visit. "When I walked into his office and introduced myself," she said, "he didn't say much. He just asked to see my driver's license. I guess that was to prove I was Meg Cernak."

"Bonnie better not show her face around here again," I interjected, "or she'll be arrested as an accomplice."

"By the way Jack, when are you going to repay the money I used to bail you out?"

That afternoon when I returned to the shop, I sat in my director's chair out in the gallery and sifted through the mail that accumulated over the last few days. In the stack was a letter from the United States Department of Justice and the Federal Drug Enforcement Administration. The letter informed me it was the DEA who seized my tractor. I remembered on the day of the bust someone who smoked cigars and had authority but wasn't a member of the sheriff's department or the state police. He must have been a DEA Agent. Now I understood why they were busting the growers. The county was taking money from the Federal Government. This was Ronald Reagan's doing.

A feeling of calamity suddenly came over me, and I sat back in my chair feeling panicked and overwhelmed, the envelopes on my lap sliding down to the floor. As I took deep breaths in an attempt to quiet my nerves, my eyes came to rest on an oil painting of an

Indian village hanging on the gallery wall, and looking at it somehow lessened my stress and gave me a warm, energizing feeling at the base of my stomach. The artwork showed teepees, horses, and people milling around as if preparing for battle. As I looked at it, the village expanded. It grew until it covered the entire gallery wall and came to life. I was suddenly back in 1876, viewing the Battle of the Little Bighorn for a second time as I viewed it when touring the battlefield, and I was witnessing the death of George Armstrong Custer.

Most accounts of the battle stated the Indians didn't know who he was. Of course they knew. The Indians identified all the leaders and how they operated. They called General Crook, "Three Stars," and Custer, "Pawhuska," or Long Hair. The gathering at the Little Bighorn River was not one tribe but a coming together of Sioux, Cheyenne, and Arapaho. Custer blundered and attacked an Indian village during a massive assembly, and the outcome was predictable.

Using army rifles taken from dead soldiers, the Indians concentrated their fire into a small group of soldiers with Custer. When only Pawhuska and one other soldier remained alive, he was easily overwhelmed and killed in a charge and his body desecrated. That he was left untouched was an unlikely scenario for a man the Indians reviled and was a myth created to enhance his reputation, as perhaps most of what was written about him was legend. He wore a leather coat that made him easily identifiable, and what they did to his body wasn't pretty. I couldn't watch anymore, and as I was turning away, I glimpsed an image of Ronald Reagan. What was he doing there? When I tried going back, the connection was broken, and the reason for his appearance on the battlefield remained a mystery.

━━━━⟨∿∿⟩━━━━

THE NEXT DAY, REGGIE AND I BEGAN OUR SEARCH FOR A LAWYER to defend us. The first was named Dale Berry. I instantly disliked the man and felt wary in his presence. Although his office was small and drab, he was smartly dressed in a blue suit with vest. Sitting on the corner of his desk, he looked casual. I suspected his nonchalant attitude was a façade to hide his excitement at the prospect of a new client. "How may I help you gentlemen?"

"We were arrested for growing marijuana," said Reggie.

"Oh! You're the guys I read about in the paper. Looks like you two will do a little sitting! Ha! Ha! Ha!"

After hearing his remark, I wanted to run out of his office. The last thing I wanted to hear from an attorney defending me was that I would do a little sitting, and his laughter rubbed me the wrong way, as if getting busted was a joke. Oblivious to what he said and his apparent lack of character, Reggie hired the man to defend him. Seeing that my partner was unable to make good judgments, I began to distance myself from him.

The next day, I called on two other lawyers. Both seemed detached and neither inspired me. I hadn't imagined finding someone to represent me would be difficult. The following day, I called on a law firm of three attorneys. The furnishings in their outer office were more upscale, with leather couches, designer lamps and original art on the walls. "May I help you?" asked a receptionist.

"I need to see someone about a legal problem.

"Jim Carrier is available but is out at the moment. He should return shortly if you care to wait."

He returned after a few minutes wearing running clothes and introduced himself. He was tall, athletic, in his early thirties, and without the counterfeit façade Dale Berry displayed. "If you excuse me while I shower, we'll talk right after."

I was shown into his office and checked out the certificates and diplomas hanging on his wall. While he was qualified, his youth and inexperience made me uneasy. He returned casually dressed in a white shirt and tie but no jacket. "How may I be of service?" he asked.

When I told him I was busted for growing marijuana, he asked for details and took notes. None of the others asked questions.

"What I'd like to do is read the *affidavit*. It's the written statement the police present to a judge for obtaining a warrant showing *probable cause* a crime was committed. I'll be at the courthouse in the morning and pick up a copy. The man who'll prosecute this case is Ted Zacker. Can you come back tomorrow around three?"

The next day when I entered his office, he was in deep concentration reading a document I assumed was the affidavit. He pointed to a chair and said he'd be right with me. After several minutes, he looked up still deep in thought. "I think we have a case," he said.

I believed those were the most beautiful words I have ever heard spoken and that lifted the feeling of doom I felt since the bust. My search was over. "What's your fee?"

"My fee is seventy-five hundred, and I'll need a thousand dollar retainer."

I felt shock. "The other lawyers I visited charge five thousand. Why is your fee higher?"

"Because I'm better," he said, unhesitatingly.

Jim Carrier had the spark I was looking for, and somehow the extra money and his inexperience didn't seem to matter. I noticed my hand trembled slightly when I wrote out the check from my shop account with the knowledge I didn't have the money to pay him the balance. Have faith, I said to myself. Somehow it'll all work out.

The grand jury heard my case and issued a *true bill*, which meant they believed I committed a crime supported by overwhelming evidence, and I would go to trial. The prosecution *arraigned* me the following week. My lawyer stood next to me in front of a short fence that separated the judge's bench from the courtroom. "In count one," said the magistrate, "The said, Jack Cernak, on or about the 19th. of August A. D. 1981 in the said County of Douglas and State of Oregon, then and there being, did unlawfully and knowingly manufacture marijuana."

As the judge read the long statement with the charges against me, I concentrated on controlling my fear and didn't hear all that he said until I heard him say: "How do you plead?"

I quickly refocused. "Not guilty," I replied.

Jim Carrier asked for a continuance, and the whole proceeding took less than ten minutes. Now it was official. I was *under indictment*, and with all the drama that unfolded over the past weeks, I hardly flinched when the judge said: "The crime carries a penalty of from three to twenty years in prison." I was scared, but I refused to even think about spending time in jail.

On the day before the arraignment, I talked with him at his office. "At the moment," he said, "the only thing that they know about you is that you're a marijuana grower. Begin to build a new image. Even if you and your wife have separated, bring her with you. Change that image by showing them you're a family man and have a business in town. "

While visiting the children at the Jefferson Street House that afternoon, I asked Meg if she would accompany me to the arraignment. "Good luck, Jack," she said. "I have better things to do than waste my time at the courthouse."

"I'd really appreciate if you came with me."

"I'm just too busy, and besides, I'd have to hire a babysitter."

"What if I pay for the babysitter?

"That's not enough. Jamie is dropping over tomorrow, and I need to go grocery shopping."

"What if I pay for the sitter, do your shopping for you and buy you lunch at the courthouse?"

"Now you're talking my language."

The cafeteria was already crowded when we entered at noon and with more people streaming in. Deputies Hall and Bishop entered at the end of the line. "Look who just got in behind us," I said.

She looked around slyly and spotted them. "Gee! Aren't we lucky?"

I will never know for sure if it was coincidence or planned, but the two cops sat across from us. "Well!" said Bishop. "If it isn't Jack Cernak and his wife. How are you folks today?"

Bishop was the talker. He was short and stocky, came across

friendly, and always wore a disarming smile. "We're fine," I said.

The conversation lapsed for the next few minutes as we concentrated on eating lunch and resumed afterward. "Look, Jack," remarked Bishop, his manner cordial and friendly, "you'd be doing yourself a big favor if you come clean and plead guilty. With all the evidence against you, I don't see any possibility of you getting away. You'll save yourself the hassle and expense of trial, and we'll talk to Zacker and recommend a lighter sentence for cooperating."

"You guys are so good to me."

"We saw your marijuana on a fly over," Hall interjected. "It was easy to spot from the air, and the next day, we drove up to your valley. When we found no one home, we walked up and made sure it was marijuana." What a bummer! I knew I shouldn't have gone drinking with Reggie. "If we go to trial and you're found guilty," Hall added with a vengeful tone, "we'll notify the IRS."

"Now wait a minute, Ken," protested Bishop. "Let's not be unfriendly. I'm sure Jack understands he can't get away, and if he cooperates, we could forget about the IRS. Let's give him every break he deserves."

The cop's friendliness threw me into confusion. He came across like an old friend with influence who wanted to help me out of a difficult jam. On another level, I sensed he was playing the good cop/bad cop routine. I wasn't sure what there was about him that made me want to trust him. The voice in the back of my head kept warning me he was a fraud and wanted to send me to prison for years. I said nothing but felt confused. "One more thing," he said, "off the record, where did you sell your marijuana? Off the record!" He repeated his statement and made hand gestures in emphasis.

I have to admit, I almost told him. Luckily, my paranoia kicked in at the right moment. "There is no off the record!" I replied, forcefully. A hush fell between us. We picked up our trays and walked out.

When Jim Carrier summoned me to his office the next day, I told him about the cafeteria incident with the two deputies. "It's lucky you didn't tell them anything," he said emphatically. "If you told them you sold your crop in San Francisco, they would have confiscated your truck, because it was used in the distribution of marijuana."

Jim Carrier's knowledge of the confusing legal procedures and his professional confidence gave me hope and eased somewhat the mounting pressure, but I mourned losing my tractor and was angry at the cops for confiscating it. "All they have is a picture of me riding on it." I said. "The photo could have been taken anywhere, even down in the garden. How can I get it back?"

"The only way is if we're able to *suppress evidence*. If we don't suppress evidence, you won't get it back even if you're found not guilty at trial by a jury."

"How can they impound my tractor if I'm found innocent?"

"All they need to *confiscate* is probable cause."

"It seems that the cards are stacked in the government's favor. I thought the Constitution states we're innocent until proven guilty." He looked at me thoughtfully but made no comment.

"I'll give a lawyer friend a call in Eugene," he said. "He specializes in retrieving confiscated property, but the reason I called you in is to warn you about your partner. When the government has a weak case, they'll offer one partner a deal to testify against the other. With all the evidence they've accumulated against you two, I'm sure they're feeling confident they can easily convict you both. Nevertheless, my advice is stay away from him."

I rarely saw Reggie after the bust, and when I did, he was usually with Wanda, carried a six-pack of beer under his arm, and looked depressed. The beer must not have been taking the edge off anymore, and his vibe made me uneasy.

A few days later, Buddy dropped over. He was one of the guys from the neighborhood who recently moved to Oregon after doing hard time at Mississippi's Parchman Farm Penitentiary. He wasn't bitter, only thankful he was a free man. His experience gave him an understanding of the realities I faced. Several fingers were missing

328   *John-Paul Cernak*

from his left hand he sawed off running a power saw while high on heroin. When I knew him, he smoked only a little grass and could be trusted. "What's happening, man?" I asked.

"I just came from the bar, and your partner was there already sloshed."

"What else is new? Getting drunk is all Reggie can do these days."

"Hey, man, be careful! He told me that if he was convicted, they'd deport him, but before he'd let that happen, he'd cut a deal and testify against you."

Buddy confirmed what I intuitively already knew, and whenever I talked with Reggie, he developed a hard edge about him. It would be much easier to justify his treachery if he convinced himself I was to blame for the bust. Since the arrest, he did little, except hire a lawyer who believed he would do, "a little sitting," and lose himself in alcohol. His hangdog expression projected an image of someone who had already given up.

Reggie returned to California in the middle of October, and in one regard, I felt relieved to have him gone. He was a bad vibe. Beneath his bravado and image there was little substance. Instead of working with me to get us free, the weight of his pessimism dragged me down. In another regard, I was angry he went back to California to earn money dumping the responsibility and expense of getting us freed into my lap. If a jury found me guilty, it was almost certain he, too, was headed for the slammer.

After Reggie returned to California, I knew it was also my time to go. Hidden in the valley was the five pounds of bud I had to convert into cash, but I wasn't free to travel without the court's permission. It irked me to go hat in hand before a judge and explain why, where, and for how long I would be gone.

Most days, I managed to stay positive, but when on occasion the thought of going to prison for years broke through into my consciousness, my life spiraled out of control and down into despair. On the evening before I was to travel, with the walls closing in on me, my anxiety pushed me out into the street. The evening was balmy, and I walked as if in a trance. The next thing I knew, I was walking uphill towards the Jefferson Street house. It was dusk, and I wasn't sure why I was going there. It must have been I needed to be with someone to help me through a difficult evening and was hoping to find solace with Meg and the children. She answered the door. "What do you want, Jack," her voice filled with anger and her face hard and unsmiling. "The children are asleep."

"I didn't realize it was that late."

"There is much you don't realize. You're finally getting what you deserve," and she slammed the door in my face.

With my emotions reeling, I staggered into the street feeling as if she hit me in the head with a baseball bat. I found myself walking along a wooded path next to the river but couldn't remember how I got there. It was dark, and the crescent moon hung low in the western sky. I was scared, and eerie sounds came from the woods as if spooks lurked behind every bush. I looked around nervously feeling a presence, as if I were being stalked. At that moment, I realized Meg didn't just want me convicted, she wanted me dead. I was the only person who knew what she was really like. With me gone, there was no one who could challenge her lies and expose her whoring. Death was stalking me.

—◦◦◦—

ON THE SECOND DAY AFTER THE BUST, I WAS CALMER. WHEN I returned to the valley and retrieved the box of bud off the mountain, I hid it back in the cellar where it was originally. I reasoned that for the police to come back and search again, they needed a second warrant, which was unlikely. Nevertheless, I felt apprehensive on the drive in until I opened the trapdoor and saw the box was still there. With it tucked snuggly under black plastic in the bed of the truck, I began my trip to California early the next morning, aware it was my last trip as a grower.

On the way out, I stopped and checked my mail at the Tiller

post office box. When getting back behind the wheel, a sheriff's vehicle was parked under a tree a short distance off. Bummer! The judge must have alerted them I was going to San Francisco, and the bastards were stalking me. Feeling such fear, I struggled to breath and almost hit the panic button. If I made a dash for it and got away fast, maybe I could lose them on one of the back roads leading into the mountains. Luckily, I quickly realized there was no chance my little pickup could outrun their powerful machine. Chanting as loud and as fast as possible, I slowly pulled out onto the highway and watched in my rearview mirror the black and white following behind. At the edge of town, they turned on their siren and flashing lights. All was lost, and after finding the box in the bed of my truck, I would face additional charges. Contemplating the fastest and the least painless way to end my life, I pulled over. But they zoomed past and disappeared into the distance, my heart pounding and gasping for breath.

The next evening, with the sun hitting the horizon and the surrounding clouds ablaze, I reached Pacifica and Rick's house high on the bluff overlooking the sea. He answered the door. "Jack! What a surprise. What's new?"

"I was busted," I said.

CHAPTER 18

It was a difficult Christmas possibly more difficult for Little Annie than for me. She missed her Papa. It seemed Meg gave Paul all her attention, and the little girl was left on her own. During visits, I saw pain and sadness in her eyes that dumped me into despondency and seemed to substantiate my worries about Meg's failure as a mother. I met a woman at the bar, and we became lovers. She was a beautiful person, but because of my troubled mind, a relationship never developed. Lying just beneath the surface was a strong undertow of fear pulling me down, and my only escape was sleep. The one positive that came from the bust was that it shook me out of my lethargy, and for the first time in months, I felt alive. I didn't know how, but somehow I would win.

Jim Carrier began talking about the motion to suppress evidence that he scheduled for early March. With the trial a little more than two months away, he did little in preparation, and I couldn't.blame him. I hadn't paid him anything on the balance. After receiving a phone call on a Tuesday morning a couple of weeks after the New Year, I went to the courthouse for permission to travel. I was gone several days. At my return, I scheduled a meeting with my lawyer. He was concentrating on a document when I entered. "Have a seat, Jack. I'll be right with you. I have a few things to finish."

I sat impatiently holding a brown paper bag tightly in my lap. After a few minutes, he looked up. "You wanted to see me this afternoon? You know the motion to suppress evidence is coming up soon, don't you?"

I stood and dropped the bag on his desk. Stacks of hundred dollar bills spilled out. He looked at me with surprise. When Rick handed me the sack full of money, there wasn't any possible way to express my gratitude for his coming through for me when I needed it the most.

⚯

1982

MOTION TO CONTROVERT THE STATEMENTS IN THE AFFIDAVIT and proposal to suppress evidence in the light of excised information. The Honorable Judge, Lyle M. Bevens of the Douglas County Superior Court presiding. Case #F-81-566. There was no jury for the motion to suppress evidence. The magistrate would decide it.

Although he was an older man, possibly in his middle to late sixties and seemed detached, I received a good vibe from him. Throughout the proceedings, he said little, and I wondered if he was listening or spaced out thinking of something more pleasant. In the wood-paneled courtroom were a bailiff and the court stenographer. Paper came out of her little typing machine like a tail. Sitting next to us at a table was Prosecutor Zacker and a female assistant. Out in the gallery were four or five people I assumed were witnesses. Among them were Deputies Hall and Bishop. How I understood the proceedings was that my attorney needed to show that a judge issued a search warrant from an affidavit presented to him by Deputy Hall that contained assumptions, inaccuracies, and false statements and that the grounds on which it was granted never existed.

In a way, everything was reversed. Instead of me being on trial, the police were. The prosecutor was Ted Zacker, a short, slight man, and I could see that he chafed at the idea he would have to defend the police actions in court. He looked angry and moved papers around on his desk with quick motions. His assistant, a nice-looking woman, did her best to ignore him. On the other hand, Jim Carrier looked focused and relaxed. I sat at the table next to him feeling all eyes were watching me.

The first witness to testify was Sergeant Kenneth Hall. The bailiff swore him in, and the tall red-headed cop gave an account of his qualifications and of his expertise in identifying drugs.

"During my ten and a half years in law enforcement," he began, "I received numerous in-service training hours in the area of narcotics and dangerous drugs. I attended the Oregon Basic Police Academy, and an eighty hour in-service training in "Operation Sinsemilla Strike Force" in Mendocino County, California, which included aerial observation of growing marijuana."

He went on for another five minutes naming all the workshops and classes he attended that aided in his identification work. I wanted to yell out to him to get on with it already. Even Zacker looked annoyed at his long list. When he finally finished, everyone in the courtroom seemed to take a long, deep breath, and the prosecutor began his questioning. "Tell us, Deputy Hall, on what grounds did you apply for a search warrant?"

"On August 17, 1981, at 11:00 AM, while flying over the Ash Creek area of Douglas County, at an altitude of 4200 feet above sea level or about 2000 feet above ground height, I identified growing marijuana plants."

"Did you do anything else to verify that it was marijuana?"

"The next day, at about 11:00 AM, Deputy Bishop and I drove to the location and identified it as the same seen from the overflight. I observed a footpath leading up the mountain to the growing plants and that it originated across the roadway and in close proximity to a residence and barn-like structure. It was reasonable to believe that the persons living in the residence were responsible for growing and tending to them."

"What did you find when you executed the search warrant?"

"When we arrived on the morning of August, 19, 1981, a Mr. Reginald Wickham was asleep in the yard in his sleeping bag, and Mr. Jack Cernak was in the residence. On the mountainside, we found a hundred and seventy-seven growing marijuana plants in four different sections. We found fifteen plants hanging in the residence and ten large black plastic bags filled with marijuana weighing approximately seven pounds each in the barn-like structure under a trapdoor. We found several ounces in baggies and numerous seeds in jars, photos of plants growing in their greenhouse, and photos of themselves. We found correspondence from previous years that talked about harvesting their dope crop, with weather records and the type harvested. Also found were numerous business cards that read—For Oregon's finest, call Jack—with Cascade Clear and Tiller Killer hand written."

"Your witness," said Zacker.

I was devastated. It wasn't until I heard him describe all the evidence the police gathered against me that I fully understood the gravity of the situation and its implication in sending me to prison. How could anyone possibly overcome all the evidence?

Jim Carrier arose, buttoned his suit jacket and asked his first question standing at the table. "Deputy Hall, did the land on where the plants were growing belong to Mr. Cernak?"

"No," he responded. "It was government land."

He slowly walked up to the witness stand."Were the growing plants visible from the road?"

"No, they were not."

"I have no further question but remain available for cross-examination."

Jim Carrier's first witness was James G. Fleming, an investigator for the Douglas County Public Defender's office. He testified about a case similar to mine where he performed an aerial search to identify growing marijuana. "The pilot," he said, "was instructed to make several passes at altitudes 800, 1000 and 1700 feet with an air speed of seventy miles per hour. I viewed the area from 800 feet and could see trees, brush, road, vehicles, and houses, but it was impossible to see individual trees and could only see clumps of brush. This phenomenon was more pronounced from higher altitudes. The day before my flight, I made an excursion over the property on foot and placed two bright, yellow drums next to tall gateposts. When I flew over, I could barely discern the bright, yellow drums, and I could not observe the fence posts at all. In my estimation, it is impossible to observe marijuana plants from the air going seventy miles per hour at 800 feet let alone from higher altitudes.

"Your witness."

"I have no questions," answered Zacker.

Jim Carrier next called Merle Benson to the stand, a self-employed private investigator. His testimony was similar to Fleming's, but that he actually flew over the Ash Creek area and said that it was impossible to identify marijuana from the height and speed Deputy Hall claimed to have observed it. The next bit of evidence, however, was more revealing. "On November 18, 1981," he said, "I had occasion to speak with Sergeant Hall and questioned him concerning the language in his affidavit." 'That at about 4:30 PM, I drove to the location of the marijuana and identified it as the same seen from the over flight.'

"Detective Hall," he continued, "stated that prior to the issuance of the search warrant, he did not identify what he saw during the over flight as marijuana. What he told me was that he merely drove to the general area but did not observe any plants from the ground location."

As I followed the proceeding carefully, it seemed the deputy perjured himself by lying under oath. Jim Carrier turned slowly and looked for a long, penetrating moment at the red-headed cop sitting at the prosecutor's table but said nothing.

"Did you physically inspect the mountainside where the plants were growing?" he asked, resuming his questioning of the private investigator.

"I did."

"What did you observe?"

"I inspected the growing area and the forest above and observed that the forest was full of paths, and someone could easily be entering the growing area from above."

"Were the plants visible from the road?"

"Thick shrubbery prevented anyone from seeing them, and they could not be seen by the occupants of the dwellings below."

"Your witness," he said.

"I have one question," said Zacker. "Were the paths in the woods as well worn as the path that led up from the road?"

The private investigator paused before answering. "That's something I couldn't tell you. I'm not sure what you mean by well worn."

The judge broke the proceedings for lunch, and the session resumed sometime after 1:30. Jim Carrier recalled Deputy Hall to the stand for cross-examination.

"Merle Benson testified that while flying over the Ash Creek Area, it was impossible to identify marijuana on the ground at the height and speed you were flying. How could you be positive that what you saw was marijuana?"

"From all my training," Hall quickly retorted, "I felt positive it was."

"Mr. Benson also testified that the forest was full of paths and someone could enter the growing area from above. Could it be possible someone else was tending to them?"

"I don't see how that was possible," Hall replied, unambiguously.

My lawyer hammered away. "Were you able to obtain fingerprints?"

"No. There was nothing that would lend itself to finding fingerprints," he replied, less stridently.

"Did you interview any of the neighbors?"

"No, I didn't," replied Hall almost meekly.

"So, in fact, you didn't get their names and don't know if any were ever convicted of growing marijuana?"

"No, I didn't."

"In your affidavit, you wrote: 'About 4:30, I drove to the location of the marijuana and identified it as the same seen from the over flight.' But you neglected to specify how you saw them. Then you wrote: 'I observed a footpath leading up the mountain to the growing plants, and the footpath originated in close proximity to the residence and barn.' Did you walk up the mountainside and trespass?"

"Well, no. We didn't actually walk up to see the marijuana and didn't trespass, but we saw the path leading up the mountainside."

Jim Carrier introduced photos into evidence taken in front of the barn that showed the path was not visible from the road unless he trespassed. As Hall walked back to the prosecutor's table, he seemed a little shaken.

My lawyer's next witness was a man named Jerry Wilson who Deputies Hall and Bishop also arrested for growing marijuana. "Tell the court what happened."

"On September 29, 1981, Deputies Hall and Bishop came to my home on Crocker Creek and seized six small marijuana plants growing behind my house. To my surprise, they also seized sixty-eight alleged marijuana plants growing in a creek bed. They left this receipt." He handed it to Jim Carrier. "I couldn't believe it. I didn't know anything about the marijuana they claimed to have seized down in the creek. I saw the plants before and thought they were just some kind of weed. I later had the opportunity to review the police report on my case and discovered that the plants after testing were not marijuana. Anyone who knows anything could see that they weren't the same."

As he finished his statement, he pointed to Deputy Hall sitting at the prosecutor's table. Zacker turned and glared angrily at the deputy. Even the Judge, who seemed disinterested until then perked up.

In an attempt to mitigate the damning account of seizing weeds, Zacker recalled Deputy Hall for redirect. "Tell us Deputy, how did you misidentify the plants you seized?"

"There are many plants that look similar, and this was one of them. It would have been more a mistake to leave them then to seize the wrong plants."

"When you raided Mr. Cernak's property, did you know that the marijuana was growing on government land?"

"There was no way to determine where private property ended and government land began, but everything we did we did in good faith."

"The evidence to establish probable cause," began Jim Carrier in his summation, "must be more than would give rise to mere suspicion." Seeing what Deputy Hall assumed was marijuana growing on a mountainside on government land from two thousand feet going seventy miles per hour with a residence nearby does not constitute probable cause. Testimony was presented that in fact the writer of the affidavit never did substantiate what he saw was marijuana. We hold that if a statement in an affidavit supporting a warrant is demonstrated to be false, and if the affiant was unreasonable in believing the truth of such information, we require that the entire affidavit be reexamined. The officer overstated the facts and therefore disrupted the normal inference-drawing process. Would the magistrate have issued the warrant had he known the plants growing on the mountainside were only assumed to be marijuana? They could have been weeds. The deputy thought he was acting in good faith, but if good faith alone were the test, the protection of the Fourth Amendment would evaporate, and people would be secure in their persons, houses, papers, and effects only at the discretion of the police."

"We do not agree," began Zacker. "On a flyover, Deputy Hall identified what he thought was marijuana, and when he executed the search warrant, it proved correct. Looking at the facts and the reasonable inferences that can be drawn from them, the impressions or opinions of the officer were not controverted by his subsequent admission he did not visually verify they were marijuana. In considering cases involving motions to suppress evidence obtained by an allegedly invalid search warrant, we must remember that the Fourth Amendment extends only to unreasonable searches and seizures. In my view, that testimony, while perhaps impeaching somewhat the credibility of the officer, did not controvert or destroy the statements in the affidavit. We must bear in mind, as recognized by the majority of cases, that in determining whether there was probable cause for issuance of a search warrant, affidavits are to be interpreted in a common sense rather than hyper-technical manner."

With the testimony and summations finished, the courtroom became still and everyone waited for the judge to speak. "Write your summations," he said, "and I will hand down a decision after a review."

He gaveled the trial adjourned.

A week later, I received a call from Jim Carrier's secretary that his summation was finished, and I could pick up a copy at the office. It was lengthy, perhaps fifty pages, and I had a good feeling about it. His writing was brilliant and reflected hours of hard work. I sensed he wanted to win almost as much as I did. I thanked my good luck in having hired a lawyer with such skill, dedication, and drive. Now there was nothing to do but wait for the judge's decision. Weeks went by, and I would be at the shop waiting for the phone to ring. Finally, after five weeks, I was called into his office. It was a dark, rainy day with a steady downpour. His two partners were in his office. Wearing dark business suits and somber faces, they looked as if someone died and were there for a funeral, mine.

"We won," said Jim Carrier, and they broke into smiles. "The judge ruled it an illegal search and seizure and a violation of the Fourth Amendment. All the evidence the police obtained during the arrest is suppressed and cannot be used against you at trial."

"How wonderful," I said, feeling more happiness and relief than I felt in months.

"It also means you'll get your tractor back, but I want to point out that although the evidence is suppressed for you, it isn't for your partner."

"Why not? We were busted together."

"When your partner said that he was only a visitor, he lost standing. They can still use the evidence against him."

"I don't understand; what do you mean by standing."

"Because you own the property, you can object to the search and seizure. Your partner would have had standing, because he was a resident but lost it when he claimed to have just arrived and was a visitor. Guests have no rights to object, and I have other bad news. Usually, when evidence is suppressed, the government will drop charges. I talked with Zacker, and he's insisting on taking you to trial."

There was no let-up. All the joy I felt moments earlier quickly evaporated. "Their evidence is only circumstantial," my lawyer quickly pointed out, "giving us a slight advantage."

That afternoon, I went to the Jefferson Street house to tell Meg the good news, and she actually seemed glad instead of showing disappointment as I thought she would.

"Congratulations on your win. Come in. The children will be glad to see you. Remember it's going to be Paul's first birthday soon, and I want to you to come over for cake and coffee."

Her attitude was so out of character that it threw me into confusion. At the party, she hinted at reconciliation. It was over a year since we separated, and I wondered why now. Several days later, she came to see me at the shop. "Over the holidays," she said, "the children missed you, and it might be okay if you came back on a trial basis."

I moved back into the Jefferson Street house the next week, and it didn't take long to discover her motives for wanting me back. She was burning out on taking care of the children, and a prerequisite for moving in was that I become Annie and Paul's nanny. My job was cook breakfast and feed the kids before going to the shop. Annie was already three and mostly dressed and fed herself. Meg cooked dinner, but the children were my responsibility until I bathed and put them to bed.

The other reason she wanted me back was that her sex drive returned, and she expected me to be her consort and keep her happy in bed. Shortly after we separated, she began to see other men. Several times when visiting the children, I felt the sharp pangs of jealousy when I saw a man leaving as I arrived, but lately, thing weren't going as well for her. She wasn't as popular as she hoped she'd be. In asking me back, she expected everything would be the same as before I left, but I no longer desired her sexually. For months after our separation, I lusted after her and would have jumped into bed at the slightest urging.

Abe Marston, Jim Carrier's partner, put it to me succinctly: "When a marriage breaks down and people seek divorce, the process is confrontational. Getting a divorce is like going to war, and unless you're prepared to do battle, you'll be taken to the cleaners."

After hearing his interpretation, I knew feeling sexually attracted to her only muddled my thinking and gave her an unfair advantage. The change came when I devised a new strategy. Whenever I felt sexual desire for her, I visualized something rotten and vile. It worked so well that in a short time my desires for her turned into disgust. When I moved back in, I was aware that I would not be able to have sex with her but believed that all I needed to do to become sexually responsive again was simply reverse the tactic.

On a morning in the second week of our reconciliation, with the shop closed and the children gone for the day, she sat on the living room couch wearing a short skirt well above her knees, and a blouse that showed ample cleavage. It was easy to understand what she wanted. Since moving in, I used every excuse in the book to avoid sexual contact and worked frantically to reverse the strategy. I felt gloom knowing I had reached the end of the line. It was now either put out or get out. I worked in the kitchen washing the dishes. "Jack," she called out, "fix me a cup of coffee, and pour yourself one and join me."

Taking out a cup, I set it on the table in front of her. She sat provocatively showing leg, and I quickly darted back into the safety of the kitchen and anxiously fiddled around hoping to buy extra time. After a few minutes, she called out again. "What the hell's taking you so long, Jack? Come join me."

"I'm almost finished," I yelled back. Leaving the protection of the kitchen, I entered the lion's den. Sitting next to her, I placed my coffee on the table in front of me and cringed when she moved closer. "You're doing such a great job with the children," she said.

"It's good to be with them again."

Although she lost some of her allure after moving out of the valley, I had to admit she looked good that morning. In a conspiratorial tone, she told me what was happening in the neighborhood in the hope of drawing me closer and having me feel part of the family again, the whole time resting her hand on my knee. "It's been a long time since we've been together," she said and moved closer still.

Nervously reaching out for my coffee, I took a long, slow drink and delayed everything. There was no way to slow Meg down once she made up her mind, and my tactic only increased her desire to get something started. The second I put the cup down, she seductively put her arms around my neck and looked deep into my eyes. "Kiss me, Jack. I've missed you and dreamt about this moment."

Hesitantly, I put my arms around her monitoring how I felt when we kissed. Since everything felt okay, I kissed her again. That was what she was waiting for and became a wildcat groping and pulling at my clothes. "Get them off," she said, her voice croaking in the throes of passion.

She stood and quickly removed her blouse and dropped her skirt to the floor. I froze watching as she reached behind her back and unhooked her bra releasing her marvelous breasts. Adroitly, she stepped out of her panties and stood before me unabashedly displaying her naked body. Overwhelmed with passion, I remembered why my desire for her was so unrelenting, and my hesitancy suddenly turned into wanting her desperately. I quickly shed my clothes, and we melted into each other's arms, our kisses burning as hot as fire. "I see you still desire me," she whispered. We kissed passionately, and as I moved into position readying to insert, she unconsciously put my hand between her legs. When I felt her wetness, my strong structure suddenly wilted, and my passion turned into revulsion.

SINCE THE BUST, I WONDERED WHAT CAUSED THE DEPUTIES TO overlook the box of bud in the cellar. One evening, during my short reconciliation with Meg, I watched TV after putting the children to bed. The late news had just come on from a local TV station, and the program opened with the newscaster talking about drug abuse. She talked first about alcohol but quickly switched to marijuana. As she talked, the station ran a video clip that almost knocked me off my chair. It was shot in the kitchen of the barn on the day of the bust. Reggie and I were already gone, and I didn't.know a TV crew had arrived. The action showed the deputies removing the ten large bags filled with marijuana leaves from the cellar. Each time a deputy below handed a bag up to the one on the floor above, they danced around showboating for the camera. They were going to be on TV and were distracted. They never looked into the box containing the bud. Thank God for TV camera crews!

CHAPTER 19

THE DOUGLAS COUNTY SHERIFF'S DEPARTMENT WAS DRAGGING its feet on returning the tractor. I suspected a few individuals in the department had their hearts set on buying it cheap when it came up at auction and were reluctant to accept the reality they lost in court. I knew it was hidden in the county's impound lot, but nobody would even acknowledge an impound lot existed let alone tell me where it was. Luck was again on my side, because the Eugene lawyer whom Jim Carrier had introduced had contacts, and I was amazed when a Federal Marshal came to help get it back. At first I was leery of having him around—suspecting chicanery by the government—but after a few days, it was obvious he came to help. His name was Nathan Crowley, and he was from San Francisco. Dressed in civilian clothes, he was a big, beefy guy, the kind you wouldn't want to tangle with. "I'll help you get your tractor back, Little Buddy," he said, after he learned I was from San Francisco.

The next day, we drove to the sheriff's department. There was no one out at the front desk. After waiting a few minutes, we walked in. The clock on the wall read 12:15. The inner office was one large room with fifteen to twenty desks, and all were empty. Everyone was at lunch. Nathan grumbled something about why everyone went to go to lunch at the same time. As we were leaving, I noticed a poster of a marijuana leaf sitting upright on a desk near the door. It read: "If you see this leaf, call the Douglas County Sheriff's Department," and stapled to the corner was my business card, "For Oregon's finest, call Jack."

Suddenly, fear washed over me. When I looked around, a copy of the poster sat on each desk, and my card was stapled on each. Now I understood why they wouldn't drop charges even if they had no evidence. I was the worst offender, arrogant and contemptuous, and I must be brought down at all costs.

—◦◦◦—

THINGS WERE NOT GOING WELL AT THE SHOP. SINCE THE RECESsion started, enough business came in that allowed me to pay my rent and stay open. As it deepened over the last several months, business stopped almost entirely. Now my small reserve was threatened, and my choices were limited after it became evident I could no longer live with Meg. Without any other choice, I closed the shop and moved back to the valley. Those were dark days for me. It took several trips to transfer my belongings, and on the last one, I stopped at the Jefferson Street house for the cats. They were dying. I wanted to return them to the valley where they could die in the forest that was their home for the first years of their lives and where they experienced joy. Sitting on the ground under the maple tree across the road from the barn, I held and stroked each, saying goodbye. Slowly, they wandered off never to be seen again, and my pain was excruciating.

Life looked bleak during those first weeks alone. Slowly, I adjusted to the solitude and began to feel as close to peaceful as the threat of going to prison for years would allow. Most nights, I sat outside watching the moon and stars on their journey across the sky as I had when I first arrived almost nine years earlier. The Spirits gave me a pass, as I now walked with impunity along the road past the orchard where I always experienced fear and was soothed by the quietness of the forest, the warm glow of the kerosene lanterns, and the howl of coyotes in the distance. I forgot how sweet the water tasted that flowed down off the mountain and how pure the mountain air was. I busied myself planting a garden using only a shovel as I had in the beginning. How fortunate I was to have.experienced that wonderful valley deep in the mountains, but I never again walked up the path to the growing area. My trial was set for the ninth of September and Reggie's was scheduled two weeks later.

⸺oᴀo⸺

Feeling an overwhelming loneliness and scared to the point of nausea, on the day before the trial, I rented a motel room in town several blocks from the courthouse and walked around for most of the day in an attempt to control my nervousness. Meg's attitude went back to what it was previously hoping I would be convicted and sent to prison. When I picked up the children the week before, she wasn't shy in her diatribe against me. "Well, Jack," she said, "I guess it's retribution time."

At my lawyer's request, I had my hair cut short and wore a white shirt and tie, sport jacket and slacks, and a pair of horned-rim glasses to complete my image of a straight guy. He thought I looked like a schoolteacher.

⸺oᴀo⸺

September 9, 1982

The Trial:

The State of Oregon v Jack Cernak. Case #-F81-566

When I arrived at the courthouse, Jim Carrier was already waiting. The courtroom was full except for the jury box. Zacker sat at the prosecutors table along with two assistants. Several people in the gallery looked like the press, and the others were all strangers. Meg did not attend. The bailiff stood and called out as the judge entered the courtroom. "Everybody rise. The Honorable Jeremiah G. Hawkins presiding."

He was tall and slim in his middle fifties, and his hair was steel gray. What distinguished him was his hooked nose that gave him a hawk like appearance and matched his name. He laid two file folders on the bench as he sat down, and I would have bet they contained a list of suppressed evidence that could not be used against me at trial. From his looking like a bird of prey and his stern demeanor, he communicated he was a hanging judge and if convicted his sentence would be harsh. In contrast to the more humanistic vibe from Judge Bevens in the motion to suppress evidence, his was cold and unfeeling.

During jury selection, both lawyers challenged prospective jurors. Zacker dismissed one woman because she felt that to convict, it was necessary the person be caught in the act of committing the crime. My attorney released one person for having strong feelings against marijuana and another, because he served on the grand jury that brought in the indictment against me. The final jury consisted of ten women and two men. Several of the women looked familiar; yet after studying each closely, I was unable to recognize any of them but fantasized at least half were growers. The judge gave instruction to the two attorneys, and it was well into the morning when the trial finally began. Zacker rose to make his opening statement.

"Ladies and gentlemen of the Jury, on August 17, 1981, on a flyover of the Ash Creek area of the Umpqua National Forest, the county sheriff identified marijuana growing on a hill. A warrant was issued, and two days later, on August 19, 1981, the sheriff found a hundred and seventy-seven plants growing on the hillside above the property owned by Mr. Jack Cernak. A well-worn path led from close by his residence to the growing plants. We feel strongly that the defendant and Mr. Reginald Wickham—who was in residence at the time—were tending and growing the marijuana. The sheriff arrested both on a charge of manufacturing a controlled substance. After you hear the evidence, I'm sure you'll feel as strongly as we do about Mr. Cernak's guilt and bring in a verdict of guilty as charged."

"Ladies and gentlemen of the jury," stated Jim Carrier in his opening statement, "My client is charged with the crime of manufacturing a controlled substance of which he is innocent, and although he is accused of that crime, it is not up to him to prove his innocence. It is the state's obligation to prove guilt, and it must be proven beyond a reasonable doubt."

The first witness for the prosecution was Sergeant Hall. The bailiff swore in the tall, red-headed cop, and Zacker began his case. "Tell the court why you arrested the defendant."

"On August 17, 1981, while Deputy Vern Bishop and I were flying over the Ash Creek area of Douglas County, we identified marijuana growing on a hillside. The next day, a judge issued a search warrant."

"Tell the court what you discovered when you served the warrant."

"When we arrived on August 19, 1981 at 5:30 in the morning, we found Mr. Reginald Wickham sleeping in the yard in his sleeping bag and Mr. Jack Cernak in the residence. Up on the mountainside, we discovered a hundred and seventy-seven marijuana plants growing in four sections. A well-worn path that originated near the residence and barn-like structure led up to the growing area. After questioning, we learned the property belonged to Mr. Cernak and that Mr. Wickham lived there for several months. We arrested them on a charge of manufacturing a controlled substance."

"Your witness," said Zacker.

Jim Carrier stood and asked his first questions standing at the table and never went up to the witness stand. "Did the land where the marijuana was growing belong to the defendant?"

"No," he answered. "It was government land."

"Was it possible they grew wild up on the mountain side?"

"No!" he answered, vehemently. "They were not growing wild."

"How could you be so sure?"

"The plants were large and healthy. I've seen lots of marijuana plants growing, and these were well tended. Some were over ten feet tall. It was obvious someone was watering them and giving them fertilizer."

"I have no further questions for now but remain available for cross-examination."

Next, Zacker brought Deputy Vern Bishop to the stand, and all Bishop did was corroborate what Hall said and added nothing new. "Your witness," said Zacker."

"I have no questions," replied my lawyer.

"The prosecution rests," said Zacker.

The prosecution's case was short. The only evidence they could present was marijuana growing on a hillside above a homestead. I'm sure they hoped Jim Carrier would make a mistake and they could slip in some of the suppressed information. When Zacker finished, it was almost noon and the trial broke for lunch. All morning, I followed the proceedings closely, as if my life depended on it, vaguely aware it did. As a free man living wild in the world, I could never live caged, and a guilty verdict would be a death sentence.

It was Jim Carrier's turn after the break. Was it possible for him to put enough space between Deputy Hall's and Bishop's testimony and create reasonable doubt? His first witness was Merle Benson, the self-employed private investigator who testified at the first trial. "Did you physically inspect the mountain side where the marijuana was growing?" he asked, opening his defense. "I did," replied the private investigator.

"And what did you observe?"

"I found the forest was full of paths and someone could easily be entering the growing area from above."

"Were the plants visible from the road?"

"Thick shrubbery grew all around, and they could not be seen by the occupants of the dwellings below."

"Are there other residences nearby?"

"Yes. There is a residence a short distance to the north another to the south.

"Your witness," he said.

Zacker stood at the table, and was about to ask a question, but with a frustrated look sat down. "I have no questions," he said.

Sergeant Kenneth Hall was called for cross-examination and was reminded he was still under oath. Like Zacker, the deputy's face reflected frustration in remembering from the first trial what was coming.

"As Merle Benson testified, the forest above was full of paths, and someone could easily be entering the growing area from above. Did you interview any of the neighbors?"

"No, I didn't," he answered, tersely.

"So, you don't know if any of the neighbors were ever convicted of growing marijuana."

"No," he said very quietly.

"I'm sorry, Deputy Hall; I wasn't able to hear you."

"No!" he said much louder and with emphasis.

"And did you get any fingerprints?"

"No," Hall said again.

"One more question. How far would you estimate, in miles, is it from Centerville to Ash Valley, where the defendant owns land?"

"I'd estimate seventy-five to eighty miles."

Jim Carrier called Wanda Jennings to the stand. "Were you working at Deer Creek picture framing shop prior to August, 1981, the shop owned by Jack Cernak?"

"Yes, I was."

"How often did you work?"

"I usually worked a few days each week."

"Did you have regular hours?"

"Not always. I came in when he had work for me to do."

"Was the defendant at the shop regularly?"

"Yes, he was there most of the time."

"When you say most of the time, you mean?"

"He was there five days a week."

"I have no more questions. Your witness."

"Ms. Jennings" began Zacker, standing at the table, "did you ever see Mr. Cernak selling marijuana out of his picture framing business?"

"No, never."

"Did you know about all the marijuana that was found on the day he was arrested?"

My lawyer stood and pointed at the prosecutor, "I object and request the jury be sequestered." Suddenly, there was electricity in the courtroom. Judge Hawkins nodded towards the bailiff who ushered the jury out and closed the door behind them. "Approach the bench," he said, looking sternly at my attorney. "Explain your actions."

"With his last question, the prosecutor was attempting to introduce privileged information."

He looked at Zacker. "When I asked if she knew about the marijuana, I referred to the marijuana growing on the mountainside."

Since I was behind them, I couldn't see their faces, but his body language was saying he didn't believe him. "Be careful, Mr. Zacker," he said, "and may I remind you, Mr. Carrier, the Fourth Amendment is to be used as a shield and not a spear." He pointed at the bailiff and the jury filled back into the courtroom. "The objection is sustained," he said, "and the last question will be stricken from the record."

"I have no more questions," said Zacker.

"The defense rests," said Jim Carrier.

"Ladies and gentlemen of the Jury," began Zacker in his closing argument standing at his table. "The facts are that on August 19, 1981, on a raid by Sergeant Hall of the Douglas County Sheriff Department, one hundred seventy-seven marijuana plants were found growing on a hill a short distance above Mr. Cernak's residence. The sheriff arrested both he and Mr. Reggie Wickham on a charge of manufacturing a controlled substance. Nearby, a well-worn path led up to the growing marijuana. Yes, there were other residences nearby, but each was a quarter of a mile away. If you lived in one of those houses and you were going to grow marijuana, would you grow it a quarter mile away a short distance above someone else's property? I think not. I am sure you will all agree it is unlikely anyone was growing except the defendant. Allow justice to prevail by bringing in a verdict of guilty as charged."

"Ladies and gentlemen of the jury," began Jim Carrier, in his closing argument, standing in front of the jury. "When the sheriff arrived, he found marijuana growing on land that belonged to the government. Below was a residence owned by Jack Cernak, and he arrested him on a charge of manufacturing an illegal substance. It's probably something I would have done if I were the sheriff. Why? Because it was easy. By golly, we have the culprit, and he was just a short distance down the hill. But not so fast! Arresting someone because they happened to be close-by doesn't prove guilt, especially in this case. Merle Benson testified that the forest above was full of paths, and anyone could be entering the growing area from above. The plants were not visible to the occupants below. Growing plants don't make a lot of noise. We must remember that Sheriff Hall testified they could not be growing wild, because, according to him, they were well tended and some over ten feet tall. When plants grows ten feet, I'm assuming it means someone is there regularly giving them water and fertilizer. But Mr. Cernak had a picture framing business in town, and as Wanda Jennings testified, he was at his shop five days each week. According to Sheriff Hall, the distance between Centerville and the growing marijuana is seventy-five to eighty miles. If he was growing the plants, just when was he tending to them? He just happened to be there on the day the sheriff arrived, and it was easy to arrest him. As for why anyone would grow marijuana above someone else's residence is because of a critical factor needed in growing anything and that is water. Water flows down off the mountain above his property. Ladies and gentlemen of the jury, the state has not proven guilt beyond a reasonable doubt, and the only possible conclusion is to bring in a verdict of not guilty."

My insides were shaking when the summations were finished. The jury was instructed to go home for the night and not talk to each other about the case. They would begin their deliberations in the morning. The bailiff let them out through the side door, and the judge gaveled the trial adjourned. "Be here by eight AM tomorrow," said Jim Carrier.

I sat in the restaurant trying to eat dinner and never felt so alone in my life. Sleep wouldn't come, so I walked for hours through the dark and empty Centerville neighborhoods, the memories and visions ghost-like vibrating through my head. Finally, around three AM, exhausted, I fell into a fitful sleep. When the motel office called to awaken me at six, I could hardly crawl out of bed. I walked in a stupor to the courthouse, my stomach in turmoil. Jim Carrier was there, and the jury already began deliberations. "Relax as best you can," he said. "It could be a while before they come in with a verdict."

"How about if I go to the coffee shop on the corner and wait there?"

"That's fine. I'll come and get you when it's time."

I was there less then forty-five minutes when Jim Carrier walked through the door. "It's time," he said. "The jury is coming back in. It's a quick decision, and I don't know if that's a good sign or not." Inside the courtroom, he leaned towards me and said quietly: "No emotional outbursts whatever the decision."

I couldn't feel the floor beneath my feet, and my whole body vibrated when the door opened, and the jury filed in and took their seats. "Have you reached a verdict?" the judge asked.

The foreman was a woman. "We have Your Honor." The bailiff took the paper and handed it to the judge.

"Will the defendant please stand."

I was trembling and feeling sick to my stomach. "What find you?"

"On the charge of manufacturing a controlled substance, we find the defendant not guilty."

Waves of relief flowed over me, but suddenly, everything came to a screeching halt when Zacker requested a roll call vote of the jury. I watched in dismay as the jurors stood and recited their

354   *John-Paul Cernak*

votes. The first was a man, and my heart sank when he said, loudly: "Guilty as charged!" The second was the other man, and he too said in a loud voice; "Guilty as charged!"

Then it was the women's turn. The first to speak was the foreman. "Not guilty," she declared, and to my relief, each of the ten women voted for acquittal. I thanked the Great Spirit. They were out in the hall waiting for the elevator. I expressed my gratitude. They smiled. The two men who voted for conviction stood in the back trying to be inconspicuous and quickly boarded the elevator to get out of sight. "Meet me at my office," said Jim Carrier.

The sun was shining, and although I felt relief, my psyche was having difficulty adjusting after so many months of holding in fear. His secretary pointed to his office. I walked in. "You sure did a great job," I said.

He looked at me and shook his head. "I don't know what to say, Jack. Everything fell just right for you. You must have friends in high places, but why I asked you to come in is to warn you to get out of town. The prosecution will subpoena you and force you to testify against your partner."

"I won't testify. I'll take the fifth."

"You can't use the Fifth Amendment against self-incrimination. It applies only when you're in jeopardy. You were found not guilty and cannot be charged again with the same crime."

I went to the Happy Hour Tavern and drank beer all afternoon before going up the hill to tell Meg of my acquittal. When she answered the door, she already knew and anger showed on her face. I'm not sure why I asked her to go out for a drink even after I saw how angry she was at the outcome. We went to a local pub. She was so uptight and unfriendly, I took her home early.

I ignored Jim Carrier's warning to get out of town and believed I was invincible and couldn't be touched. If they came into the valley looking for me, I wouldn't answer the door. Three days later, a loud knock awakened me in the middle of the night as I slept on the second floor of the new house. After being awakened at that early hour and not thinking clearly, I yelled down the stairs; "Who's there?"

"THE SHERIFF!" came a loud voice out of the darkness. "I HAVE A SUBPOENA FOR YOU!"

I had no one to blame but my own arrogance. Now it was either testify against Reggie or go to jail. I thought about what he would do if the circumstances were reversed. But it didn't matter. I wouldn't testify against him. If I did, I would never be able to live with myself. Since I wouldn't testify, I would go to jail, and it was a bitter pill to swallow after winning two trials keeping me out of prison.

The next day, I drove to Centerville to tell Jim Carrier the bad news, but before I could say anything, he pointed to a chair and said he had something important to tell me: "While on the witness stand and under oath, Deputy Hall changed his story and testified that your partner was a resident for three months. The arrest report states your partner claimed to have just arrived. I spoke with Zacker and told him what he testified and pointed out your partner was a resident. Anything said under oath supersedes all other statements. As a tenant, he had standing, and all the evidence against him is suppressed as it was for you. Zacker agreed, and he's dropping charges against him."

Although stunned speechless, I felt anger. "Did Hall lie on the witness stand under oath?"

He looked down at his desk, and when he looked up, his lips were pressed tightly against his teeth. "If your partner had just arrived, Hall would have no way of hooking the two of you together. As a resident, he might have convinced the jury you were in cahoots even though you were there only occasionally. And while I was in Zacker's office, he returned some of the evidence they had against you."

Among the evidence was a stack of photos Bonnie took, but missing were the one of me riding the tractor and the snap shot of the plants growing in the greenhouse. The most important item, however, was a copy of the land sales contract for the Jefferson Street House I didn't know the prosecution had along with a note to the IRS attached. "Your wife wasn't in the clear," he proclaimed. "If you were convicted, the sheriff would have arrested her immediately, charged her with growing, and in all likelihood confiscated your house." He sat down, signaling he was finished but quickly stood remembering something. "Oh! By the way, Jack, what was it you came in to tell me?"

On the day before his scheduled trial, Reggie came up from California. Everyone met at the bar for a small celebration. When I tried talking to him, his hard edge grew even harder, and I left in disgust.

I learned they were finally returning the tractor, and the next morning, I headed over to the Douglas County Sheriff's Department. The deputy on duty behind the front desk was a big guy and wore a handlebar moustache. The minute I entered, he launched into a loud, angry, verbal attack against me. His face was red and contorted into an ugly mask. I never saw him before and didn't know who he was. But he knew who I was. "People like you should be eliminated," he said. "You shouldn't be allowed to walk this earth. Son of a bitches like you should be ground into ashes."

Alarmed by the ferociousness of his attack, I backed away and never took my eyes off him until safely out the door. It was easy to understand the reason for his anger. With all the evidence against me, they thought they had a sure conviction. He was expressing outrage I had the audacity to escape and the frustration there was nothing they could do about it. What bothered me was his attack came while on duty, and he feared no censure. If he was capable of expressing such malice and hatred while in the department, what was he capable of doing if he confronted me somewhere isolated? I considered him dangerous as I did all the deputies who believed as he did. Although it troubled me, I wasn't surprised it came when it did. The world changed and not in a good way. What I feared the most happened. The haters were in power.

Thoroughly shaken by his attack and reeling from the incident, I went to my favorite restaurant for coffee. The eatery was just off the downtown, and it was where I usually went for lunch when the shop was open. The food was good, and everyone working there knew I was busted for growing marijuana. My waitress was Sarah. She was part owner and in her sixties, tall, slim, and attractive, and you could tell she was once a beautiful woman. "Good to see you, Jack," she said, "and congratulations on winning your trial."

"Thanks for the good vibes. How's business?"

"If more shops close, I don't know how we'll stay open. I sure hope this recession ends soon. What can I get you?"

"Just coffee today."

I sat on my favorite stool watching customers come and go, but I wasn't there mentally. I was back in the Sheriff's Department replaying the attack by the deputy. His ugly face and handlebar moustache kept flashing in my mind and feeling I had missed something important. Then, I suddenly remembered, and my breathing accelerated and felt dizzy. As I backed towards the door, a vision of a soldier flashed before me superimposed over the deputy. He was dressed in a nineteenth century military uniform similar to those worn by the troops of the Seventh Cavalry commanded by Custer. I recognized the deputy as the soldier I killed in the Battle of the Little Big Horn, and I remembered more. In that fleeting instant, I saw the soldier together with a woman. She was dressed in a hooped skirt, her hair in a bun, and it was Meg. They were married, and she was his wife.

In the next instant, I was back at the battlefield and for the second time witnessing the death of Custer. The last time I refused to watch as the Indians desecrated his body. This time, I couldn't turn away, and what I saw threw me into shock. With several arrows protruding from his mangled and debased corpse lying lifeless on the ground, an image of Ronald Reagan emerged. He was the reincarnation of George Armstrong Custer. The shock was more than my system could handle, and my head was about to

358   *John-Paul Cernak*

explode. As I was blacking out, I heard myself scream: "Ahhhhhha!"

The cry quickly relieved the pressure in my head and brought me back to awareness. When I opened my eyes, everyone in the restaurant was staring at me. Sarah rushed over. "Jack! Jack! Are you alright?"

"I'm OK, I'm OK," I said, holding my head, but I was crying and could hardly contain myself. I walked around Centerville for hours integrating what I learned. Slowly, my psyche accepted the truth of our lives, and I wondered if Meg knew. She may have not known consciously but must have had recognition on a deeper level.

—◦⁄ℓ⁄◦—

FROM AN EARLY AGE, I WAS AWARE OF THE INJUSTICES THE INDIANS suffered at the hands of the Europeans who took their land, killed the buffalo, and practiced genocide. From my first readings of the Indian Wars and in particular the Battle of the Little Bighorn, I experienced a profound dislike for Custer. I understood more where that animosity originated after learning I was an Indian in my last life and died fighting against him. It wasn't any wonder then why I felt enmity for Reagan and bristled at the mention of his name. If Custer came back from the Indian Wars a hero, as he did from the Civil War, our country's history would likely read differently. Now he was president, and I hoped and prayed his soul learned compassion— different from his last life and unlike the soldier with the handlebar moustache who was filled with hatred. Only history would give us the answer, looking closely at the man and not the myth.

I died fighting Custer in the Battle of the Little Bighorn, and although the Indians won the battle, they lost the war. In this battle, I survived, but the outcome of the struggle was still in doubt. Make no mistake, Reagan's attack against the counterculture, the liberal left, and people of color was a war. He wrapped himself in the flag and made it seem that anyone who looked and thought differently was somehow unpatriotic. Have there been other wars and additional battles in past lives that are lost to memory, and will there be more wars and further battles in future lifetimes? Is it my fate and humanity's destiny to fight against the dark forces again and again whatever name they are called?

―⊷⊷⊷―

ON MY DRIVE BACK, I SANG, WHOOPED, HOLLERED, AND EXPRESSED unrestrained joy, but beneath my jubilation, I felt a sadness. I would have to leave the valley and find a new source of income. I felt blessed as the days continued warm and sunny through the middle of October. At around eleven o'clock on my last day, I heard a coyote howl. It seemed strange to hear them during daylight. When I looked out the side door, a large male sat howling a short way up the valley. I leaned a chair against the side of the barn listening to his serenade. After a few minutes, I became aware he was retelling the story of my life in the valley, of my victories and of my defeats and of my joys and of my sorrows. I believed my leaving was temporary until then, but he was saying goodbye.

Later that afternoon, a thin layer of high clouds drifted in from the southwest. By early evening heavy, dark storm clouds moved in low and fast, and the winter rains began in a deluge. At daybreak, with my insecurities nagging me, I loaded my things into the truck, locked the barn, and drove north on I-5 through the storm's unrelenting fury. I was moving to Eugene. But how would I earn money without knowing anyone, and where would I live? When the big green sign above the freeway warned me I was approaching my exit, I brushed away my insecurities and vowed to make the most of it, whatever were the circumstances. As I headed the truck off the freeway, the rain suddenly stopped, and the sun broke through the dark overcast bathing everything in brilliant sunlight. "Far out! What a beautiful day!" I pulled up to the stop and looked around feeling positive vibes everywhere and seeing life from a new perspective. "Somehow it'll all work out," I said aloud feeling a surge of energy.

FIN